# THE LEWISTON SHOOTINGS

## AN ALL-AMERICAN TRAGEDY

## ROBERT CONLIN

**WILD**BLUE
P R E S S

WildBluePress.com

*THE LEWISTON SHOOTINGS published by:*
*WILDBLUE PRESS*
*P.O. Box 102440*
*Denver, Colorado 80250*

*WILDBLUE PRESS is registered at the U.S. Patent and Trademark Offices.*

*ISBN 978-1-960332-90-5 Trade Paperback*
*ISBN 978-1-960332-92-9 eBook*
*ISBN 978-1-960332-91-2 Hardback*

*Cover design © 2024 WildBlue Press. All rights reserved.*
*Interior Formatting and Cover Design by Elijah Toten*
*www.totencreative.com*

# THE LEWISTON SHOOTINGS

# CONTENTS

# ACKNOWLEDGMENTS

Mass shootings have become so common in the United States that we've become collectively numbed to the devastation they cause. Until they hit close to home, and the victims are people you may have seen in the grocery store, or nodded to at a high school game, or God forbid, they may be a loved one. Then, in addition to having to endure their loss, you're hounded by reporters for days and weeks to follow asking you to talk about that loss, how it's affected you and your family, *how do you feel*?

In researching and writing this book, I'm afraid I was that reporter. As hard as I tried to justify it by reminding myself that these thoughts and feelings were important in being able to show "victims" as real people, it did feel very intrusive. I could never explain that away. At the end of the day, all I could say is that the whole Lewiston story would be told by someone, and better I tell it than someone from far away who doesn't have a sense of this place and its people. Despite this inadequate explanation, people who were shattered and still grieving did talk to me. I hope I did justice to their generosity.

Thank you to *Elizabeth Seal* for talking about her husband, *Joshua Seal*, and letting his children and the world know how much he loved them and the life that they all built. She's raising their four young kids alone now. Her strength and grace in the face of such adversity is remarkable. Thank you to *Dr. Nirav Shah* for sharing his recollections of working with Josh and being able to laugh together, despite the communication challenge.

Thank you to *Arthur Barnard* for talking about his son, *Artie Strout,* and recalling the painful minutes when he heard the news after he left his son at Schemengees. Arthur shared stories about Artie and the bond he had with his wife and five children, and he opened up about the sheer frustration of engaging in the gun control debate as the father of a recent victim. He has the heart of a lion and the courage of conviction.

Thank you to *Justin and Samantha Juray,* the owners of Just-In-Time Recreation, for recalling the horrors of that night in their bowling alley, and the devastating impact it had on their tight knit community. Their determination to reopen and to help rebuild that communityis a beacon of hope to many.

Thank you to *Danielle Grondin* for her courage in talking about what it felt like to look a mass shooter in the eye, and how she and so many others have been robbed of their sense of safety anytime they venture out in public. She's not sure she'll ever go back to bowling at Just-In-Time with her friends. I hope she'll be able to one day.

Thank you to *Cara Lamb* for her courage and raw honesty in describing how Robert Card's family struggled to find a way to get him some help but found instead that local law enforcement and Army Reserve soldiers didn't have the same level of concern. She spoke up because she wants these institutions to learn from their mistakes and remember that public safety is far more important than jurisdictional disputes and face-saving measures.

Thank you to *Sean Hodgson* for talking about his long friendship with Robert Card. Because of his substance abuse and mental health struggles, he's been dismissed as 'unreliable' by several actors in this story. After hours of conversations, he seems far more believable to me than his detractors. Hopefully, Sean will find some peace and a way to rebuild his life.

Thank you to *Nicole Herling* for talking about watching her brother's decline and desperately searching for a way to help him. The Card family has demonstrated incredible courage and empathy toward the victims' families and the wider community as they deal with their own grief. Their efforts to work on behalf of soldiers to increase mental health access and improve training methods speak volumes about their character.

Thank you to *Shannon Houlihan* for talking about the work environment at Four Winds Hospital, to *Dr. Michael Harvey* for sharing his expertise about the link between hearing loss and mental health, and to *Pine Tree Society* and *Grace Clooney* for providing ASL interpretation for the author in his conversation with Elizabeth Seal.

Thank you to my good friend, *Michael Peterson*, for slogging through a rough draft and offering his sage advice on the book's structure, and to my mother, *Jean Conlin,* who helped edit and proofread the manuscript, and refrained from writing, "were you drunk when you wrote this?" in the margins, like she has in the past.

Finally, thank you to the people of Lewiston and the region for demonstrating that empathy, compassion, and resilience in the darkest and most difficult of times is the true measure of a community's worth. It won't ever be on the *Coolest Small Cities in America* list, but Lewiston is number one in the hearts and minds of the people who know it best.

*The eight 160-foot spires of the Basilica of Saints Peter and Paul tower over the densely-populated neighborhoods adjacent to New England's second-largest church. (Photo by Robert Conlin)*

# PROLOGUE

By the time the sun rose at 7:08 on the morning of October 25th, 2023, the pulse of daily life in Lewiston, Maine, and its sister city of Auburn on the west bank of the Androscoggin River had already begun its rhythmic beat in the predawn darkness. It was a Wednesday, the middle of the work week, and traffic had picked up on Lewiston's main arteries of Lisbon, Sabattus, Webster, and Main Streets, and across the Longley Bridge connecting the twin cities.

The delivery trucks for the daily newspaper, the *Sun Journal,* crisscrossed the city, filling the racks at gas stations, supermarkets, and small neighborhood variety stores like Webb's Market on Pine St., the Corner Variety on Lincoln, and Speakers Variety on Spruce. Lewiston's venerable newspaper can trace its roots back to 1847—remarkable local longevity in an age of corporate media consolidation. It's printed in South Portland now, but its ink is still dedicated to delivering local news from A to Z.

The delivery trucks for another Lewiston institution—Lepage Bakeries—made their own rounds from its Cedar Street location, carrying its Country Kitchen and Barowsky baked goods to stores all over northern New England, as they've done since 1903.

Despite the late October date, drivers could roll down their windows and hang out an arm for a bonus tan. The thermometer would hit 68 degrees later in the day and climb into the 70's for the following three. The combination of colorful fall foliage and warm temperatures was an anomaly in decades past, but it's becoming more common as the climate in Maine warms.

The clock would go back one hour for daylight savings in four days; a welcome change for early risers like newspaper and bakery delivery drivers, but a slow elevator descent to the bottom floor for everyone who hates driving home in the dark just after the 8-4 p.m. work shift ends.

But thoughts of that could wait. It was a beautiful day in Maine's second-largest city. The middle-aged Auburn couple who appeared in a photo on the front page of the *Sun Journal's* local section that morning splitting two cords of wood for the cold temperatures that would eventually arrive could finish it off, have it stacked by day's end, and still have time to enjoy a cold beverage while watching the sunset.

Over at Simone's hot dog stand on Chestnut Street, they'd be prepping menu items, making sure that there were plenty of 'Lewiston Lobsters' (red-dyed hot dogs) ready for the lunch rush. It's been a family-owned business for 115 years, so they'd be able to do it with their eyes closed.

Around the corner a way, the doors of the Franco Center on Cedar St., would soon swing open to welcome French language class attendees. The center is housed in the former St. Mary's Church, and just down the block from the shuttered L'ecole St. Marie School, both of which were the heart of the city's predominantly Franco-American civic life until they closed in 2000.

And soon the phones would start to ring at the Immigrant Resource Center on Lisbon St. The center provides housing assistance, legal resources, and mental health support for Lewiston's newest immigrants, most from Somalia and other African countries. In one of the whitest states in the nation, Lewiston's 6,000 plus African refugees have helped to write a new chapter in the American immigrant story.

Halloween was less than a week away, and the decorative ghouls and witches, grinning pumpkins and scythe-wielding zombies that stalked the shadows of Lewiston's imagination wilted as the sun rose higher behind the eight majestic spires of the iconic Basilica of Saints Peter and Paul Catholic Church on Bartlett Street. If those 170-foot-high spires were to ever disappear, Lewiston would be as unrecognizable as Paris without the Eiffel Tower.

Two miles north at Just-In-Time Recreation Center on Mollison Way, the close-knit staff would be making sure the pinsetter machines on each of its thirty-four bowling lanes were working properly, food was prepped, and beer kegs primed for the influx of league participants later in the day, and rental shoes and bowling balls were cleaned and ready to go.

Four miles south of them, the equally tight-knit staff at Schemengees Bar & Grille on Lincoln St. would be setting up for the lunchtime crowd and readying the pool tables and cornhole lanes for a busy night of league play. It's not an easy name to pronounce, but that didn't matter to its many dedicated regulars who gathered there after work for a fun time out with friends.

No one could know during that ordinary October day that the pulse of daily life in Lewiston and the surrounding area would be on life support just an hour after sunset that very evening. No one, that is, except the man who would be responsible for making sure of that.

*Robert Card Jr.'s property on West Road in Bowdoin in December, 2023. He left from here for the 30-minute trip to Just-In-Time Recreation Center in Lewiston on October 25th. His ex-wife, Cara Lamb, put up the plywood on the window after authorities had completed their search and collected evidence. (Photo by Robert Conlin)*

# THE ROAD FROM PARANOIA TO INFAMY

To the sixty million or so Americans who live in areas defined as "rural" America, the town of Bowdoin, Maine doesn't look much different from their towns in Pennsylvania, or Oregon, or Iowa—except for the hills. There are no mountains in Bowdoin, but there are 3,100 residents and lots of hills.

The sparsely settled roads in the forty-nine-square-mile town are home to small ranch houses, double-wide modular homes, weathered Cape-style houses with peeling paint, and single-wide trailers. Most of the visible roadside lots have barns or outbuildings of some kind. There are four small churches of various denominations, one small convenience store, one K-5 school for just over 200 students, and small businesses advertising land excavation, trash hauling, plumbing and heating services, land surveying, tire sales, and various other services and commodities.

Over on the western side of town a few miles away from the store and school—the epicenter of town if you can call it that—is the appropriately named West Rd. It's not far from the humming Interstate 95 traffic that slices along the western edge of Bowdoin, but it's far enough away and there's plenty of trees to buffer the sound. These trees, mostly conifers, with some deciduous mixed in among them, are thick enough along the road to induce a slight feeling of claustrophobia as you drive along. Not enough to feel your chest tighten with anxiety, but they crowd the pavement like parade-watchers on stilts, blocking out most of the light and ambient warmth of a sunny early winter day.

At the high point of the road, a gap in the trees provides a view of rolling fields and distant hills on the western horizon. It's just a short way down from that scenic spot to a two-acre cleared lot in the woods containing a shabby white single-wide trailer, next to a newer-looking, blue two-bay outbuilding on a slab.

The trailer is oriented east to west, so only a short end faces the road. The one window on that end is boarded up with plywood, giving it the look of an abandoned property. With all the trees surrounding the site, it's deeply shaded, even on a bright day. There are no signs of life, no indication that anyone lives there. There's certainly nothing to suggest that it was the most infamous home in Maine for weeks, if not longer.

The now-empty trailer was once Robert Russell Card II's home. The forty-year-old native of Bowdoin was known to be reserved and private, but he had shifted the country's focus onto this quiet farming community in a very dramatic way for forty-eight hours. If anyone had ever suggested to a resident prior to October 25th, 2023, that a massive law enforcement presence would flood the town, and that heavily armed tactical SWAT teams and armored cars and helicopters with blinding searchlights and bullhorns would shatter the tranquility of this country road, they'd be the laughingstock of town. But no one is laughing here now. It's deep in shadow and eerily quiet. It feels haunted.

Before Card left the trailer in the early evening of October 25th, he wrote a note to his eighteen-year-old son, Colby, disclosing his phone and banking information, and left it out to be seen. Colby still hasn't read it. To this date in May 2024, the Maine State Police (MSP) haven't allowed him to. Card also left his cell phone, with a message that he had written three days before and clearly intended for law enforcement to see. He set the phone down at 6:05 p.m. in the spot where officers from a tactical squad found it later that night.

*"I'm having issues. I've had enough. I'm trained to hurt people,"* the message read.

That night he was wearing his charcoal-colored tactical pants, a brown sweatshirt, and light brown military-style combat boots. He loaded a Ruger SFAR-10 semi-automatic rifle, a Smith & Wesson M&P 15 semi-automatic rifle, a Smith & Wesson M&P .40 caliber handgun, and magazines and clips of ammunition into his white 2013 Subaru Outback.

If he went straight to his destination without stopping, he was about a thirty-minute ride away. The sun would have just been setting. He would have taken a right out of his driveway onto the heavily wooded West Road and followed that for a couple of miles, then turned left onto Route 197, a busy two-lane road that would have had a steady flow of traffic that time of day. He would have then branched left onto Rt. 9/126 after a couple of miles, in the direction of Lewiston in neighboring Androscoggin County. Then he would have followed that road for another six miles into the town of Sabattus along the way, the landscape changing from the farms, fields, and rolling hills of Bowdoin and Litchfield to small businesses advertising auto repair and detailing, car washes, coffee and donuts, fortune telling, laundry facilities, and more. He'd have driven past a small strip mall in Sabattus that contains a Chinese restaurant and a nightclub and lounge called Mixers, which is housed in a nondescript, low-slung building with a tiny sign affixed with its name over a single door. Card was known to frequent Mixers. Somehow, he got the idea in his head over the previous year that people there were calling him a pedophile and they were spreading the rumor online. This wasn't the only area business he believed was doing that either.

Back up Rt. 197 in the opposite direction, the people at Gowell's Shop 'n Save supermarket in Litchfield, where he would stop in to buy beer and groceries, were also referring to him as a pedophile, he thought. He planned to take care of that at both places, but not on this night. On this particular night, he was going to two places in Lewiston where he was convinced they were spreading the same rumors, or even worse.

Card would have crossed the Lewiston city line, then veered right through close-quarter residential neighborhoods with compact houses and tidy yards. He would have then wound through these streets for another couple of miles, before taking a sharp right and turning onto Mollison Way, the short main road for the Fairgrounds Business Park. As the name implies, the business park was the former site of the Maine State Fair, which ran every summer from 1881 up until the 1970s, when encroaching commercial development, neglected racetrack facilities, and declining attendance led to its eventual closure.

Now it's home to several healthcare clinics and companies, a Maine Department of Motor Vehicles branch office, a methadone clinic, an Italian restaurant, a Subway sandwich shop, and a bowling alley in a sprawling building at 24 Mollison Way. That's where Robert Card was headed when he turned down the one-hundred-yard-long entrance road, drove around to the back side parking lot and entrance to Just-in-Time Recreation Center, and parked his car.

Night had fallen, but pole-mounted halogen lights in the lot cast enough light to easily navigate toward the entrance of the bowling alley. The oversized parking lot was nowhere near full, but there were still plenty of cars already there. Enough to carry the roughly sixty people inside, including nearly twenty kids, some of whom came to work on their bowling skills in a practice session run by a longtime customer and his wife.

A small sign indicating the entrance to *Just-In-Time Recreation* is mounted on the beige-colored building near the door. It contradicts the large letters that spell out

*Sparetime* on the side of the building facing Mollison Way. The owners, Justin and Samantha Juray, had bought the bowling alley in 2021 and changed the name, but they never got around to changing the letters out front, and people used the two business names interchangeably.

The entrance door opens into a foyer with a large plate glass window facing the parking lot. A few steps through that, and the glass-fronted door that opens to the interior is right there. If you came in blindfolded, you'd still have a good idea where all the action was located, because bowling alleys tend to be noisy places. With twenty-two lanes of ten-pin and twelve lanes of candlepin—a regional New England game played with a grapefruit-sized bowling ball and tall pins shaped like candles—Just-In-Time is no exception. The 30,000-square-foot building is wrapped in metal siding, which amplifies the sound of an average size thirteen-pound bowling ball striking pins. Add the conversation, laughter, and crosstalk between dozens of people, and the noise emanating from Just-in-Time carries easily into the foyer.

Card would have been familiar with all these details because he had bowled there several times before. Sometime just before 6:55 p.m. he swung open the door, walked in, and raised the Ruger SFAR-10 (small frame automatic reloading) rifle to his right shoulder. He didn't even bother looking at the camera he knew was there.

In the next fifteen minutes, he would forever change the lives of the family and friends of the eighteen people he killed at the bowling alley and at Schemengees Bar & Grille across town, as well as the thirteen he wounded and the dozens upon dozens of survivors who witnessed the carnage.

He also forever altered how Maine residents think about their safety. In that short time span, he flipped the script. Mainers don't like to be told how to think, but Robert Card II accomplished doing that to them in mere minutes. He spat in their face and told them to forget their foolish, naive notion that, "It won't happen here." Because it can, it did, and he made it happen.

# "9-1-1 OPERATOR, WHAT'S YOUR EMERGENCY?"

The Lewiston-Auburn 9-1-1 Emergency Communications System is housed in a building in Auburn, the twin city situated just across the Androscoggin River from Lewiston. It's the third-busiest of the twenty-six Public Safety Answering Points (PSAF's) in the state of Maine in terms of call volume. On the night of October 25th, it was the busiest by a country mile.

The first calls came in at 6:55 p.m. from Just-in-Time Recreation Center at 24 Mollison Way (*some conversations have been condensed and are time-stamped to the second.*)

\* \* \*

**6:55:31**: *There's a guy shooting.* (From a person locked in an interior office)

**6:55:31**: *There's been a mass shooting at Just-In-Time. I'm at the front desk. He just walked out my door two seconds ago.* (From Just-In-Time co-owner, Samantha Juray)

**6:55:32**: *There's a guy in here shooting people with a gun. A bunch of us just ran out the back door.*

**6:55:37**: *Someone's got a gun in the bowling alley. A couple of shots fired.*

9-1-1: *Anyone injured?*

*I don't know. We just booked it the fuck out into the woods. Some people know who has the gun.*

**6:55:37:** *We just heard gunfire. Bowling alley. Mollison Way. Lewiston*

9-1-1: *Anyone injured?*

*I don't know. I'm not going out there.*

**6:55:58:** *I've got a bunch of kids in the back. It's kids' bowling practice night.*

**6:56:** *Shooter. There's a shooter. I have a kid. He's bleeding. He's been shot in the arm.*

**6:56:** *We're in the back. I heard shots and I saw the gun and I was next to the office so I grabbed my four-year-old and ran in.*

9-1-1: *Help is on the way.*

*It's so quiet out there.*

**6:56:43:** *Is the police here at the door? I hear voices. I don't know who's there.* (From a woman who was hiding in a back room with an injured boy.)

9-1-1: *I don't know who's there.*

*Find out because they're trying to get in and we're scared.*

9-1-1: *Okay.*

*I need fucking proof before I open that goddamned door.*

*Yes. yes, pray, pray. You're okay. I need to find something clean. My coat is the only thing...Has the shooter been detained?*

9-1-1: *Not as of yet, no.*

*Jesus Christ. That's why I'm not opening the door.*

9-1-1: *That's right, do not open that door for anyone until we're sure who it is.*

\*\*\*

The first Lewiston Police Department officers officially responded within four minutes of the first call. A few off-duty police officers who were at a nearby firing range training for an upcoming firearms proficiency test were said to have arrived at just about the same time, although their arrival time has never been officially noted. These officers, both on duty and off, would be the first of hundreds of law enforcement officers—local, county, state, and federal—who would descend on Lewiston and surrounding towns in the hours and days to follow—over 400 in all by the time it was over, according to the Maine State Police inquiry four months later.

As they encountered survivors who had fled the building and were running down Mollison Way towards Main St. (Route 202) a few hundred yards away, these early first responders would get a clearer picture of the horror that had just taken place inside the bowling alley.

It's more accurate to say they would get a rudimentary stick-figure picture: *man, gun, shots, casualties.* It had happened so suddenly, so violently, and completely out of context, that eyewitness accounts of what had transpired contained tiny snapshots taken while glancing from under a table or over a shoulder, in the mad dash to escape.

With this scant information to go on, officers raced into the parking lot and looked for a way into the building. They did so with the assumption that the shooter—or perhaps shooters, because no one could definitively say there wasn't more than one—was still inside. They would also learn from fleeing survivors that the lanes were packed with bowlers that night and that eighteen kids, some of whom they had grabbed and pulled out an exit door on the opposite side from the entrance door, were among them.

Unlike so many of the mass shooting incidents we've become familiar with, the responding officers didn't wait for orders from higher-ups. They didn't set up a perimeter and wait for an on-scene commander or a heavily armed tactical team to arrive. Instead, they took immediate action, with little regard for their own safety. The first wave of law enforcement officers arriving at Just-In-Time swore an oath to serve and protect, and they clearly upheld it that night.

Some found their way into the building through the entrance door, others through a rear door fifty yards away, and with service weapons drawn and tactical stances engaged, they approached a crime scene that most had trained for, but few had imagined they'd ever encounter.

Unexpectedly, Just-In-Time co-owner, Samantha Juray, unlocked the entrance door to let them in. A former EMT, she had witnessed and survived the carnage, and then her muscle memory kicked in and she went on autopilot, despite having changed careers long before that. The smoke had barely cleared, and she began assessing the dead and injured, checking for signs of life.

"He's gone," she said to the police officers as she unlocked the door. "He left a couple of minutes ago. I watched him go and locked the door behind him."

His victims lay where they had been executed. Michael Deslauriers II and Jason Walker, both fifty-one, were closest to the entrance. Lifelong friends and longtime bowlers at Sparetime and then Just-In-Time, the two men had been bowling with their wife and their life partner at a lane close to the front door.

To the right of the entrance, William Young, forty-four, and his son, Aaron Young, fourteen, lay dead near the lane where Aaron had been bowling in the youth clinic run by Robert Violette, seventy-six, and his wife, Lucille, seventy-three. Aaron was an enthusiastic participant in the weekly sessions, and his father brought him every Wednesday and Saturday and watched with pride as he developed into a skilled competitor.

The Violettes' bodies were close by. Robert had been fatally shot when he stepped in front of some of the kids to shield them from Card. Lucille was shot nearby. She survived initially, but she died of her injuries in the ambulance on the way to the hospital. Both avid longtime bowlers, they loved the kids who flocked to their practice sessions over the years, and the feeling was mutual from both the kids and from the large extended circle of friends they had made over the decades.

Thomas Conrad, thirty-four, was Just-in-Time's manager. He had started just months before, but his get-things-done attitude, his dedication, and his easy rapport with customers had already made him invaluable to the Jurays. He had just served a customer a beer a few seconds before he was shot, exchanging pleasantries as he often did. It would be his last conversation on earth.

Tricia Asselin, fifty-three, was a part-time employee who basically grew up in the bowling alley. She'd worked every position there, and when she wasn't working, she'd often be bowling with the friends she had made there over the years, which was what she was doing that night. She was calling 9-1-1 on her cell phone when Card gunned her down near the front desk. According to Staff Sgt. Sean Hodgson, Card's Army Reserve colleague and longtime friend who bowled with him at Just-in-Time, he had previously witnessed Card making a pass at Tricia earlier in the summer, and she rebuffed him, saying, "Not tonight honey."

Over at the back door that so many survivors had fled through, Thomas Giberti, a seventy-nine-year-old former manager of the bowling alley, who knows every inch of the

30,000-square-foot building like the back of his hand, lay in the doorway. He had been shot seven times in both legs while he ushered kids out the door to safety, but he survived.

Gavin Robitaille, sixteen, had been bowling with his mother and brother when a bullet tore through his arm. A sophomore at Edward Little High School in Auburn, Gavin was a pitcher on the school's baseball team. Incredibly, while some of the Robitaille family was at Just-In-Time, his father and grandfather were four miles away at a sports bar and restaurant that would soon become as horribly familiar as the bowling alley.

As the police cautiously made their way through the building, they became conscious of all the survivors who were crouching behind the ball returns, flattened to the floor under benches, curled up in tight balls behind tables that had been flipped over, pressed up tight against each other in distant corners of the candlepin lanes, huddled in a utility room and walk-in cooler, even wedged in behind the pin-setting machines at the end of the lanes.

While they processed those dissonant images, their focus was on determining where the shooter was and whether he had left the property. Samantha Juray saw him exit the building and locked the door behind him. But where did he go?

Was he lying in ambush outside somewhere, ready, like so many mass shooters are, to die of suicide by cop, and take a few with him?

Or did he sneak back around through another door and re-enter the building? Some of the officers had been there before for work or play, but they didn't have a blueprint in front of them to refer to all the entrances.

Or had he circled around the building so that he could attack the fleeing survivors from the rear as they ran towards the lights of nearby businesses and the steady flow of evening traffic on busy Main Street?

In the feverish chaotic aftermath of the shooting—already the worst in Maine history—it was anyone's guess who he was and where he was going. Within minutes, they would get the answer to the second question. Not long after that, a manhunt would reveal the answer to the first.

*The open farmland and fields around Card's hometown of Bowdoin, Maine. Card would have driven down this road on his way to Just-In-Time Recreation Center in Lewiston. (Photo by Robert Conlin)*

# A PLACE CALLED HOME

Robert Card II, Robbie as he was known to the family, grew up with his parents, Robert Sr. and Janna, his older brother, Ryan, and his younger sister, Nicole, on the family farm on Meadow Road, a hilly country road that slices through the town from Rt. 125 in the north to Rt. 201 in the south.

Because it connects these two busy regional roads, there's more traffic on it than you would expect to see on a road that's flanked by wide open fields, small ponds, scattered houses, and woods. Of course, that's all relative to where you live and how you define heavy traffic. The fact that there are no traffic lights in Bowdoin probably puts that in perspective.

Perched at the top of a long slope bounded by fields on both sides, the small Cape-style farmhouse that the Card kids grew up in looks no different than many of the others in town. Built in 1961, it was painted white at one time, but it's been so faded by weather and time it's hard to tell now.

At 850 square feet, it's a small house for a family of five. There are three bedrooms and two bathrooms, a mud room on one side, and an attached garage on the other. An old basketball backboard is still mounted to the front of the garage, but the hoop has broken away, and the asphalt driveway is cracked and sprouting weeds; the one-on-one games that the brothers once played are a distant memory.

Out in the small front yard, a rusted swing set, a fallow vegetable garden, some garden ornaments, and a birdbath endure the hardship of another winter. Come spring and summer, the air in the yard and fields around will hum and buzz with the sound of birds, butterflies, bees, and bats when night falls, but it's quiet in mid-winter and the sound of an approaching car carries from far off.

The house is situated on 2.3 acres according to the town land maps, but the Cards own hundreds of acres of land on either side of the house, across the street, and in other locations in the town. The family's roots in Bowdoin are deep and go back generations, and their land holdings reflect that.

The Card family isn't material rich, but they are land rich, even if much of the land is working land and not ideally located to sell to a developer to slap up a community of cookie-cutter houses. Not that they'd want to. That might be some landowner's dream, but that's not something the family would be inclined to inflict on their fellow citizens of Bowdoin.

Back when they were younger, the Card kids did chores to keep the family's dairy farm up and running. Over the years, the family transitioned to raising cattle for beef, and, like most farms in the state, a variety of other agricultural products to make ends meet. Maine farmers tend to wear lots of hats and are used to taking off one and putting on another multiple times during a workday.

There are an estimated 150,000 miles of rock walls snaking through the fields and woods in New England, but that's not because farmers liked building them. The receding glaciers of the last Ice Age made the job of turning the soil here a hellish undertaking, and it proved easier to stack the rocks up and build a boundary with them than it was to haul them away. Bulk crops like field corn, wheat, or soybean aren't suited for Maine's topography or soil, so instead, the state's farmers cobble together a living growing potatoes, blueberries, sweet corn, or apples. Or they might run dairy farms, poultry and egg farms, raise cattle for meat, grow organic vegetables, tap maple trees for syrup, and sell the hay from their fields for a little extra income. There are other specialty farms too, including mushroom and hemp, hops for the burgeoning craft beer brewing industry, sheep or alpaca farms, even ostrich and buffalo farms—and of course in a state whose heritage is roped to the sea—oyster, mussel, and seaweed farms.

Back in the day, the Card family used to run a small sawmill as well, cutting down the trees on the property, but they quit that years ago. That's another natural commodity that Maine has in abundance though, and many other landowners have kept up the practice. In fact, with 89% of its landmass blanketed by forest, it's the most heavily wooded state in the country, and lumber products continue to be one of its most valuable exports.

You don't get rich stitching together a living off the land in a small town in Maine. But you do create another kind of wealth, and when you plant roots in a place like Bowdoin and stay for a long time, your family name carries some currency. That's certainly true of the Card family. It's hard to know how much this will change after what a native son did on October 25th, 2023. There's no doubt that the family and town's history post-2023 will always be tied to that date. As for the spoken history of the Card family in town, only future generations will know the answer to that. It's a question that hangs like a millstone around the neck of a proud family whose son, brother, and father did a horrific thing that they'll never fully understand. The immediate family will suffer the impact the most, but it will reverberate throughout the extended family as well. Card's siblings, Ryan and Nicole, are both married and have children. The family tree extends its roots even deeper into the community with aunts, uncles, cousins, etc.

They're all struggling to come to grips with what Robbie did, while also grieving the loss of the person they remember, not the one who did this terrible thing. They know the pain he's caused so many others is indescribable, and nothing they can say or do will change that.

Some are relying on their spiritual faith to get them through. Others don't have that, and they're simply not equipped to deal with the emotional fallout, especially as the months go on and the steady drip of revealing news about the response of local law enforcement and the Army Reserve continues.

On a Saturday morning in mid-March of 2024, nearly five months after the shootings, the *New York Times, Boston Globe, Associated Press, CBS, NBC, CNN,* and countless others have published lengthy stories about an interim report released by an independent commission formed by the Maine governor to examine the details of the crime. This came a week or so after the results of Card's brain study were released by the Concussion Legacy Foundation on behalf of the family, which also received national media coverage.

So, it's unlikely that Bowdoin residents will ever hear the family's name and not automatically think of what Robert Card II did to all those innocent people in Lewiston and why he did it. In small towns like Bowdoin, residents can lay low, especially in the winter, and stay under the radar if they're so inclined. But there is an opportunity to rub shoulders with your neighbors if you want at church, Bowdoin Central School activities, the annual town cleanup, or civic gatherings, like the annual town meeting every March.

There are also weekly selectmen's meetings on Mondays at 6:30 p.m., where a three-member elected board oversees the affairs of the town. There, in the simple white Bowdoin Town Office building, the board discusses everything from a telecom tower proposal to the deadline for printing the town report, to a letter a resident sent objecting to the location of the snow plow turnaround. Or they might get a report from the Road Commissioner, which is arguably the most important job in town. It's by far the one with the biggest budget. The job was held by Wendall Card Sr., a distant family relative, for many years before he passed away at age eighty-one in June 2023.

His son, Wendall Jr., stepped into the position. He's as dedicated to the job as his father. Even if he has nothing to report, he'll come in to say so, as he did on February 6th, 2023, which the selectmen's meeting minutes indicated with the note, "Jr. Card just came in to check-in. He has no issues."

He was back again on October 30th, just five days after his relative committed his horrible crime. This time it was to talk about the sand and salt contract for the upcoming winter, and to explain that the truck driver who was hauling the salt to the town's sand and salt shed inadvertently opened the tailgate while he was driving down the road, dumping some of the contents onto the pavement. The same driver then took down some electrical wires when he raised the dump bed.

The official meeting minutes don't reveal any of the off-color comments about that driver's abilities that surely followed. Nor do they mention any discussion, if any occurred, about the events of October 25th, or the death of a native son two days later. Like the suppressor Robert Card tried to buy in August, the shock was probably very effective at dampening any public discussion in town. Plus, true Mainers don't like to air their dirty laundry in public.

For a small town that rarely got a mention outside the town limits, 2023 put Bowdoin on the map for all the wrong reasons. It happened twice, in fact. The first time was April 18th, when thirty-four-year-old Joseph Eaton shot his parents and their friends, a couple in their sixties and seventies, to death in the family home on a quiet back road. After gunning them down, he drove to an overpass above busy Rt. 295 and shot at passing cars, striking one and wounding a family of three inside.

Eaton had been released from Windham Correctional Facility only four days before, after serving a sentence for aggravated assault. His mother, whom he described as a "saint," had picked him up at the prison, bought him some new clothes, and brought him home. After he killed the four of them, he left a note and posted a rambling Facebook video alluding to the trauma he said he suffered as a result of being molested as a child.

It was a shocking multiple murder in a state that rarely sees them. The Eaton murders received heavy local media coverage and ultimately sparked a renewed call for tighter gun control laws, even though Eaton had stolen the guns used in the shootings from his parents' friends, and no law could have prevented that. Ultimately, a legislative bill proposing background checks for private gun sales died in the Maine Senate months later before the Lewiston shootings.

Twenty-two Mainers killed at the hands of two Bowdoin men in a single year. It sounds like the plot twist for a Stephen King horror story, not reality. As far as years go, it was an unbelievably bad one in the small town. But it was even worse in Lewiston.

# "WE HAVE ANOTHER ACTIVE SHOOTER AT SCHEMENGEES"

David and Kathy Lebel have owned Schemengees Bar & Grille in Lewiston for over twenty-five years. If they had a nickel for every time someone asked, "Where did that name come from?" they might be retired by now.

The answer is they inherited it when they bought a Lisbon pool hall for $25,000 in 1998 and moved it to Lewiston. The previous owner apparently bore an uncanny likeness to the actor, Eugene Levy, who was one-half of a fictional polka-playing duo called the Schmenge Brothers. He and the other half, John Candy, were popular late-night comedy show guests for the five or six years they kept the act running.

In 2007, the city of Lewiston bought out the lease from their early Lincoln Street location and floated them a block grant loan for a new location in order to build a storm cistern between the street and the Androscoggin River. After a long search for a location, the Lebels moved Schemengees to a new site a couple of miles up the street.

The site is located on a long straightaway on Lincoln Street, which runs parallel to the Androscoggin River, just a long cornhole bag toss away from the low-slung, long rectangular building. Painted light blue, the building was formerly a machine shop, which explains why it looks like it was plucked from the BIW shipyard in Bath and dropped on the spot. After the Lebels bought the 7600-square-foot building, they didn't do much of anything to the outside, but inside they added a full-sized kitchen, a dining room, and a full comfort food menu.

In addition to the ten professional pool tables they installed, they also added sixteen dart boards, and then, as the game gained in popularity, several cornhole boards, pitch boxes, and electronic scoring machines. Between all that and the twelve big screen TVs showing sporting events of every kind, it didn't take long for the new Schemengees to become a popular destination, no matter that most people still had a hard time pronouncing the name.

They also added a colorful twelve-foot-high, sixty-foot-long mural of various scenes of dogs as comic book-style pool hustlers. Painted by a famed local artist, the panels that make up the mural depict bulldogs lining up a shot, others watching with cigarettes hanging out of the corner of their mouth, and one ripping the felt cloth of a pool table with his cue when he leaned into the break. The mural belongs in the Louvre of pool hall art museums.

Just like Just-In-Time Recreation Center four miles across town, the business bread and butter for Schemengees was their leagues. Their members were the people who helped keep the lights on; the faithful who would show whether it was a cold, snowy January night, or a miserable, rainy October evening. It didn't matter whether they shot a ball, tossed a bag, or threw a dart; league night was a guaranteed couple of hours every week to play a game you enjoyed, have a couple of beverages, and spend time with friends while doing it.

On Monday nights, it was game-on for the dart league and the inhouse eight-ball pool league. Tuesday night brought a cornhole league, and Thursday night the independent billiard league. Wednesday night, the tail end of hump day for the mostly working-class patrons at Schemengees, was a second slot for the cornhole league, as well as the Maine Valley Pool League, which drew teams in from Lewiston/

Auburn, Brunswick, Waldoboro, and elsewhere in southern, central, and mid-coast Maine.

Some of the players in the cornhole league were affiliated with the American Deaf Cornhole Association, others with the regional New England Deaf Cornhole League. Cornhole has become a popular sport for deaf people across the country. In Maine's tight-knit Deaf community, many had gone to school together at the Baxter School for the Deaf on Mackworth Island near Portland, so gatherings like the cornhole league were a great way for them to stay connected to each other.

The Wednesday night cornhole league at Schemengees kicked off at 6:30, the pool league at 7:00. By the start of the pool league, the dinner rush was usually winding down, but the bartenders, and oftentimes Schemengees' manager, Joe "Cue Ball" Walker, would be pulling pints of the twenty-two beers on tap.

On Wednesday, October 25th, just after 7:00, while the pool players were lining up the eight-ball and doing their best to avoid a scratch, and the cornhole players were doing their best to land an "airmail" or "cornhole" and avoid throwing a "grasshopper" or "screaming eagle," a white 2013 Subaru Outback with a distinctive black bumper pulled into the crowded parking lot.

The man who got out had been there many times before. He played in cornhole tournaments there for years. Though he wasn't particularly well-known, he did form some relationships there. In fact, he had met a woman there the year before at a competition and they had dated for a few months until they broke it off the previous January.

He wasn't dressed for a night of cornhole though. On this night the man who got out of the car was dressed in dark tactical-style pants and a brown sweatshirt. He removed a Ruger SFAR semi-automatic rifle from the car and made his way to the entrance. He left the car engine running. Then, as friends ate, drank, chatted, and competed inside, he calmly opened the door, stepped inside, and opened fire.

The first call that came into the Lewiston-Auburn 9-1-1 Emergency Communications Systems left little doubt about what was happening: (*Some conversations condensed*)

\*\*\*

**7:07:20:**

*Get to fucking Schemengees Bar & Grille right now. There's a shooter.*

(The dispatcher yells out, presumably to the other dispatchers in the room.)

*Hey, we have another active shooter at Schemengees. We're getting 9-1-1 calls flooding in now for that.*

**7:07:20:**

*I'm in the field hiding. I have a man that looks like he's shot to me. He looks like he's at least in his thirties. I think he's deaf. He's been shot in the arm.*

*9-1-1: Use a piece of cloth, wrap it around tightly and form a tourniquet until the ambulance can get to you.*

**7:07:20:**

*Schemengees Bar & Grille. There are many people injured.*

*9-1-1: Are you injured?*

*No, I'm not injured. I'm right next to someone who is injured though.*

*9-1-1: Okay, where are you?*

*Under the pool table.*

9-1-1: *Where are they bleeding from?*

*Uh, I really can't tell. It's dark in here.*

9-1-1: *Okay. I need you to grab a dry clean cloth, if you can find one. If not, honestly any cloth will do at this point. I want you to wrap up wherever he is bleeding from, keep pressure on the wound. Where are you located?*

*I'm right next to him. I'm under the pool table right now.*

9-1-1: *Under the pool table?*

*Say that again, I'm talking through my watch.*

9-1-1: *No, that's okay. Under the pool table with wounded, understood. We have officers en route, okay.*

*All right. Thank you.*

**7:08:16:**

9-1-1. *What's the address of your emergency?*

*Schemengees Bar and Grille, Lewiston, Maine. Active shooter,*

9-1-1: *Okay. Can you give me a description of the person?*

*Uh, tall, white, male, uh, dark clothing, hooded, jeans. That's all I could get. He walked in the door.*

9-1-1: *Okay. Anybody hurt that you know of right now?*

*I have no idea. I'm outside. Bullets are still going off right now. I would assume there's people dead.*

9-1-1: *Okay. All right. So we're going to be on the way over there, okay? Where are you right now?*

*I'm outside by the dumpster. I can't leave. My keys aren't here.*

9-1-1: *Okay. We have help on the way, okay?*

*Okay. He's still—he's still shooting. People are hurt.*

9-1-1: *How many—how many total?*

*I have no idea.*

9-1-1: *How many shots have been fired?*

*(Whispering) I'm sorry, hold on—probably twenty.*

9-1-1: *Okay. All right. We're on the way, sir, okay?*

**7:08:16**

9-1-1. *What's the address of your emergency?*

*I don't know the address, Schemengees Bar and Grille, Lewiston.*

9-1-1: *Okay. Do you have a description of the person?*

*Uh, no. I've been—I've been hit though.*

9-1-1: *Okay, where?*

*Uh, love handle. I think it's a graze.*

9-1-1: *Where are you located?*

*I'm in the parking lot. I need to find my wife.*

9-1-1: *Where in the parking lot? Are you near a vehicle, so I can get you help?*

*Yeah, red, red Silverado. There's no power.*

9-1-1: *Okay. Where is that person now? Still inside?*

*He took off, uh, uh, east towards, uh, I don't—I don't know which direction he went. He went up the hill.*

9-1-1: *All right. I want you to stay with me, okay?*

*Yup. I'm with you. I don't think I'm—there's a couple guys performing CPR on a gentleman right now. I need to find my wife. Is there—is it okay to go inside?* (To victim who approaches in the parking lot.)

Second Victim: *I don't know. There's a lot of people hurt inside.*

9-1-1: *How many?*

Second Victim: *The lights are out.*

First Victim: *The lights are out. I don't — hang on —*

Second Victim: *There's a lot.*

9-1-1: *Okay. Do you have an approximate of how many?*

First Victim: *Uh, one, two, three, four, um, five in the parking lot. I don't—I don't know how many more. Can't see anything.*

First Victim: *You okay?* (To Second Victim)

Second Victim: *Shot twice.*

Second Victim: *Me too.*

9-1-1: *Okay. How many people inside? You said there's five victims in the parking lot, how many inside?*

First Victim: *Uh, there's three people in the parking lot right now and, uh, there's twenty-two teams of two players playing cornhole.*

Second Victim (To First Victim): *Are you shot?*

First Victim: *Yeah, babe, I'm good. I'm good. I don't—I don't know. There's a lot—lots of casualties. I don't—I don't know how—a lot.* (To 9-1-1) *But, I have an officer here.*

9-1-1: *Okay. I'm going to let you go, okay?*

\*\*\*

Only a minute had passed between the first call from a survivor hiding under a pool table next to an injured man and the call from the injured victim in the parking lot. "He took off east, he went up the hill," the parking lot caller told dispatch.

As Card raced out of the parking lot and pointed the car toward his next destination, he left a horrifying scene of bloodshed behind. Ten people were dead or dying at Schemengees, ten others wounded. On its own, it would have been by far the worst murder scene in Maine history. Coupled with what he had just done at Just-In-Time minutes before, it became one of the worst in American history.

The bodies he left behind weren't statistics on a page though. To the rest of the world, they're now known as the "18 Lewiston shooting victims," just like the "58 Las Vegas victims," the "49 Orlando victims," the "27 Newtown victims", the "21 Uvalde victims," and so forth. But when it happens in your own backyard, those numbers have names. The names had lives, and they left behind lots of people who loved them and now grieve for their loss.

There at Schemengees, they were fathers, husbands, sons, and brothers. They had girlfriends and wives, sons and daughters, started and raised families, worked to support them, endured hardships, experienced triumphs and failures, wrestled with their own demons, loved their people the best they knew how.

And they had all come to a funky-looking, oddly-named restaurant and sports bar on the banks of a river in a Maine city that has weathered its own storms to spend time with their friends. That's where a deeply paranoid man finished doing what he had been telling people he was going to do. He "took care of it."

He shot and killed Joe Walker, the beloved fifty-seven-year-old manager of the restaurant who confronted Card and paid with his life. He shot and killed Keith MacNeir, sixty-four, who was celebrating his birthday by visiting his son from Florida. He was sitting at the bar, waiting for him to return from a union meeting.

He shot and killed Payton Brewer-Ross, a forty-year-old pipefitter at Bath Iron Works and the father of a young daughter, who had been playing cornhole with friends, and he shot and killed Ron Morin, fifty-five, the father of two, a longtime Coca-Cola employee and an avid athlete and cornhole player.

He shot and killed Joshua Seal, thirty-six, a father of four young children and a well-known ASL interpreter who had been playing in a cornhole league, and he shot and killed Seal's deaf friends, Bryan MacFarlane, forty, a commercial truck driver and avid outdoorsman, Stephen Vozzella, forty-five, a U.S. Postal Service employee and the father of two, and Billy Brackett, forty-eight, a multi-sport athlete, baseball coach, and the father of a two-year old daughter.

He shot and killed Artie Strout, forty-two, the father of a blended family of five kids who was playing pool in the Wednesday night eight-ball league. His father, Arthur Barnard, had just left the table ten minutes earlier. One table over, he shot and killed Maxx Hathaway, thirty-five, who was raising two young girls with his wife, with a third on the way.

When he was done, he left just as quickly as he came. Minutes later, overwhelmed Maine law enforcement officers would be frantically trying to find out who he was and where he had gone.

## Robert R. Card

April 4, 1983

Rob, Boob, Bob, Card

*Make your own rules.* –Varsity Blue. Watching varsity soccer and add activity's that followed. On beach w/ our cooler -PD RT GS KC KO RC JO SL. ? hunts-KC SL PD RC. Party's you should remember who U R. Football game's Junior's VS. Senior's. Paint ball games- RC PD MD GS JF KW TF SP NH LB MC JD CB. Friendly's crew you know how to make the best out of a bad situation. Car shopping. Swimming at the worst times- RT KC RC PD GS MH. Chilling at RT'S. Card's hill. RT's summer school trip. tennis ball baseball games at PT's. Pond hockey. Camping. Halloween. Corey water's house. Video games- MLB99, tony hawk, cruise n' world, James Bond 007. 41/2 ft I suite you.

*Robert Card Jr.'s senior yearbook photo for the Mt. Ararat High School Class of 2001.*

*Card and his son, Colby, at his wedding. He and his ex-wife, Cara Lamb, married in 2005, then divorced in 2007. Colby, now 18, lives with Lamb in a small oceanfront town on Maine's mid coast. (Photo courtesy of Cara Lamb)*

# FIRST SIGNS OF TROUBLE

Up until the beginning of 2022, there didn't seem to be anything much different about forty-year-old Robert Card II to most in his immediate circle of family, friends, and acquaintances.

For a man on the cusp of middle-age, he was in decent shape. He was six-foot tall and probably a few pounds overweight. Sitting in the cab of a truck for eight hours or more a day for fifteen years didn't help. He wasn't the same trim, handsome guy that his teenage sweetheart, Cara Lamb, married in 2005, but he hadn't gone to fat like so many guys his age either. He was starting to drink too much though, and that was bound to catch up to him at some point. But he was still active. Like so many men who grew up in rural Maine, he liked to spend time outdoors, to fish, hunt, go four-wheeling in the woods, and snowmobiling in the winter. He played in horseshoe and cornhole leagues too.

The ramshackle single-wide trailer he lived in on a wooded lot was only five miles from his family's home. Next door to the trailer is a large house he built single-handedly when was still married. The trailer was supposed to be a temporary home. He planned to move into the house with his wife and son, but the marriage ended abruptly, and he eventually sold the house and stayed in the trailer.

Card had a habit of bouncing from one driving job to the next for years when he signed on as a driver for a recycling company named Maine Recycling in Lisbon in February

2022. With a fleet of trucks, over one hundred trailers, and 50,000-square-feet of processing area, the company is one of the largest recycling businesses in New England, sending out drivers to pick up returnable bottles and cans at beverage distributors all over the northern tier of the region.

He would show up in the morning for work, get his pickup assignments for the day, then climb in the cab of his company truck, hitch up to a fifty-five-foot trailer parked in the overflow lot on the fifteen-acre facility, and head out on the road. By all accounts, it went well for the first half of the year, and it seemed like his job-hopping habit might come to an end.

But Colby, who had been living with him in his trailer, started dropping hints to his family that his father wasn't doing well, and it was beginning to concern him. That concern was heightened when Card asked him to move out so he could move his friend, Staff Sgt. Sean Hodgson, into his room.

It initially came as a surprise to Colby, but the warning signs had been present for months. He and his father were close over the years. They enjoyed fishing together in the many nearby lakes and streams, and they also spent time playing in horseshoe and cornhole tournaments in the area. But over the previous months, his father began to draw away from him and the rest of the family. He seemed to be receding inside himself, putting up a wall behind him as he did. That wall was the seemingly insurmountable belief that people were referring to him as a pedophile nearly everywhere he went. By the time he told his son to move, he had almost completely bricked himself off from his family.

The only person he allowed inside was Hodgson. Card and Hodgson had served together in the Army Reserve since 2006. They first met in the 439th Quartermaster Company unit based in Somersworth, New Hampshire, which is just over the border with Maine, and then for the last six years in Bravo Company of the 3-304th.

They bonded quickly, Hodgson said in a phone conversation in mid-March of 2024. They partied together in bars in Dover, New Hampshire, and discovered that they had mutual interests in cars, working with their hands, and bowling. The fact that they were both honest, no-bullshit kind of guys was probably the glue that held their friendship together, Hodgson said. He called him "Sergeant Card," Card called him "Hodge," and they would be in and out of each other's lives for the next seventeen years, depending on circumstances. With Hodgson now staying in his bedroom, Colby went to live with his mother in a coastal town about a forty-five-minute drive away.

Sitting in a bakery/coffee shop located just a five-minute drive from where the two first met as teenagers while working at the now-defunct Friendly's Restaurant in Brunswick's Cook's Corner, Cara Lamb talked about their relationship, and then the acrimonious sixteen years that followed their divorce.

They met when they were both teens working at a Brunswick restaurant. He was a year older, tall and handsome, and she was "young and dumb," and in puppy love. She went to Brunswick High School, and he went to Mt. Ararat in Topsham, but that wasn't the only difference between them. Cara was adopted by a family who owned a local lumberyard for generations, while he came from a farm family. Everything he and his siblings had, they worked for. His father, who also worked for a local electrician, preached the value of hard work and self-reliance, which meant that if any of them wanted to go to college, they would need to pay for it themselves.

This difference in their backgrounds was something he would never let her forget, Cara explained. It didn't matter to him that she is hard-working by nature, and her personality is about as far from entitled as any you can imagine (the author's opinion, not hers). She works in the kitchen of another area restaurant now, she's inked up, swears more than a sailor, and tells it as she sees it. She'd be the last asked to join a sorority, which would probably be just fine by her.

But still, back then she thought she was in love, and they dated for a few years before marrying the same year she gave birth to Colby. It didn't take long for her to realize she had made a mistake, especially when she would suggest they go to marriage counseling to try and get past their differences, and he would wave her away, asking what he would learn that he didn't already know.

He was incensed when she eventually told him she wanted a divorce, Cara said. Over the sixteen years since his opinion of her never changed. He could just never let go of the anger he felt at her for severing their relationship, she said. Their post-divorce years were bitter, and they never really improved. But they raised their son together— although she would contest the use of the word "together" to describe their parenting approach.

The last time she saw him was in early summer of 2023 at Colby's high school graduation. He still wouldn't look in her direction or speak a word to her. This was a good thing too, because just a few weeks earlier she and Colby had spoken to a Sagadahoc County sheriff's deputy about the mounting evidence that he was having some kind of psychotic break. Neither one of them wanted him to know they had spoken to law enforcement about him for fear he would explode.

That conversation happened on the morning of May 5th, 2023, when Colby and his mother went to see the school resource officer at Mt. Ararat High School. The officer, Gabrielle Mathieu, is a member of the Topsham Police Department assigned to the school. A graduate of the police academy seven years prior, she replaced a forty-seven-year-old officer in 2021 after his arrest and subsequent guilty plea to a misdemeanor assault charge in relation to a sexual relationship he had with a student at the school. He ultimately resigned from the force and was decertified as a police officer, and Matthieu took his place.

Although it's located in a Maine town with a population of under 10,000, Mt. Ararat High School, which is named after the 240-foot hill behind the school, isn't immune to big city violence. At the beginning of the school year, a group of parents sent a letter to the school's principal expressing concern over violent incidents involving students, including one in which a student pulled a gun on another at the local fairgrounds.

Officer Mathieu would be the first Maine law enforcement member to hear of Card's increasing paranoia. Given that he lived in Bowdoin, she called the Sagadahoc County Sheriff's Office and asked that they come and talk to Colby and his mother at the school office.

Deputy Chad Carleton, a fifty-three-year-old officer in the office's patrol division, answered the call later that morning. Carleton began his very detailed 1300-word incident report by saying that he sat in Mathieu's office and "learned a bit about Robert's life."

Together with his mother, Colby told Carleton and Mathieu that around the end of 2022, his father began hearing voices when they were out in public. When he would tell Colby that people were talking about him, his son tried to assure him that no one in their vicinity was even looking at them, let alone talking about him.

The comments he thought he was hearing were always derogatory remarks about him being a pedophile. Colby said this continued for months, and when he stopped by his father's trailer in Bowdoin a couple of weeks before, he got very angry and accused Colby of saying similar things behind his back.

Cara confirmed his account, saying that she was concerned about Colby spending time with him, especially since he had gone to his brother Ryan's house and taken possession of ten to fifteen handguns and rifles that were stored there. Although he hadn't seen his father do anything threatening with the guns, Colby said, he and his mother did not want him to know that they had spoken with law enforcement for fear it would aggravate the situation.

They told Carleton that the extended Card family was aware of his deteriorating mental health, but their efforts to talk to him and get him to seek help were in vain because he was locked into denial. Because he was resistant to any offers of help, and they didn't want him to know about their discussions with the SCSO, Carleton said they all agreed that the "best avenue of getting Robert some help" was to talk to his Army Reserve command. Cara agreed to reach out to Card's sister-in-law Katie, a registered nurse and trusted friend of Robbie's, and after Carleton gave Cara his card they parted ways.

Carleton then began making calls to the Army Reserve Center in the small southern city of Saco. The sheriff's deputy connected with an administrator at the center, who then provided him with the cell number for First Sgt. Kelvin Mote, a senior NCO in the 3-304th who was Card's Bravo Company squad leader. Mote is also an Ellsworth police officer, the administrator told Carleton, adding that various members of the unit were aware of Card's deteriorating mental health and were concerned for him.

After leaving Mote a voicemail, Carleton called Cara Lamb back to update her, and she in turn told him she spoke with Ryan Card, his brother. He told her that he was aware that Robbie was drinking heavily and had made "angry threats about having to shoot someone."

Carleton ultimately spoke to First Sgt. Mote and the Bravo Company soldier mirrored Colby Card's account of his father's behavior, saying that he had accused members of the unit of calling him a pedophile. Still, he told Carleton, he wasn't aware of how bad Card's condition was, and he was happy Carleton called when he did, because the unit had an upcoming training session that would involve using firearms and grenades. He would call Captain Jeremy Reamer, his commanding officer, Mote said, and "figure out options to get Robert help."

Deputy Carleton then fielded a call from SRO Mathieu, who asked him to call Ryan Card. When he did, the forty-year-old former U.S. Army Ranger told the deputy that he hadn't been aware that Robbie had taken the guns from the family home, and he was concerned about the volatile mix of his brother's heightened paranoia and the firepower he now possessed.

Ryan then told Carleton that his brother's paranoia had started in earnest back in January, right around the time that he started using hearing aids. It had gotten progressively worse since. Robbie had just told him that day that he was going to hire a lawyer to "deal with the people" accusing him of being a pedophile.

The deputy then offered to go with Ryan to speak to Robert, but, like Colby and Cara Lamb, Ryan was concerned that the presence of law enforcement would "exacerbate the conversation." Instead, they agreed that involving Robbie's Army unit was the best idea and that Ryan would contact Deputy Carleton if he believed his brother was an imminent danger to himself or others.

Intrigued by Ryan Card's mention of the hearing aids coinciding with his brother's paranoia, Deputy Carleton went online and did some research. His finding: "I found that hearing loss induced mental illness is a documented condition that can project itself in paranoid behavior."

The next day, Carleton called Cara Lamb to see if she had an update. She told him that Ryan and his sister, Nicole Herling, had gone to see Robbie the night before and spent about ninety minutes with him. He answered the door holding a handgun and complaining about people casing his house.

But otherwise, the conversation went well, Cara recounted, and he agreed that he would go see a doctor about the paranoia and "voices he was hearing." Nicole, Cara told Deputy Carleton, also had a nursing background, and she too had "done some research on the hearing loss/ mental illness connection and believes there is likely a connection."

Their conversation ended with Cara telling the deputy that Ryan and his sister would make sure their brother went to the doctor and that the family wanted to stress that they didn't want Robbie to know they had been talking to law enforcement and the Army. Carleton said he would pass the word.

Deputy Carleton concluded his lengthy interaction and subsequent report by calling First Sgt. Mote to fill him in on everything he had learned. Mote, in turn, assured Carleton that "their plan was to sit down with Robert in the near future and see if they could get him to open up about what has been going on."

The deputy's last sentence in the report was, "I specifically warned [Mote] about the fact Robert had allegedly answered the door with a gun in his hand."

*Army cadets engage in live fire grenade exercises at West Point. (Photo courtesy of Department of Defense)*

# PART-TIME SOLDIER

After graduating from high school, Card had gone off to the University of Maine-Orono to study engineering. Orono was about a two-hour drive from Bowdoin. It would be the first—and ultimately last—time that he would put some distance between himself and his hometown for a prolonged period. It wouldn't last long though. He was back home after a year. The stress of having to pay his own tuition and keep up with classwork was too much, so he returned to Bowdoin ready to pull the pin on Plan B, which was to enlist in the Army Reserve. Not only would he make some money and accrue some benefits that could help with college down the road, but he would also be answering the call to serve that resonated in the country after the 9/11 attacks on the World Trade Center towers and the Pentagon building.

Like everyone else who enlisted in the Reserves at the time, he was told that deployment to a combat zone was all but guaranteed. The war in Afghanistan was well-established by 2002, and the Bush Administration was making its pitch to invade Iraq in front of the United Nations General Assembly by then as well. Why Reserves instead of active duty? After all, his older brother Ryan had opted for Army active duty and ended up doing four tours in Afghanistan and Iraq with the elite 75th Rangers Regiment.

Well for one, he and Cara were an item, and leaving Bowdoin meant leaving her. Secondly, he wasn't the hard-charging guy that his brother was. He was quieter and more reserved; he would be the one to snuggle up with his mother as a little boy and watch TV, while Ryan would be outside raising hell of some kind. The Reserves just seemed like a better fit for Robert, Cara believes.

The Army Reserve force was formed in 1920, right after the end of World War I hostilities. It was created as a stopgap measure to maintain a ready fighting force after the Army released three million soldiers from service between 1918 and 1919. It's been dismantled, reorganized, reshuffled, and tinkered with ever since, but Reserve soldiers have been engaged in almost every military conflict we've been involved in since its inception.

By the time that Card signed an eight-year enlistment contract in late 2002, it had a complement of 205,000 soldiers in 379 units across the country. The Reserves are often confused with the Army National Guard, but the Guard operates in every state in the country and is commanded by each state's governor, with limited federal intervention, whereas the Reserves are under direct operational command of the U.S. Department of Defense.

Reserve members are expected to attend drills one weekend a month at their unit's facilities and an annual two-week continuous training exercise. This schedule is the reason why they've been referred to as "weekend warriors." The term might sting new members, but if they're smart, they learn to laugh it off and take advantage of the health insurance, educational assistance, skills training, and discounted pricing for goods at military commissaries that come with enlistment.

Reserve soldiers certainly don't join to get rich. A first-year private with full drill attendance makes just over $4,000 annually, while a Sgt. First Class with twenty years of service—Card's status when he died—earns just shy of $8,500. Still, as little as those amounts might sound to many, it helps pay the bills for the mainly working-class Americans who enlist in our country's armed forces. All

Reserve recruits attend the same basic training as active-duty soldiers. Their boot camp isn't dumbed down or any less physically demanding, and the drill instructors whose job it is to break a recruit down and then help build them back up, don't soften their language or demeanor for a 'weekend warrior.'

In December 2002, as winter in Bowdoin settled in for a prolonged stay, the nineteen-year-old boarded a commercial aircraft for the first time in his life for the trip to the milder climate of Fort Benning (renamed Fort Moore in 2023) on the Georgia-Alabama state line for ten weeks of basic training. In addition to providing basic training for 80,000 recruits per year, the base, one of the Army's largest and most crucial to its mission, also trains the Army's Airborne and Rangers, and hosts the Officer Candidate School (OCS).

After completing basic and officially becoming a U.S. Army soldier, Card went to the Quartermaster School at Fort Gregg-Adams in rural Virginia. Like Fort Benning, the Army renamed the base in 2022 from its original name of Fort Lee. There he would spend eleven weeks completing his Military Occupational Specialty (MOS) training.

He had opted to become a Petroleum Supply Specialist. That MOS pretty much guaranteed that he would never see combat if called to active duty. The Army's description of this job says it requires "the handling and distribution of petroleum products. A Petroleum Supply Specialist supervises or receives, stores, accounts for and cares for, dispenses, issues and ships bulk or packaged petroleum, oil and lubricant products." Short of lighting it afire, that accounts for pretty much everything one can do with a petroleum product.

Like every job in the military, that MOS, no matter how mundane, serves an important purpose. History-shaping battles have been won by the armies who found a way to provide a steady stream of ammunition, fuel, food, and other essentials to their troops. Fuel is clearly crucial for tanks, aircraft, supply trucks, and any number of other pieces of machinery that support and move an army.

"My men can eat their belts, but my tanks got to have gas," famed World War II General, George Patton, told General Eisenhower as his Third Army tore through Europe at a breakneck pace.

But for the individual soldier assigned to the unit, it's primarily a rear-echelon position, which means that if they ever ended up in a combat theater, they would likely be out of harm's way. Of course, there's no guarantee, and fuel trucks and depots are prime targets for enemy long-range ordnance, but the odds of returning home from a combat deployment unscathed are more in their favor than those of an infantryman.

After PS training, Card came back home to Maine to settle into the one weekend a month, two weeks a year rhythm of an Army Reserve commitment. The Reserves are constantly disbanding, consolidating, or relocating units and unit members, so transfers are not uncommon. When the Somersworth, New Hampshire unit, currently home to the 716th Engineer Company, relocated, Staff Sgt. Card found himself back in a unit on home soil. This unit, Bravo Company of the 3rd Battalion/304th Regiment of the 104th Training Division, is based at the Lt. Colonel Charles Butler Reserve Center in Saco. Lt. Colonel Butler, a West Point graduate, received the Distinguished Service Cross in 1950 for leading a rescue mission to save a trapped American unit in the Korean War. He was later killed in combat in Vietnam in 1973. The 3-304th is one of three battalions that make up the 3rd Brigade, which has its headquarters at Fort Belvoir in Virginia. The 104th Training (Leader) Division is based at Joint Base Lewis-McChord in Washington state.

Saco is a small city on the southern coast about an hour's drive southeast of Card's hometown of Bowdoin. Situated eighteen miles south of Maine's largest city Portland, Saco has a population of 20,000. It was, in its heyday, a thriving industrial center, with sawmills, textile mills, iron foundries, and leather goods manufacturers sited near the mouth of the 136-mile-long Saco River and the power-generating Saco Falls, where it empties out into the Atlantic.

Like Lewiston, Saco and its sister city of Biddeford attracted generations of immigrants to work in the mills, including a sizable French-Canadian population. Also, like Lewiston, the loss of the manufacturing base struck Saco and Biddeford hard. It's a familiar tale for river mill cities and towns all over New England. From Nashua, New Hampshire, to Winooski, Vermont, from Holyoke, Massachusetts to Pawtucket, Rhode Island to Waterbury, Connecticut, the story is of boom to bust, and for some, a resurgence.

Both Maine cities have rebounded in the last decade. Saco maintains its working-class patina, but the mill renovations and the new restaurants and shops that have settled in its downtown have given it a spit and polish shine. Many of the mills now house small start-up businesses, condos, microbreweries, restaurants, and other commercial ventures.

Saco is also home to the General Dynamics Armament Systems plant, where the defense giant makes its Gatling guns, M2A1 .50 caliber machine guns, MK 47 40mm grenade launchers, and other weapons systems. The company is the city's largest employer, and with its massive Bath Iron Works shipbuilding plant churning out Navy destroyers in the city of Bath up north, one of the state's as well.

The seventy-four-man Bravo Company has participated in leader training at West Point for over a decade. The Army's historic military academy sits high on a bluff overlooking the Hudson River, about fifty miles north of New York City. It's one of the U.S. military's most iconic and historically relevant places. Since 1801, it has welcomed cadets to its brick-lined campus, many of whom would go on to become household names. That includes Generals Eisenhower, Patton, McArthur, Grant, and Lee—as well as seventy-six Medal of Honor recipients.

There, Bravo Company would fulfill their annual two-week commitment by training an average of 1200 cadets in the use of small arms, grenades, anti-tank weapons, and machine guns. Many of these cadets would end up assigned to lead small infantry fighting units, where mastering these combat skills is essential for survival.

Which means Bravo Company performed an important mission. On paper, they might not have appeared to be overly qualified, but looks can be deceiving. Army Reserve soldiers might be 'weekend warriors,' but that doesn't mean they always were. Bravo Company has several former active-duty soldiers who served combat deployments to Afghanistan and Iraq and then transitioned to the Reserves and law enforcement positions in civilian life. For example, their senior NCO was an Army Ranger who was heavily engaged in the 1993 firefight in Mogadishu, Somalia that was memorialized in the movie, *Black Hawk Down.* A number of other Bravo Company soldiers served on active duty and had combat deployments as well. These soldiers include the Sheriff of Oxford County, a deputy in the Androscoggin County Sheriff's Department, a lieutenant in the Brunswick Police Department, a corporal in the Ellsworth Police Department, a Maine State Police trooper, and a Rockland patrol officer. Bravo Company's commanding officer serves in the Nashua, New Hampshire Police Department.

With his MOS as a petroleum supply specialist and his civilian career as a truck driver, Card, on the other hand, didn't appear on paper to be as qualified to train cadets in the use of weapons. Particularly with grenades, which is ultimately what he ended up doing for a number of summers at West Point.

In a conversation in mid-March of 2024, his longtime friend and Bravo Company soldier, Staff Sgt. Hodgson, emphasized that reservists like he and Card were soldiers first, MOS second. They had been highly trained in combat tactics, weapons handling, marksmanship and all the other skills regular soldiers have, he pointed out.

As for Card's training experience at West Point, it's important, because there are valid questions about whether his longtime exposure to concussive grenade blasts was a cause of the traumatic brain injury (TBI) he was diagnosed with after his death. That injury, in turn, might have contributed to his increasing paranoia, auditory hallucinations, and ultimately, his homicidal impulse.

Every West Point cadet must throw at least one live M-67 fragmentation grenade during training. With 1200 cadets rotating through training every year, Card and his colleagues at the grenade training range would have been exposed to thousands of explosions during the eight years he was said to have participated in AT.

Could that exposure have been a reason for his hearing loss and a contributing factor to his mental health crisis? According to a *New York Times* report, a colleague of Card's in the same grenade-throwing training unit had to be pulled off the range in 2022 because of concerns over his mental health.[1] He was subsequently sent to a psychiatric hospital. As of December 2023, eighteen months later, he's still there, according to a family member of the soldier the Times reporter spoke to.

The Army isn't talking about anything related to Card. Given it's looking at the prospect of multiple lawsuits over their knowledge of Card's rapidly declining mental health in the months before the shooting and his threats to shoot people, it's easy to understand why they're so reticent. Especially since in April 2023, the U.S. government agreed to pay $144 million to the families of the horrific

---

1. *New York Times,* Did Army Blast Exposure Play a Role in Maine Gunman's Rampage? 12/11/2023

2017 Sutherland Springs, Texas shooting to settle lawsuits brought against the Air Force. This settlement offer came after a federal judge levied a $232 million judgment against the service. The judge found that they failed to notify the FBI on multiple occasions about the shooter's history of violence while he was stationed at a Texas air base. Had they done so, that information would have been entered into the National Instant Criminal Background (NICS) system and he would not have been able to legally purchase firearms, which may have prevented him from going on to kill twenty-six victims attending Sunday church service.

In the months after the Lewiston shootings, the Army has done what institutions tend to do when they feel threatened by the prospect of potentially damaging information seeing the light of day: They've slow-walked the release of records that they're legally obligated to provide under the Freedom of Information Act, and they've sought refuge under the cover of claiming they are conducting their own independent review.

In late February 2024, they finally released Card's service records, which included details about annual evaluations, promotions, and reenlistments, showing he received consistently exemplary annual evaluations praising his professionalism and ability to lead his squad. The records revealed he received an $8,000 reenlistment bonus in 2013, and in 2020 was promoted to Sergeant First Class.

His last evaluation in April 2023 was especially positive.

*SFC Robert Card is a consummate professional. He demonstrates the ability to train future leaders with great care for their safety and well-being. SFC Card has excelled as a squad leader, mentoring his troops to be among the best. SFC Card should be sent to his NCO system and promoted with his peers.*

What isn't mentioned in any of the records they released is his well-documented descent into paranoia in the last year of his life. There's no mention of the increasing fear his fellow soldiers—some longtime friends—had of him throughout 2023, including at the time of the writing of this evaluation. His immediate superiors were equally aware of Card's disturbing behavior. His April 2023 evaluation was submitted with the knowledge that his behavior was becoming a cause of great concern within the unit. It would have been written by Card's direct supervisor, First Sgt. Mote, and signed off by a "Senior Rater," in this case, Captain Jeremy Reamer, Bravo Company's commanding officer. Glowing assessment aside, their concern would deepen in the next six months as Card spiraled out of control. For the most part, that concern would stay in-house, surfacing only when his paranoia was too evident to conceal. By mid-September, the soldier who was recognized for "his ability to train future leaders with great care for their safety and well-being" became the soldier who everyone was afraid to be around.

# MAINE'S GUN CULTURE

Maine's national image may be its rocky coastline, lighthouses, and lobster rolls, but its 6000 lakes and ponds, 31,000 miles of rivers, and 17.5 million acres of forest land also make it a sportsperson's paradise. It's been that way since the state was established in 1820 as part of the Missouri Compromise, and given its distance from population centers, its 611-mile border with Canada, and its comparatively harsh winters, it will likely stay that way. Even with a predicted influx of new residents moving from regions more adversely affected by climate change, it will still be a great place to camp, fish, hike, canoe, kayak, and of course, hunt. As iconic an image as the lobster is for the state, L.L. Bean hunting boots, moose, and whitetail deer certainly rank near the top of answers in the Maine association word game.

As it was for the native Eastern Abenaki tribes who lived in Maine for 12,000 years before the arrival of Europeans, hunting has long been a way of life in the state. Outside of the state's few cities, it's embedded in the local DNA, passed down through the generations. In the leadup to November 2nd and the opening of deer hunting season for firearms, terrain gets scouted, blinds and stands go up, pulses quicken, and blaze orange vests and hats fly off the shelf faster than they can be stocked.

So, it should come as little surprise that Mainers are fond of their guns. To suggest banning some of them, or restricting access, or regulating any more than they already are is like suggesting taking nine-irons and drivers from golfers, rods from fishermen, or tents from campers. Let's just say that it wouldn't go over well at a Saturday night bean supper in Jackman, for example.

That's not to say all gun owners in Maine are hunters. In fact, the Rand Corporation research group estimates that 48% of 1.36 million Maine residents own a firearm, the sixteenth highest gun ownership rate in the country per population. With 207,000 paid resident hunting licenses issued in 2021, that works out to roughly 1 of every 3.5 Mainers using their firearm to hunt. While hunting made generations of Mainers comfortable with guns, there are plenty of Maine gun owners who purchased a firearm not to hunt, but to shoot targets or skeet at one of the dozens of rod and gun clubs around the state, or to blast away at cans out in a gravel pit or at rotting Halloween pumpkins lined up along a tree break. Or they might not even shoot at all, and simply keep a gun to protect themselves and their families. Despite having the lowest violent crime rate in the country, that is a talking point for firearms manufacturers and gun advocacy groups, and it resonates with some Mainers.

Everytown for Gun Safety, a prominent gun control advocacy group with an emphasis on producing data, ranks the state 25th overall for its gun control laws. It's a surprisingly high ranking, considering it gives Maine a 20.5 out of 100 overall score. In a state where gun ownership is freely accepted, you can expect that the laws in place to regulate it are fairly loose compared to most states with a legislature led by a Democratic-majority and a Democratic governor.

For example, Maine gun owners are not required to register their weapons, nor do they need a license or permit to own them. State law allows open carry everywhere but bars, schools, universities, courthouses, federal buildings, and state parks, and concealed carry does not require a permit. Private sales background checks are not required, there is no restriction on magazine capacity, owners are not required to report if their gun is lost or stolen, and there is no law enforcement notification requirement if a prohibited person tries to purchase a firearm.

Then, of course, there's the state's first-in-the-nation yellow flag law, its watered-down version of the red flag law used by twenty other states in the country. Although it's a stopgap measure that provides more benefit than the non-existent mental health reporting requirements of eleven other states, its efficacy has been called into question in light of the Lewiston shootings.

In addition to the wide acceptance of gun ownership in the state, another reason for Maine's less restrictive gun laws is one that was on almost every Mainer's lips when they heard about the shootings: *I thought it would never happen here.*

On October 17th, 2023, just eight days before Robert Card went on his rampage, the *Lewiston Sun-Journal* printed a front-page article touting newly released FBI statistics that showed Maine had the lowest violent crime rate in the country in 2022. The state's homicide rate of 2.2 per 100,000 population was nearly three times lower than the national average of 6.3. The national average for the other official violent crimes of rapes, robberies, and aggravated assaults was more than three times higher than Maine's.

Having a high rate of gun ownership and the lowest rate of violent crime is proof positive that Mainers are responsible gun owners, gun rights supporters say. They claim that gun control advocates fail to acknowledge that, and in doing so, relentlessly attack the Second Amendment rights of gun owners and try to solve the problem of gun violence with a one-size-fits-all approach. Consider Justin Davis, the state director for the National Rifle Association, and the interview he gave to *The Daily Wire* in April 2023 on Maine's lack of gun control and the low crime rate

*Maine has the lowest rate of violent crime in the entire nation.*

*Not one of the lowest, but the lowest. And, with the odd exception of slipping to number two here and there, that ranking has remained a constant for decades. This level of safety has been achieved with what most gun control groups call the weakest gun laws in the county. Desperate to prop up the 'you can't be safe without surrendering your rights' narrative, a handful of Maine politicians are pushing big-city gun laws guaranteed to sacrifice your freedoms and make it more difficult to defend yourself, your loved ones, and your homes.* [italics added]

Like so many other Maine residents when it came to mass shootings, it appears that Davis had a full-blown case of "it will never happen here-itis." It's hard to fault people for having that mindset. There were more murders in an average ten-day period in the city of Chicago in 2022 than there were in the entire state of Maine for the year. In fact, there were only nineteen homicides in Maine in 2022, which is one victim more than the number of people Card killed in a fifteen-minute span on October 25th, 2023.

In an October 17th, 2023 *Sun Journal* article, Darcie McElwee, the U.S. Attorney for the District of Maine, took note of the shooting that previous April that killed four people in the town of Bowdoin, and injured three more on a highway south of town when the gunman randomly opened fire from an overpass.

"We did see some very public violence, and that jarred us, because it's something we're not used to seeing," she told the paper. A Maine native herself, McElwee recognized that Maine wasn't immune to random senseless shootings. Little did she know what was to come just over a week later.

There were some who knew that Maine's perceived immunity to mass shootings would inevitably wear off at some point, and it wasn't if, but when, it would happen.

Like Professor Michael Rocque, a sociology professor at Bates College, which is located just two miles from Just-in-Time Recreation Center. Professor Rocque has researched mass shooting incidents extensively, and he had publicly predicted before the Lewiston shootings it was only a matter of time before Maine joined the ranks of mass shooting sites in the United States.

As gun rights advocates like to point out though, it's not the gun, but the person who commits the crime. True enough, but if you want to own a gun, you need a place to buy it. That's not a problem in the state of Maine. According to Bureau of Alcohol, Tobacco, and Firearms data, there are 474 federally licensed firearms (FFL) dealers in the state. That's one for every 35.4 people per 100,000 population, the 13th highest rate in the United States. For perspective, Wyoming is number one at 97.4 per 100,000, while New Jersey is 50th at 3.5 per 100,000. Not all these FFL dealers have storefronts though. In fact, most don't. Some are inactive, some work the gun show circuit, others are pawn shops that are required to obtain a license to trade in firearms. It's hard to know how many actual gun stores there are in the state because the ATF database doesn't provide that breakdown.

That's true on the national level as well, where claims by gun control advocates that there are more gun stores in the United States than McDonald's, Subway, and Wendy's fast-food restaurants combined get passed around on the media grapevine. It's a headline-grabbing claim, but they're counting FFL dealers, some with post office boxes listed as their address, not storefronts where people can walk in and shop for a firearm. But there's no question it's simple to find one. Of the 474 FFL dealers in Maine, it appears that roughly sixty have a physical location where someone could walk in and purchase a firearm. That figure comes from a roundup of gun stores listed on an online Maine hunting guide. Of the twenty FFL dealers in Lewiston and the five towns that touch its borders, the guide shows eight physical stores.

Like everyone else in the United States who purchases a firearm from an FFL dealer, Maine gun buyers are first subject to a criminal background check through the National Instant Criminal Background Check System (NICS), which is run by the FBI and operated out of a gargantuan 500,000 square-foot building in the hills of West Virginia. The NICS system was created in 1993 as part of the Brady Act, which mandated federal background checks on firearms purchases. It was named after James Brady, the White House press secretary for the Reagan Administration who was shot and injured in the 1981 assassination attempt on President Reagan.

Since then, it's served as the proverbial safety net for the balancing act of providing the public some level of safety, while respecting citizen's rights under the Second Amendment of the Constitution.

The mandatory background check process is fairly straightforward. To purchase a weapon from an FFL dealer, the purchaser has to fill out ATF Form 4473, which the dealer then electronically submits to the FBI to run through the NICS system. Form 4473 asks several very specific questions related to eligibility.

Depending on a variety of factors—including whether the applicant has a common name which could be confused for another applicant, whether a misdemeanor arrest was recorded properly by the law enforcement agency and adjudicating court, or even what day the application is submitted (Black Friday 2023 saw a record 215,000 background requests, for example)—a determination can come back in as little as a few minutes, or it may take the entire three-business day window allotted to the FBI to complete the check.

If the check isn't completed by then, the purchaser is automatically allowed by law to complete the transaction and take possession of the firearm. This three-day loophole is sometimes referred to as the "Charleston loophole," and its existence has been fiercely debated since 2015, when a virulently racist twenty-one-year-old man in South Carolina, Dylann Roof, was allowed to buy a firearm because his check had not been completed in time. He took possession of the handgun he purchased and then shot nine African-American churchgoers to death. Roof had been previously convicted of illegal possession of narcotics and the transaction would have been denied had it been processed in time.

According to NICS officials, that was one of many times the three-day window has slammed shut before a background check can be completed. In just one example, in a 2022 report, officials claimed that the Department of Homeland Security failed to respond to 59% of NICS inquiries in a two-year span from 2019-2021, resulting in hundreds of transactions proceeding without completed checks.

Since it was fully implemented in 1998, NICS has run 465 million background checks on gun purchasers from all over the country from its 100,000-square-foot computer room. In that time, it has issued 2.3 million denials nationwide for reasons such as previous felony criminal convictions, domestic violence conviction, an ongoing protection order, illegal possession of a controlled substance, dishonorable discharge from the military, or having been adjudicated for mental health reasons. In 2022 alone, NICS processed 32 million background checks nationwide, and issued nearly 132,000 denials. In the same calendar year, the system conducted 114,090 Maine background checks and issued 705 denials.

Buried in that mountain of background checks would have been one for a forty-year-old man from the small Maine town of Bowdoin to purchase a Ruger SFAR-10 semi-automatic rifle in July of 2023. He had no felony convictions or other disqualifying factors, and was, in fact, an active-duty Army Reserve NCO with a spotless record of twenty years of service. Given that, he cleared the background check, and the transaction was completed.

The next month, the same man tried to purchase a suppressor, or silencer as they're commonly called, from a gun store in Auburn. To do so, he had to fill out a separate Form 4473, because a suppressor is subject to the same background check as a firearm. On this form, he checked off the box that asks if an applicant has ever been committed to a mental institution.

A positive answer to that question is a disqualifying factor. The man had been committed to a twenty-day stay at a psychiatric hospital in upstate New York and had been released just the day before. His honesty was the only reason the transaction was denied, because his stay at the hospital hadn't been reported to the system. As it turns out, it wasn't a question of Card's honesty as much as it was the fact that his friend, Hodgson, advised him to check the box, because knowingly providing a false answer on the form is a felony offense, Hodgson told a commission panel established by Governor Mills in April, 2024.

This very limited look at these two transactions underscores what many believe are the inherent flaws in the NICS system. To lawfully deny a transaction based on the disqualifying factors, that information has to be entered into the system. To be entered into the system, it has to be reported properly—by law enforcement agencies, military branches, adjudicating courts, mental health facilities, etc. His involuntary stay at the Four Winds Hospital in Katonah, New York could have triggered that state's red flag reporting requirement, but that didn't happen. The only reason Card was unable to purchase the suppressor was because he self-reported. That level of honesty is surely the exception, not the rule.

The last two decades of mass shootings have left a trail of unreported disqualifying factors that should have prevented perpetrators from obtaining a firearm. That's not counting the loopholes that make buying a firearm at a gun show or in a private sale no more difficult than sending a text message, agreeing on a price, then meeting in a shopping mall parking lot to complete the transaction.

For example, the Virginia Tech shooter who killed thirty-two people in 2007 on the school campus had been ruled a danger to himself and others by a court, but that was never reported to the FBI to be logged into the NICS system. The 2017 Sutherland Springs, Texas church shooter should have been flagged multiple times by the Air Force for assault convictions and threats, but that never happened, which allowed him to clear background checks to purchase weapons used in the killing of twenty-two churchgoers. Due to his drug convictions, Dylann Roof should have never been able to purchase the .45 caliber handgun he used to murder nine people. The list goes on.

The failure of thousands of disparate institutions across the country to report disqualifying factors is troubling to say the least, but at least somewhat understandable. With a patchwork of various state laws dictating reporting standards, and HIPAA laws restricting the sharing of mental health information, it's hardly a surprise that countless transactions slip through the cracks. Only thirty-nine states have mental health reporting laws. Five permit reporting, but don't require it. Three require reporting to a state agency, but not the FBI. And three states—New Hampshire, Montana, and Wyoming—don't require any mental health reporting at all.

In 2022, NICS created a new file for Extreme Risk Protection Orders (ERPOs), also known as red flag orders. These are for orders issued by an adjudicating criminal or civil court restricting firearms for someone deemed a danger to themselves or others. But only twenty states currently have red flag laws. Of the remaining thirty, twenty-eight of them—Maine included—don't have the law, but vow to honor ERPOs issued by the others. Two states—Oklahoma and West Virginia—have anti-ERPO laws and won't honor the orders issued by other states. Ironically, West Virginia's economy benefits enormously from hosting the 3,000 FBI personnel who staff NICS and six other federal criminal information programs in Clarksburg.

That's just a few of the many choke points that restrict the flow of information needed to maintain an effective NICS system. Given the scale of the decentralized law enforcement, judicial, penal, and healthcare systems in the country, it's plainly evident that a quick fix isn't in the cards. There's no way of knowing how many disqualifying cases go unreported across the country because there's no centralized database. But what excuses are there for highly centralized, hierarchical institutions like the Department of Defense (DOD) who do not have an effective means of sharing information about their prohibited personnel? Why do the Army, the Navy, the Air Force, and the Marine Corps—all of which fall under the umbrella of the Department of Defense—fail miserably in meeting the reporting standards?

A 2017 DOD Inspector General's report laid bare the military's apparent inability to comply with reporting disqualifying factors to the NICS system. The Air Force failed to report in 14% of its cases, the report said. The Navy and Marine Corps were equally remiss in 36% of their cases, and the Army failed in a staggering 41% of its cases. If they can create branch-wide standards—and penalties for failing them—for everything from how to properly attach ribbons to a uniform to how to address a commanding officer, why can't they do the same for complying with standards that are designed to keep the public safe?

Coming as it did right before a bipartisan Senate bill called The Fix NICS Act of 2018 was introduced, the 2017 report revealed the giant holes in the system in the wake of the Sutherland Springs shooting. The Fix NICS Act called for penalties on federal agencies who failed to report relevant records, and offered incentives to states to improve their reporting. It was one of the rare gun-control bills that was backed by the NRA.

Senator Collins of Maine had jumped on board early in the bill's development by addressing a letter to the Secretary of Defense calling for a comprehensive review of the military's reporting system. As a 2017 *Time* article pointed out, researchers who had looked closely at the DOD's system a couple of years earlier had determined that the problem was that there was no standardized system of tracking prohibited personnel across all four branches. Instead, each branch relied on their own internal system, and generally had low-level employees inputting information, with very little in the way of checks and balances.

It was the second attempt to address flaws in reporting to the system in just over a decade. The 2007 NICS Improvement Act called for federal agencies to report prohibited persons to the Attorney General no less than quarterly. The legislative name change from "Improve" to "Fix" is probably a good indicator of how well the first attempt worked.

Has the second worked? There's ample evidence that state mental health reporting has increased sharply, and virtually every federal agency has made some progress. A 2022 Department of Justice report said overall records submissions to the NICS system increased 45% from 2018 to the end of 2022. By the end of the year, the three databases scanned by a NICS background check contained over 121 million records in total. Of the forty-five federal agencies the DOJ scrutinized in its semi-annual report, only one was not in compliance with the records submission requirements mandated by the Fix NICS Act. That agency was the Department of Defense.

Sometimes, federal agencies make every effort to comply with NICS reporting requirements, only to fall victim to the partisan warfare that so often defines gun-related policy. The Social Security Administration, for example, had barely implemented an Obama-era requirement to enter the names of everyone who was adjudicated mentally incapable of handling their financial affairs to NICS, but one of President Trump's first policy decisions was to remove that requirement in early 2018. He did so despite his oft-repeated claim that mental health issues are the major drivers of mass shootings.

That same issue arose again in 2023, when Republican Senator John Kennedy of Louisiana proposed an amendment to abolish the VA rule that mandated that veterans who have been adjudicated as mentally incompetent and needing assistance to manage their VA benefits should lose access to firearms and be reported to the NICS system. Military.com reports that there are 109,000 veterans who are affected by the rule.

The VA argued against Kennedy's amendment, saying that there was a correlation between suicidal ideation and the inability to manage benefits, and that lifting the rule would jeopardize veterans at risk and hamper its ability to reduce the number of veterans who commit suicide by gun. Also arguing against the abolishment, Connecticut Senator, Chris Murphy, (D) added that nearly one-third of the estimated 109,000 affected personnel have been clinically diagnosed as schizophrenic.

Despite their argument, the United States Senate voted, 53-45 in favor of abolishment. The vote took place on the afternoon of October 25th, 2023, just hours before Sgt. First Class Robert Card, an Army Reserve NCO who was clearly in the throes of a mental breakdown, went on his rampage. Maine Senators, Susan Collins and Angus King voted to abolish the rule. Two weeks later, the two sent a request to the Inspector General of the Department of the Army asking them to conduct a comprehensive review of the Lewiston shooting. They asked specifically for a review of the Army's policy of determining when to invoke a state's crisis intervention law to temporarily remove firearms from a soldier who is a danger to themselves or others, and for an explanation of what circumstances trigger the Army to report its personnel to the NICS system. The Army IG has agreed to that request.

However, neither Senator King nor Senator Collins nor their staff have responded to multiple requests for comment by the author on how they can begin to explain that review request considering their VA rules vote on the same day that one of their constituents was gunning down eighteen others in cold blood.

# THE YELLOW FLAG LAW

The halls of the ornate 1820's-era Maine State House in Augusta are bustling from January through June, teeming with elected officials, aides, lobbyists, news reporters, advocates for everything from climate change activists to the Girl Scouts, engaged Maine citizens attending committee hearings in person, school kids on guided tours, and tourists on days when inclement weather forces them inside.

Maine has a part-time legislature consisting of 151 members of the House and thirty-five Senators. There are also three non-voting House members representing the Penobscot, Passamaquoddy, and Houlton Band of Maliseet Indians, an arrangement that reflects the state's troubled history with its native citizens.

These legislators don't do the job and make the trek to the small city of Augusta for the money. For their efforts, they're only paid $27,000 annually, plus a meager $70 per day for lodging and $50 a day for food if they're from far-flung places like Madawaska, an Aroostook County town nearly five hours drive away. They're in line for a proposed pay raise to $45,000 though, which will be the first since 1999.

Like legislators in the other forty-nine states, they know that most of the work they do will fly under the radar for a majority of the public. Your typical public hearing for say, the Health, Insurance and Financial Services Committee, or the Appropriations and Financial Affairs Committee, will draw interested parties only, with maybe a stray spectator or two who came in by accident and are waiting for a break in the action to discreetly slip out.

If they're on the Criminal Justice and Public Safety Committee or the Judiciary Committee it's a different story. Every hearing day is game day for the thirteen legislators of these committees. This is the State House big leagues; the New York Yankees and Boston Red Sox of Maine politics, drawing sellout crowds while the other committees play to empty seats. The forty or so chairs in their assigned hearing rooms are routinely filled as legislators hash out proposed bills presented to the committees. They may be discussing expunging past marijuana convictions, approving a new District Court judge, or making yet another attempt to improve conditions at the Long Creek Youth Development Center, the state's only juvenile detention facility.

Among the myriad of issues they'll deal with over the course of a legislative session, there's one that's guaranteed to pack the room. When it's open for debate, spectators too late to grab a seat will have to wedge into the room, cheek to jowl, twisting their bodies sideways to try and find a pocket of space, and avoid elbowing their neighbor as they comply with the reminder to turn off their cell phones.

That issue is guns. If the proposed legislation has anything to do with "controlling" guns, be it an outright ban, a restriction, or a modification, you get the sense that some spectators would camp out in the marble hallway the night before if it were allowed. Thankfully, it isn't. Once the legislators finish with their interminable back and forth discussion, sticking for the most part to party lines, they open the floor for the public testimony part of the hearing. This is when anyone who feels like it—and remembers to bring thirteen copies of their thoughts on the subject to hand out to legislators—gets to go up to the lectern and have their say. Some strident and forceful, some trembling with nerves, they represent the 'for the people, by the people' model of our political system, and serve as a reminder that democracy can be both uplifting and a messy and tiring business.

The 2018 public hearing for LD 1884, *An Act to Create a Community Protection Order to Allow Courts to Prevent High-Risk Individuals From Possessing Firearms* in the Judiciary Committee hearing room is a good example. The bill was sponsored by then-Senator Mark Dion (D-Portland), the former Sheriff of Cumberland County, Maine's most populous. It was essentially Maine's attempt at creating a red flag law, which would have allowed family or other household members and law enforcement to petition the court for a temporary order to remove any guns from a person who presented an imminent or substantial high risk to themselves or others.

Other than a few provisions here and there, the bill mirrored red flag laws that have been enacted in nineteen other states in the country. The temporary order could be granted *ex-parte*, which means the subject of the order did not need to be notified beforehand, and it would last up to twenty-one days. In that period, the court was obligated to hold an evidentiary hearing to determine whether such an order could be extended for an additional six months.

The bill's co-sponsor was former House Speaker, Sara Gideon (D-Freeport), who gained brief national prominence with her run for U.S. Senator Susan Collins' seat in 2020. She was roundly defeated in that race, despite raising $68 million, the vast majority of which came from outside the state. She's dropped out of media attention for the time being, but her husband is in the news cycle now; he's an attorney representing some of the families of the Lewiston shootings in pending lawsuits.

For that bill's public hearing, sixty-one people offered testimony for or against the proposed legislation. Many were representing organizations—Maine Chiefs of Police Association, the National Rifle Association, the Maine

Psychological Association, Gun Owners of Maine, and the Maine Gun Safety Coalition, for example.

Many more were private citizens from all over the state. They came from the blue-collar paper mill town of Rumford, from the tony Portland suburb of Cape Elizabeth, from Beals, Surry, and Ellsworth on the Downeast coast. They were all massed together in a cramped, stuffy Victorian-era room, built back when a seasoned gun owner firing a Springfield Model 1816 rifle could squeeze off two to three rounds a minute, talking about laws that regulate weapons like a Ruger AR-10 semi-automatic rifle capable of firing 700 rounds a minute. Given all the arguments for and the arguments against the dozens of proposed gun-related bills over the years, these legislative discussions and public testimony are predictable.

As soon as a speaker says, "I stand in support of this bill," you know you'll hear about the litany of mass shootings in the country; Sandy Hook and Parkland, Uvalde and Las Vegas and Sutherland Springs, and well, stick a pin in a map of the United States and there's been a mass shooting within a hundred-mile radius of most of them. As soon as a speaker says, "I stand in opposition to this bill," you know you'll hear about the Second Amendment, about the lack of due process, about "the person kills, not the gun," about a mental health crisis that's causing all these shootings.

But LD 1884 threaded the needle between these two standpoints, and after a suggestion by then Attorney General, Janet Mills, to close some gaps in the ability of a court to remove weapons from people in outpatient mental health programs, the amended bill passed both the House and Senate and made it to the desk of Governor Paul LePage. A Lewiston native who traveled a hard road from childhood abuse and homelessness to the State House, the staunchly pro-gun and unashamedly blunt Republican vetoed the bill. He cited the lack of due process—the *ex-parte* provision in which a judge could prohibit a person from possessing firearms without their knowledge or their ability to contest. Procedural due process is entitled to every citizen, and it falls under the protection of the Fourteenth Amendment of the Constitution. This argument is still embedded in legal challenges to red flag laws. In fact, two New York Supreme Court justices cited that state's law as unconstitutional in a 2023 decision for that very reason, a ruling which has been appealed by the state.

With Senator Dion's bill dead in the water and the legislative session ending, the 128th Legislature would fail to pass a meaningful gun control law, something they had hoped to do in the wake of the Parkland School shooting in Florida earlier in the year. But then a newly-elected Governor Mills seized the reins, and one year later gun control advocates could claim a victory—of sorts.

When it comes to the issue of guns, Governor Mills has had to walk a very fine line since assuming office in 2018 and winning reelection against former Governor LePage in 2022. A native of the central Maine town of Farmington, she is a trailblazer in many respects. In addition to being the state's first female governor, she was also the first female criminal prosecutor in Maine and the first female District Attorney in New England.

Governor Mills grew up surrounded by hunters, and her early record as a state legislator representing her hometown reflects the influence that's had on her career as a politician. Maine ranks sixth in the nation for hunting licenses per capita (15.1 per 100) and is number one east of the Mississippi. Once outside of the metro area of Portland and some of the more upscale coastal towns, the percentage of the state's population that hunts goes up. Like other rural areas, in Franklin County, where Farmington is situated, camo and orange is the outfit of choice during the season. Like most urban areas, that outfit is more out of place in Lewiston, where residents tend to skew more to the left on gun control issues.

In her first three terms in Maine's House of Representatives, Mills received an A or A+ grade from the National Rifle Association, no small achievement for a Democrat. But, as a candidate in the Democratic primary governor's race in 2018, she was supporting calls for bans on assault rifles and high-capacity magazines. Predictably, her grade from the NRA plummeted to an F. Did Governor Mills really support those bans, or did she just say that to gain favor with voters to win the Democratic nomination?

Well, in a 2022 survey that the Sportsman's Alliance of Maine (SAM) presented to the candidates in the governor's race, she claimed to be opposed to a red flag law, opposed to background checks for private sales, and opposed to bans on assault rifles and high-capacity magazines. SAM is an influential organization in the state. It's been the public-facing voice of Maine's 300,000 hunters and outdoorsmen and women since 1975. It's decidedly less combative than the NRA, but it's no less effective in protecting gun owner's interests in the state. In fact, it's helped to "defeat hundreds of anti-Second-Amendment gun control proposals," SAM points out on its website, and it led efforts to amend the Maine Constitution to "guarantee the right for law-abiding citizens of Maine to own firearms, including the right that it shall never be questioned."

In her survey response to SAM, Governor Mills wouldn't be the first Maine politician to say one thing and mean another. She's a political pragmatist who grapples with the issue of gun control like Muhammed Ali did when he was up against the ropes; 'rope a dope,' bob and weave, slip the punch, win the round.

But then, so do the state's elected officials in Washington D.C. Congressman Jared Golden, who represents the "purple" second congressional district, was one of the few Democrats to oppose an assault rifle ban. One day after the shooting, the Lewiston native tearfully renounced that position, saying, "I had a false confidence that our community was above this, and we could be in full control." And of course, as noted in the previous chapter, Senators King and Collins have both toe-tapped their way around gun control issues.

Back to Augusta and the 2019 attempt to salvage the red flag law that Governor LePage had vetoed. Working directly with David Trahan, the executive director of SAM, and legislators from both sides of the aisle, Governor Mills helped craft a new bill and shepherd it through House and Senate votes, before signing it into law in June of that year. With the exceptionally cumbersome legislative title of, *An Act to Enhance Personal and Public Safety By Requiring Evaluations of and Judicial Hearings for Persons in Protective Custody Regarding Risk of Harm and Restricting Access to Dangerous Weapons,* the law cried out for a shorter, punchier name.

So, it became known as the yellow flag law, Maine's modified version of the red flag law. It was, and still is, the only state legislative attempt in the country to provide the due process that red flag opponents call for, and still serve as an effective tool in increasing public safety. At least that was the idea. With the requirement that a mental health professional make the call that a person presented an imminent risk of harm to themselves or others before someone's weapons could be removed, the major sticking point that a gun owner could lose the right to possess firearms without due process was removed.

Curiously, what seems to get little to no mention in the uproar about due process and Second Amendment rights is the fact that the state has had a statute for over twenty-five years that restricts firearm access for Maine adults in an *ex-parte* process. It's a civil protection order, or Protection from Abuse (PFA) orders as they're called in Maine. Recipients of PFA orders are barred from possessing firearms for the duration of the order, typically one to two years, but sometimes longer. There's a strong correlation between firearms and domestic violence homicides, so the PFA restriction has enjoyed universal support, including from SAM. In fact, a June 2024 ruling by a gun-friendly U.S. Supreme Court in a New York case affirmed that position.

But there are serious flaws in the Maine law that are ignored, including the fact that statutorily expanded definitions of abuse now include financial (i.e. withholding credit cards), and emotional (i.e. verbal abuse), are considered no different than documented physical abuse, threats, or intimidation in the eyes of the PFA law.

The PFA weapons restriction provision also doesn't consider the issue of false allegations of domestic abuse, which many legal practitioners engaged in the family law system—Maine judges included—quietly acknowledge is widespread, especially in divorce cases involving child custody and shared property. That knowledge has been deliberately concealed from the public by legislators however, and the end result is an untold number of weapons restrictions based on false allegations.[2] While this restriction has the full backing of SAM and other gun rights advocates, the prospect of a gun owner suffering a full-blown mental health crisis losing their right to possess a semi-automatic rifle capable of firing 700 rounds a minute draws their fervent opposition. It's an interesting paradox.

And so, Maine ran the yellow law up the pole, and politicians from both parties touted the state's pragmatic approach as a model of less restrictive gun control legislation that other states would do well to adopt. As the events of October 25th, 2023 demonstrated, it also created too many hurdles for local law enforcement to overcome. That's changed somewhat in light of the Lewiston shootings, but it still puts a heavy burden on law enforcement to clear those hurdles.

---

2. Maine Commission on Domestic and Sexual Abuse Report Pursuant to LD 1143, 2010 (minute notes on subcommittee meeting 12/9/2009 and survey results obtained in an FOAA request)

*Eight people died in the bowling alley, seen here from Mollison Way with the center's old name still mounted on the exterior. The entrance to the building is on the back side. (Photo by Robert Conlin)*

# "I'LL SEE YOU IN HEAVEN"

Samantha Juray had just gone into the kitchen directly behind the front desk at Just-In-Time Recreation to check on late dinner orders of chicken wings, burgers, nachos, and other menu items when she heard a loud banging noise. Thinking it might have been a balloon bursting or a piece of machinery breaking, she flung open the door to check.

She saw a dark-haired bearded man standing a few yards away. He was dressed in dark pants and a brown sweatshirt. Inexplicably, he was holding a rifle, the barrel pointed down towards the floor. He was having some kind of problem with it, she could tell.

Her brain scrambled to process the image in front of her. What was this man doing? Why did he bring a paint gun into the bowling alley? As she did, on the periphery of her vision, she saw two longtime bowling friends, Jason Walker, and Michael Deslauriers II, advancing towards him from the lanes over to the left of the desk. They were both hunched over and obviously in heightened states of alert.

Jason was headed directly towards him, while Michael swung around to approach him from the rear. They didn't say a word to each other that she heard but seemed to be working in tandem. Which wasn't surprising, because the two men, both fifty-one, had been best friends since kindergarten.

As they neared the man, Samantha saw something she'll never be able to erase from her memory. Jason tried to kick the rifle from the man's hands, but he was able to swing the barrel up and shoot him multiple times. Michael had gotten close enough to reach out and touch Card, but he then swung around and fired multiple rounds at him too. The lifelong friends both fell to the floor near each other. They grew up together as close to blood brothers as two unrelated men can be, and they died the same way.

Samantha's brain recorded a visual picture of the man as this happened. His eyes were stone cold dead, his face a blank mask. After a frozen moment of shock and disbelief, she spun around and ran back into the kitchen, grabbing two of the young kitchen staff and shoving them into the walk-in cooler with the admonition, "Stay here, do not come out, and do not open this fucking door for anyone. No one!"

The encounter was done, and over sixteen seconds after Card had walked through the door of the bowling alley, Kathleen Walker, Jason's wife, explained in a Facebook post four days before Christmas. The tight-lipped Maine State Police (MSP), lead investigators in the case, had notified her and Michael's partner, Stacey Cyr, of the details.

*After 8 long weeks, we were finally able to speak to officials from the Maine State Police about the evening of October 25, 2023. Since that fateful night, we have suspected that our significant others, Michael Deslauriers II and Jason Walker, best friends since kindergarten, died trying to save others. In the meeting, the State Police confirmed this to be true.*

The two couples were on lane sixteen that night, the lane closest to the door, bowling together as they often did. It was a normal session up until then. Two-and-a-half hours earlier, they had received a cheerful greeting from the Violettes when they came in the front door of Just-In-Time, and then a big bear hug from the manager, Thomas Conrad. Surrounded by friends, they were laughing and having a great time, she explained, and were just starting their third frame when they heard a single rifle shot.

Jason looked over towards the door, and then instantly screamed, *"GET DOWN, GET DOWN!"* He had always been fiercely protective of his wife and two sons. She knew instantly that he was serious. Stacey dove under the small table bowlers use to tabulate scores. Kathleen curled up around the ball return, which offered scant protection, but was the only object close enough to provide some kind of cover.

Maine State Police told her that Card's rifle had jammed after a single shot, which is why when Samantha Juray saw him, he had it pointed at the ground and was fiddling with it. Only nine seconds had elapsed since he had entered. It's apparently a common enough problem with the Ruger SFAR that there are YouTube videos addressing the issue, and online message boards like RugerForum.net have numerous complaints of similar jams with the rifle. Despite all the acclaim the weapon received from publications and web sites covering the gun manufacturing industry when it was introduced in late 2022, complainants say that a faulty gas regulator design causes the rifle to jam with certain types of ammo. Ruger is said to have since updated the regulator.

For all the talk of Card's firearms expertise, and the fact that he helped train West Point cadets for over a decade in handling and firing the Army's standard-issue, gas-operated Colt M4 carbine, it's surprising that he would not have recognized the possibility of a jam and made sure to field-test it before setting out on his carefully-planned mission. He had owned the rifle for nearly four months by that time. This is especially noteworthy considering a report that the Maine State Police released in early June 2024 indicating that Card had gone to a gun range earlier on the day of the shootings. One of the 3,000 heavily redacted pages the agency released to comply with FOAA requests, the report noted that he went with an unnamed friend, who said that he left because Card's demeanor was concerning. It's not clear who this friend was.

Michael Deslauriers and Jason Walker, a former member of the Maine National Guard, recognized the gun jam instantly and they closed the gap between themselves and Card and made their charge only seven seconds after the first shot. Tragically, it took Card slightly less time than that to clear the jam. Completely defenseless, they lunged at him in a desperate attempt to disarm him before he could hurt their wife and partner, friends, and the eighteen kids who were in the building. He shot Jason in the leg, and then pivoted and fired two shots at Michael. Then he turned back to Jason, shooting him in the head, and then firing two more bullets into his body. Kathleen Walker said later at a state inquiry that Jason had bullet graze wounds in each of his palms as well. Their incredibly selfless act of courage provided more time for the people in Just-In-Time to recognize what the sound of that single shot was, and to react any way they could. Kathleen, Stacy, their four combined children, and their circle of family and friends find some solace in that fact.

Kathleen's Facebook post on the shooting ended with a note on their grief but also about the impact of the two friends' bravery that night.

*It will never be known just how many lives could have been lost that night had these two brave lifelong friends not found the courage to confront this mentally disturbed man and attempt to disarm him. The critical seconds that Jason and Mike were able to occupy him provided time for others to hide, escape and find safety. We could not be prouder of their selfless acts of bravery.*

After killing Walker and Deslauriers, Card spent the next thirty-two seconds shooting people inside the bowling alley, the MSP told the women. Many of those who made it out or managed to find cover inside were able to do so because of the actions of the two men.

Justin Juray knows exactly what they mean. Because he was one of the lucky ones who was able to take advantage of their ultimate sacrifice. Had they not done what they did, the memorial that hangs on the wall of a refurbished Just-In-Time would likely be inscribed with many more names.

Justin was bowling with his father on a lane adjacent to the two couples. An avid bowler long before he was the owner, it was one of the perks of the job that both he and Samantha took advantage of when they could. Like Samantha, he was mystified by the sound of the first shot. As the business owner, his first thought was that a piece of machinery had come to a sudden and drastic end. In an industry with thin profit margins and expensive machinery, a sound like that could only mean bad news. He was standing on the platform that leads down to the lane when he heard the sound and looked over to see the barrel of a rifle pointed at the ceiling. A protruding section of the wall prevented him from seeing who was holding it. He found himself stuck in the spot for a few seconds trying to fathom what was going on. Then he saw muzzle flashes, and almost simultaneously clusters of people running for the single exit door some one hundred feet away.

Justin grabbed his father, who suffers from several health ailments and pushed him towards the door. He heard the first shot, but he doesn't remember hearing any more, not because there weren't any, but because his brain was trying to process so much disconsonant information, they simply didn't register. In the commotion of the race to the exit, he remembers things seemed to happen in slow motion. Then suddenly, he and his dad were stumbling out the door and running away from the building. Ahead of them, a ragged line of people were sprinting towards Mollison Way and traffic, lights, people, safety. In his mind, Justin's plan, if you could call it that, was to follow them. But his father, breathing hard and laboring, headed towards a nearby fence and dropped down at the base of it underneath a tree. Knowing it would be futile to try and get him up, the sturdily-built Justin laid down on top of him. He was instantly afraid that the shooter was going to see a bunch of targets out in the open and come out and mow them down. With no other way of protecting him, Justin covered his father as best he could. As waves of panic and fear washed over him, his thoughts flipped to his wife. Samantha, his best friend, his partner in life and business, was still inside. She had brought him a drink and was headed back towards the front a minute before the first shot rang out. He was sure she was dead. Laying there on top of his dad, he began to cry.

Danielle Grondin had come to bowl in the league with her partner, a Department of Defense analyst who had just returned from an assignment in an East African country after getting stuck in the middle of a military coup. After longtime employee Tricia Asselin gave her boyfriend a hug, Danielle went over to the small bar to get a beer and banter with Thomas Conrad, the manager of the bowling alley.

She had just sat down at a table near the lane and taken a sip of her beer when she heard the first shot. She looked over to see a man near the entrance with a rifle in his hands. It was pointed at the ground as he was doing something to it, then he raised it and she saw a green laser dot dancing on the rug. He was very calm and methodical. Maybe he's playing one of the arcade games located to the left of the entrance, she thought. Then he fired again.

She dropped to the ground, but her partner yelled, "No, get the fuck up and run!" A long-time gun owner, she looked over to see that the man was having issues with the rifle again. Her partner grabbed her and pulled her with him as they made a mad dash for the exit door at the far end of the building.

Tom Hatfield was with his girlfriend for his second week of bowling in the Apple Valley Golf League. They were bowling on the same lane against Tricia Asselin, who not only was a good friend of his, but also an employee at the golf club as well. He was standing in the lane, a ball in his hand, when he heard the first shot echo through the building. His girlfriend asked, "Is that a balloon?" He looked over and saw the rifle and the silhouette of the man holding it. He was clearly having a problem with it, Hatfield recognized. He dropped the bowling ball in his hand and ran towards the door. His girlfriend dove under a table.

Tricia Asselin's cousin, Tammy Asselin, was with her eleven-year-old daughter, who was bowling in the practice session with the Violettes, when the first shot went off. She froze, her brain unwilling to acknowledge what she could clearly see in front of her. She eventually was able to dislodge herself from the spot and follow the staggered groups of people dashing for the door as Card wrestled with the gun jam.

It was only when she was outside that she realized that her daughter was not with her. She panicked, and for the next hour she frantically sought information from anyone and everyone. Her phone was still inside, so she had no idea whether her daughter was trying to contact her. Finally, she got word that she had made it out with some other kids and some adults who led them to safety. Her daughter was able to reach her grandfather, telling him, "Pepe, I'm not dead."

It was a family affair for the Asselin's that night at Just-In-Time. Tricia's sister, Bobbi Nichols, joined her for the first time to bowl in the league. Tricia was a hugger, Bobbi said, so it took a while for her to greet everyone and introduce them all to her sister. They were bowling in separate lanes, and Bobbi would roll her frame, then go over to Tricia's lane to watch her. When she walked over to her lane just before 7:00 p.m. she found that Tricia had gone to the front desk to check on reports of a lane malfunction, despite the fact she wasn't even on duty. Bobbi heard the first shot just then, and as the reality of what was happening sunk in, she was pulled into the current of people making a dash for the door.

Two-and-a-half hours later, Samantha Juray came out of the building into a parking lot jammed full of emergency response vehicles and delivered her the horrible news. "I'm so sorry, she didn't make it," Samantha told her. Later, in the haze of her grief, Bobbi Nichols discovered the shooter was Robert Card II. She and Tricia had grown up in Bowdoin and knew the Card family. In fact, they had lived on West Road, the same road Robert's trailer was on.

After the shooting stopped and they caught a glimpse of Samantha Juray locking the door behind the departed Card, Kathleen Walker and Stacey Cyr got up and ran down the lanes towards the back of the building, as several others were doing. But not before seeing some horrifying images of the carnage he left behind.

Stacey said she saw the bodies of her husband and his best friend up near the entrance, and knew they were both dead. She looked down on the floor next to the table she had been hiding under to see the Violettes both crumpled to the floor and lifeless. Just a few minutes before, she had shared a laugh with them as they watched the antics of one of the boys bowling with the couple in their youth practice session.

As they approached the door out of the building, they saw a man lying near the entrance who had been shot multiple times. Next to him, another man was tending to a teenager who had been shot in the arm. They went out the door, not having a clue where the shooter had gone, and ran to a parking lot across Mollison Way.

Kathleen recalled later in the inquiry that she exchanged smiles and greetings with the Violettes and a hug with Thomas Conrad, then bowled with her husband of nearly twenty-seven years and his lifelong best friend. Two hours later, all five of them would be dead.

Their families came just minutes after they called them from the parking lot. The first officers to respond were still searching around the building for signs of the shooter when they reached the scene. Kathleen's twenty-four-year-old son screamed that he needed to see his father but was prevented from doing so. Desperate to reach him, he sent a text to his unattended phone: *I'm sorry I wasn't there for you. I love you and I'll see you in heaven.*

# LAWLESS LOOPHOLES

The Lewiston Armory is a massive brick colossus of a building from a bygone era. It was built in 1923 for the sole purpose of providing training and storage for the Maine National Guard, but Lewiston city officials and residents were so enamored with the building, they voted to keep it and rent it out to the National Guard for its monthly drills.

In the century it's looked over the city blocks of the Webster Street neighborhood just north of downtown, the Armory has served as a time capsule of Lewiston's history over the last hundred years. Its massive main hall has hosted military drills and ceremonies, traveling circuses, home shows, and boxing bouts featuring world champions like Joe Louis, Sugar Ray Robinson, Jack Dempsey, and Lewiston's own world featherweight and lightweight champion, Joey Gamache.

It's played host to basketball tournaments, roller derbies, and the Harlem Globetrotters, famous musicians like Buddy Holly, Jerry Lee Lewis, Jimi Hendrix, and Freddy Mercury and Queen on its stage, held beauty pageants, marching band drills, dance recitals, and for three decades, the Gamache Boxing Club down in the depths of the basement. In 2020, the Armory served as a COVID-19 shelter.

On October 26th, 2023, it opened its doors to the Red Cross, the FBI's Victim Services Division, grief counselors and other social work professionals and became the Family Assistance Center to help families of the victims and survivors of the mass shooting cope with their shock and grief.

Five months later, on March 23rd and 24th, 2024 it hosted the forty-sixth annual Twin Cities Gun Show, an event that raises money for youth and veterans' groups in the Lewiston-Auburn region.

The Twin Cities show is one of fourteen gun shows in Maine that are listed on the 2024 calendar on a website called Gun Show Trader. Nationwide, the site lists 1852 gun shows across the U.S. for the year. The ATF agency estimates of the number of gun shows nationally have ranged from 2000 to 5000 over the years, an estimate obviously too wide to cite with any degree of certainty. One thing that is certain is that they range from relatively small gatherings in towns and cities across the country, to mega-shows that bring in thousands of vendors and tens of thousands of attendees.

The Wanenmacher's Tulsa Arms Show in Oklahoma, for example, features 4,200 tables of gun-related merchandise in an eleven-acre room. It's billed as the world's largest gun show and draws crowds of up to 40,000 for the one weekend in April it's held. Another, the Nation's Gun Show in Chantilly, Virginia offers 1,400 tables of modern rifles, shotguns and handguns, antique firearms, ammo, accessories, knives, swords during the seven times a year, three-day sessions it's held. Compared to these, gun shows like the Twin Cities Show are like small town yard sales selling goods piled on rickety card tables, with hand drawn signs stuck in the ground down the road with an arrow pointing to their location.

One thing that they virtually all have in common though, is that the vendors behind those tables will consist of a mix of FFL dealers who make a living selling gun-related goods, and private sellers who dabble in the business of selling gun-related goods, but don't rely on gun sales as their principal source of income. At least that's what they would claim if officially asked. Because the former group is required by federal law to submit a record of the transaction and a completed ATF Form 4473 for a NICS background check on the buyer, while in thirty states, Maine included, the latter group can accept payment, hand over the firearm, and call it a day. No paperwork, no background check, no problem.

That, in a nutshell, is the infamous "gun show loophole," the subject of hundreds of proposed state legislative bills across the country over the years, and at least nine proposed federal Congressional bills in the last twenty years. All of those federal attempts have failed, while the most recent of Maine Democratic legislators' attempt to require mandatory background checks for gun show purchases failed in 2023. Seven years earlier, in a 2016 referendum, Maine voters rejected a call for universal background checks (UBC) by a 52% to 48% margin. The results skewed along the urban/rural divide in the state. For instance, Lewiston residents voted overwhelmingly for, while Bowdoin (Card's hometown) residents voted overwhelmingly against.

When it comes to the call for UBC, supporters of gun owner's rights must feel like the defenders of the Alamo, facing wave after unrelenting wave of attack. In testimony opposing LD 168, the failed 2023 Maine UBC legislation, one resident of the aptly named town of Mexico, Maine summed up the prevailing sentiment of gun owners.

*The only way to enforce universal background checks is to implement a gun registry. Gun registries are unconstitutional and I do not support LD 168. Our guns are none of your business. My rights do not stop because people are scared. Our second amendment rights are here to protect the scared people in the event a scarier situation were to ever happen.*

A woman from Card's hometown of Bowdoin spoke from the opposite side of the spectrum.

*I've heard on numerous occasions that Governor Mills won't support universal background checks in Maine until we have a mass shooting...I am here to urge you to act before such a tragedy occurs.*

The state Senate killed the bill in late June, roughly four months before the shooting this woman feared came to pass. She'll get the chance to speak again however, because Democrats in Augusta have reintroduced similar legislation in 2024.

Twenty other states have managed to pass legislation that requires background checks for private sales. On the federal level, in August 2023 the ATF suggested an amendment to the 2022 Bipartisan Safer Communities Act, the only real substantive federal gun legislation created in years. Passed in the immediate aftermath of Uvalde, it requires background checks for any buyers under twenty-one, provides money to states to implement red flag laws, and delivers billions of dollars in grants for mental health crisis intervention programs.

The ATF amendment would clarify the definition of what it means for a person to be "engaged in the business of dealing in firearms." As it's now written, FFL licensing requirements state that a person whose main source of income does not come from selling firearms would be exempt from needing to obtain one, and therefore exempt from the need to submit a transaction for a NICS background check. That standard was established with the Firearm Owners Protection Act of 1986. Prior to that, the definition was selling four or less firearms a year.

The amendment says "all persons who devote time, attention, and labor to dealing in firearms as a regular course of trade or business to predominantly earn a profit through the repetitive purchase and sale of firearms" would be required to obtain an FFL license.

In the ninety-day comment period that followed the proposal, over 300,000 people weighed in with their opinion. Needless to say, gun rights advocates view this rule change as an overreach by the ATF, and an attempt to usurp the legislative process. Should the proposed rule change be implemented, it will certainly face challenges in court.

It's a major concern for the people in the thirty states without UBC who sell firearms as a secondary source of income. If implemented, they'd have to go through the same process as other FFL dealers, and they'd have far more paperwork to complete. Given that there's absolutely none required now, any paperwork would probably feel like a burden. Without conducting a survey, it's hard to know how many of them would acknowledge that this minor inconvenience is worth it to keep firearms out of the hands of people who aren't supposed to have them.

While the viewpoints from both sides are crystal clear, the actual impact of a UBC for private sales at gun shows, online stores, and any place where there's a transfer of a firearm, is less clear. One major reason for that is there is an appalling lack of government data and research available to make that determination—or many others involving gun-related issues.

For example, a 500-page 2020 RAND Corp. report titled, *The Science of Gun Policy,* studied eighteen common gun control-related policies and concluded that there wasn't enough data and research to determine whether they worked as intended. The only definitive conclusions they could make was that safe gun storage laws prevent juvenile deaths, and that the removal of concealed carry restrictions has led to an increase in homicides. The common consensus identifying the major reason for the lack of government research into gun violence is that the NRA has been pushing back against it for decades, at least as far back as 1993 when it lobbied lawmakers hard for the passage of the Dickey Amendment. That amendment essentially threatened the Centers for

Disease Control and the National Institute of Health with cuts in funding if it engaged in gun research. This came after CDC money helped fund a study that determined that the presence of a firearm in a household increased the risk of homicide. Duly chastened, the CDC's spending on gun violence research plummeted 96% over the next twenty years. The NIH discontinued its funding on gun research for years as well. Our ability to fully understand one of the leading causes of premature death in the country has been hampered ever since.

Michael Bloomberg, the former New York City mayor and Democratic presidential hopeful, has tried to change that by investing at least $50 million into Everytown for Gun Safety, a prominent gun control advocacy group with a heavy emphasis on data-driven policy. But they have skin in the game, so, while their methodology and data collection methods appear to be top-notch, their findings will always be suspect to many.

What little federal government research there is on gun show sales comes from an ATF report that concludes that 3% of the guns used in crimes that it traced from 2017-2021 were purchased at gun shows from FFL dealers. It was unable to determine what percentage of purchases come from unlicensed private sellers for the simple reason that they don't need to fill out any paperwork, hence there's no paper trail to track.

As a result of this lack of clear data, much of the evidence offered is anecdotal. As is often the case with anecdotes, they can have more of an impact than data and statistics. Unfortunately, these gun violence-related anecdotes are drenched in blood, but the visceral reaction they provoke often fades with time—until the next one.

Take for example the horrific mass shooting in the Canadian province of Nova Scotia in 2020, where a local dentist, dressed in a police uniform and driving a police replica car, went on a shooting rampage over the course of thirteen hours. By the time he was eventually shot and killed, twenty-two other people lay dead. Three of the guns he used were illegally purchased at a gun show in Houlton, Maine from a private seller.

Or the supermarket parking lot in Bath, a half hour or so drive from Lewiston, where in 2015 a man selling a 9mm handgun to another in a private sale accidentally shot and killed his girlfriend, the mother of their two children, when he was showing the buyer the weapon.

Or an apartment in South Portland in 2010, where a vivacious twenty-five-year-old woman named Darien Richardson was shot in a home invasion, and later died of her injuries. The same gun used to kill her was used in a Portland murder the next month. Police were able to determine that the gun had been purchased from an FFL dealer, and then resold at a Maine gun show, but the trail went cold, and her murder is still unsolved. Darien's parents later started a gun control advocacy group called Remembering Darien. In 2021, they helped craft a proposed UBC bill called "Darien's Law," but that proposed legislation died without a full vote.

While the debate over gun shows rages on, private gun sales in classified ads and online shopping marketplaces seem to fly under the radar. One major seller, for example, is *Uncle Henry's,* Maine's venerable swap and sell guide. First published in 1969, it was a must-have purchase at gas stations and convenience stores for decades, and from Kittery to Caribou, lines would form on Thursday afternoons when it rolled off the press. For Mainers cooped up indoors during the long winters, an Uncle Henry's road trip to go look at a barn full of old boards for sale, or a collection of Cabbage Patch dolls, or a 250-pound anvil for him and a wedding dress only used once for her, or any of the thousands of other items listed (*"Almost Everything Under the Sun"* is its tag line)—was a great way to pass a day.

For gun enthusiasts, *Uncle Henry's* was, and still is, a gold mine. Given its online presence, the print guide isn't as ubiquitous as it once was, and the number of ads overall has diminished as Facebook Marketplace and Craigslist have risen to prominence. But if you want to buy a gun from a private seller and skip the UBC, you can still find one in *Uncle Henry's*. In a 2016 report, Everytown said it scrutinized forty-four months of the guide and determined that it averaged 2,300 private gun sale ads annually over that period, for a total of 8,000. A more recent casual, methodology-free scan by the author produced results in line with those findings.

In his testimony to the independent commission looking into the Lewiston shootings, Sagadahoc County Sheriff's Deputy, Chad Carleton, said he looked at *Uncle Henry's* the morning before he came in to testify and spotted eight private sales for AR-15 semi-automatic rifles, a similar type of firearm to what Card used during his rampage. His point was that all the discussion about red card laws versus yellow card laws is overshadowed by the fact that anyone who has been adjudicated as mentally incompetent and had their weapons taken away could easily find another without submitting to a background check. That's a point that Arthur Barnard, the father of Schemengees victim, Artie Strout, makes to anyone whenever the discussion comes up.

*Uncle Henry's* is clearly not the only platform for private gun sales, but for Maine-specific sales it's the most prominent. Nationally, online sites like Armslist.com connect firearms buyers and sellers, some FFL-licensed, but many not. Armslist says it has 45,000 guns for sale at any given time. As one of the nation's largest firearms marketplaces, it is a frequent target of gun control advocates and their lawyers. So much so that the site maintains a legal defense fund and makes public pleas for donations to help stave off lawsuits. So far, it's managed to keep its portal open, and in doing so, has established a lucrative business.

The company offers buyers a $7 per month premium account, while sellers pay $30 per month to maintain an account. While the company is privately-owned and does not share its user numbers and annual revenue, a Wisconsin District Court maintained in a 2021 ruling that Armslist had 1.2 million private sellers alone.

The company has been sued in multiple states and prevailed every time. In 2012, the Brady Campaign filed a lawsuit on behalf of a Canadian woman who was killed by a stalker who was prohibited from owning a firearm. He purchased the weapon on Armslist. A similar case was filed in 2021 in Wisconsin by the family of a woman killed by her estranged husband with a gun that was also illegally purchased on the site. Both courts ruled that the people's elected representatives, not courts, should decide gun public policy.

If a prohibited gun buyer is averse to shopping at gun shows or in classified or online marketplaces, there's always the prospect of making a "straw man" firearms purchase. That's simply finding someone who isn't prohibited from buying a gun to make the purchase for them.

A 2020 ATF report on gun traces by law enforcement determined, for example, that seven percent of the guns used in crimes in Massachusetts recovered by law enforcement came from "straw man" purchases in Maine. The state, because of its fairly lax gun laws, regularly shows up as the point of purchase of a gun used to commit a crime in all the New England states, the report noted. Most of those fly under the radar. Some of the larger "straw man" transactions end up in the headlines. In November 2023, a month after the shootings at Just-In-Time and Schemengees, a Lewiston man was sentenced to ten years in federal prison for illegally obtaining thirty-six firearms through straw man transactions. A convicted felon, he paid others in drugs and cash to make the purchases for him.

In April 2023, a woman from the town of Turner, just outside of Lewiston, was charged with purchasing fifty-five guns from three FFL dealers in Maine for a street gang in Los Angeles. One of the guns was traced to an arrest in Los Angeles shortly after the weapons were transferred to gang members. It's not a recent problem either. A decade earlier, a pawn shop worker in the city of Brewer was charged with illegally transferring sixteen guns to a Connecticut street gang.

Of all the gun-related legislation presented to the Maine Legislature in 2023, only one bill was passed by the House and Senate and signed into law by Governor Mills. LD 22 increased the jail time for people convicted of transferring firearms through "straw man" purchases. It was a modest victory in a year that shattered Maine's self-image as a state that would never suffer the trauma of a mass shooting.

*Sgt. First Class Robert Card II, left, in a grenade training pit at West Point. His Army Reserve Bravo Company, 3-304th Regiment, 104th Training Division trained Army cadets there every summer for two weeks. (Photo courtesy of Department of Defense)*

# "THEY'RE SCARED I'M GOING TO DO SOMETHING. I AM CAPABLE"

In the last conversation that SCSO Deputy Sheriff, Chad Carleton, had with Army personnel in early May of 2023, he was assured by First Sgt. Kelvin Mote that he and Bravo Company's commander, Captain Jeremy Reamer, were going to "sit down in the near future" with SFC Card and work out a plan to get him the mental health help he so clearly needed.

First, Sgt. Mote had thanked Carleton for bringing his attention to how much Card needed that help, especially because the unit's annual two-week training session at West Point was scheduled in just two months' time. There's little doubt that he recognized that Card could be a liability if something wasn't done.

All of this leads to a very obvious question: Was there any attempt within the unit to get him that help before they left in early July? Both Mote and Reamer provided the answer when they testified at the independent commission under subpoena in early March 2024: no, there was not. The impact of this failure to develop a plan to get Card help became clear, because the events that led to his twenty-day stay at a psychiatric hospital in Katonah, New York were consistent with the behavior that had been the cause of concern earlier. Card arrived at Camp Smith, a New York National Guard base located in Cortlandt on Friday, July 14th. The next evening, he and his fellow soldiers went to a convenience store to get some beer. While they were in the parking lot, he once again latched on to the idea that they were calling him a pedophile. It was there and then that he shoved a longtime friend and fellow Bravo Company soldier, Sgt. Daryl Reed, telling him to stop calling him that name.

In addition to Reed, Staff Sgt. Christopher Wainwright, the Oxford County Sheriff, and Cpl. Matthew Noyes, an Androscoggin County Sheriff's Deputy, were also with him in the parking lot, and then in the car on the ride back to the hotel. On the way back, Card muttered that he "would take care of it" several times, according to an email that First Sgt. Mote wrote to the SCSO on September 15th when he requested that they conduct a welfare check on him. When his fellow soldiers asked what he "would take care of," he didn't respond.

The information that follows is from the Facebook page of the wife of Sgt. Daryl Reed, who was not only with Card that night, but was his friend of ten years. Through screenshots of text messages she exchanged with her husband in real time, Sgt. Reed's wife provides a detailed timeline of the events that brought him to the hospital.

She posted these texts five days after the shootings with her husband's blessing, she says, in the hope that "maybe something can be done to prevent a tragedy like this from happening again." Given the Army's reluctance to discuss anything to do with Robert Card, you would think that they would have ordered Sgt. Reed to have his wife take down the posts. She claims they haven't done so though. In fact, her husband testified in late April 2024 under subpoena at the independent commission hearings.

*"I thought he was going to punch me in the face and I was going to have to tackle him and fuck him up. But I really don't want to hit him. He really has lost his mind,"* Sgt. Reed told his wife in a text a couple hours after the incident at the convenience store.

After arriving back at the barracks, Card complained to his colleagues that the front desk clerks were "saying bad things about him," Sgt. Reed told his wife. By 10:30 p.m., he had barricaded himself in his room and wouldn't open the door.

*"They're calling the MPs now. This is so fucked up right now…The 1SG and the MSG are trying to talk to him. He won't open the door. He's had so many guns I would not put it past him to bring one."*

The 1SG he's referring to is First Sgt. Mote. The MSG is Master Sgt. Yurek, a Brunswick, Maine police officer. Combined with Wainwright and Noyes' earlier interaction with Card at the convenience store and on the ride home, that makes four Maine law enforcement members who witnessed Card's unraveling that night.

Based on their years of friendship and service together as weapons training instructors, it's not a stretch to believe Sgt. Reed was stating a fact when he said in his next text to his wife: *"He had a $10k scope that can see at night too."* It's unclear whether that statement was meant to indicate the past or the present, but it's an ominous fact, nonetheless. Other unit members would refer to the scope as costing between $14,000 and $20,000. Whatever the price, it was clearly a high-quality piece of equipment, and it would prove to be a source of concern to law enforcement later when they were frantically searching for him. After failed attempts to get Card to open the door, Reed tells his wife that the MPs (Military Police) had been called, and they would come with breaching tools to force the door open. After that, he said, his friend of ten years would be on the receiving end of necessary force.

*"The MPs are going to go in and rock his fucking world. They don't mess around with this shit. He's going to lose this battle if he doesn't open the door. They'll take him to the hospital right after this. I did a few of these when I was an MP."*

The text thread ends with a few comments from Sgt. Reed about possibly videoing the encounter at the barracks door and about his scouting exits in case he needed to run. The final exchange has Reed's wife urging him to go to his own room, and then telling him she was going to bed because she had to get up to take their daughter to her basketball game in the morning.

They resume texting the next morning at 11:00, when Sgt. Reed tells her that the New York State Police (NYSP) just interviewed him, and that, *"they're about to go get him. They just want to interview his brother or his son for more information before they do."* Directly after, he says, *"We're taking him to the Keller Hospital now. We have a police escort. 1SG, me and [redacted] are riding with Card and the police are in the front and the back in their cars."* Card refuses to talk, Reed says. He just stares at the floor of the SUV as they make the forty-five-minute drive to the Keller Army Community Hospital, which is located on the grounds of West Point.

At one point, Sgt. Reed tells his wife, *"He doesn't seem mad. He seems sad."*

*"He's probably embarrassed. Have you guys told him you just want to make sure he's ok and safe?"* she asks.

*"Yeah. He's crying now. It's making me sad."*

Bravo Company's command called in the NYSP when they were informed that they were the agency with jurisdictional authority over Camp Smith, a New York National Guard base. State national guard units report to the state's governor rather than the Department of Defense. The specifics about the NYSP involvement with Card became clear in February 2024, when a Portland TV station obtained and aired a ten-minute video of two troopers interviewing Card in his Camp Smith barracks room on July 16th. It became crystal clear when the NYSP complied with an FOI request from the author and released the incident report written by responding trooper, Anthony Clevinger.

Before they spoke with Card, the troopers spoke at length with five members of Bravo Company who witnessed Card's behavior. He had arrived the day before in a rental car, they said. After checking in, he joined them at an outdoor swimming pool and drank some beer. He seemed more quiet than normal and off-kilter then, they noted, but the real indication of his state of mind happened later at the convenience store.

After a long discussion with the other Bravo Company members, the troopers went to Card's room and knocked on the door. Surprisingly, he opened it within seconds of the pair announcing themselves. It was dark when he first opened it, before he flipped on a light switch. He was bare chested, wearing a pair of dark shorts with bright yellow letters spelling ARMY. One of the troopers suggested he put on a shirt, and then Card pulled open the door and they walked in. He sat on his disheveled bed in the spartan, Band-Aid-colored cinder block room, a framed photo of the Statue of Liberty on the wall behind him. He was gaunt and pale, his cheeks sunken, his hair shaved close to his head. It's a chilling video, in part because it's the first time that most of us have heard his voice and seen him as someone other than a mass shooter in a grainy video still with a high-powered semi-automatic rifle raised in a shooting position.

He sat passively as one of the troopers tells him that the guys in his unit are genuinely worried about him, so they've come to check on him. "What's going on?" he asks.

*"I flipped out on someone messing with me and they're cowards and ran away. I didn't do anything wrong. I wasn't physical with anyone."*

He goes on to explain that everyone is talking behind his back. He had to quit his job, he said, but the same thing is happening at his new job.

*"Everyone is fucking with me. It's getting old. I know it's happening. I watch and listen to people, that's what I do."*

When they ask him to elaborate, he tells the troopers that he got hearing aids about three months before, but the voices calling him a pedophile started three months before that. He got the hearing aids, he said, because people would be talking and looking at him, but he wasn't able to hear them.

*"I was pretty invisible. Now everyone knows who I am."*

The troopers are polite and supportive. They tell him that they've been asked by his superiors to take him to the Army's Keller Community Hospital back at West Point.

*"Are you willing to do that?"* they ask.

*"If it's command directed I guess I have to. Will it do anything? No. I'd rather people stop fucking talking about me. I'm a private person. I don't like my private shit out there."*

*"Well, it's just that the guys are really worried about you."*

For the first time in the conversation, Card becomes animated. He bounces on the mattress and then rubs his palms together vigorously, like he's trying to warm them on a cold day.

*"Cause they're scared I'm going to do something. Because I am capable."*

The troopers show alarm for the first time. Their response is instantaneous.

*"What do you mean by that?"*

Card's expression instantly switches off and goes blank.

*"Nothing."*

The troopers escorted the vehicle that took him to the Army hospital. The trip occurred with no incident they note in closing the incident report. On that benign note, that was the end of their involvement. It took a total of three-and-a-half hours.

What the troopers didn't do was forward the report to the NYSP Bureau of Criminal Investigations (BCI) to review for a possible ERPO (red flag) order to have his personal firearms temporarily removed. To do that, they would have had to have concluded that Card was suicidal, homicidal, or had placed others in reasonable fear of physical harm. Instead, they decided that his behavior didn't meet the threshold.

It's a process that New York authorities have become much more familiar with in the last two years. Since New York Governor, Kathy Hochul, had amended New York's red flag law in 2022 to require the State Police to seek an ERPO if they think one is needed, the number of orders across the state had doubled. The governor's executive order amending the state's red flag law came just four days after a May 2022 mass shooting at a Buffalo supermarket killed ten people. The shooter in that case had openly vowed to commit a racially motivated mass shooting before carrying it out.

Had the troopers thought that Card's behavior rose to the qualifying standard and forwarded the report to the BCI, and had the BCI agreed and issued an order, it could have been forwarded to Maine authorities to initiate the removal of his firearms. But given the involvement of the Army and jurisdictional questions, it's anyone's guess as to whether that process would have happened.

So, SFC Card was "command-directed" to Keller Hospital, which means he was involuntarily hospitalized, as is clear in the video. The shaken Bravo Company soldiers joked later about how it was an annual training they wouldn't forget, and they resumed their duties while their colleague underwent his first hours in a psychiatric hospital.

Later that evening, Sgt. Reed sends a text to his wife explaining that he got a hold of [redacted], who said he was going to try and talk to Robert Card Sr. back in Bowdoin and get him to remove his son's guns, presumably so he wouldn't have access to them when he got home. The Card family's deep-rooted concern about Robbie's descent into psychosis would escalate as soon as they got word that he had been committed to a psychiatric hospital, but there was also some hope that maybe now he would get the help he desperately needed.

*Card taking a selfie in the bathroom of his trailer. He texted this photo to his best friend, Sgt. Sean Hodgson months before the shooting, along with a chilling statement about "taking people out."*

Sgt. Reed's wife wasn't so sanguine. Late that night her husband texted her a photo of a soldier dressed in his combat fatigues with an assault rifle slung across his chest. He's taking a selfie in front of a mirror. He's clean-shaven, with a tight military haircut, but the bathroom where he's taking the picture is a mess. The small vanity surrounding the rusted sink is covered with bathroom items and the dingy floral wallpaper looks to be circa-1950.

It's Robert Card II. He's looking down at the camera, his eyes are hooded and inscrutable. He sent the photo to [redacted], who then sent it to Sgt. Reed. Reed's wife said Card texted his friend a message accompanying the photo that said he, *"could take out as many people as he wanted to easily that were talking about him, or something like that."*

*"Where was that taken?"* Reed's wife asks her husband. He doesn't answer. Instead, he says he has to cut it short,

and their exchange ends. Card's image is embedded on the screen like a dark spirit who will haunt people forever.

In answer to the question as to whether 3-304th leadership should have allowed him to attend annual training in July 2023 knowing what they knew about Card's alarming mental decline and vague threats of violence, a senior Army Judge Advocate General (JAG, the military's legal branch) officer who asked that their identity not be revealed, explained it to the author like this.

*"He might not have exhibited concerning behavior during battle assembly (weekend drill), but if he did, a commander is required to conduct an inquiry, which could take up to thirty days, unless urgent circumstances required expedited action."*

Although First Sgt. Mote had been made aware by SCSO Deputy Carleton of Card's condition in May, the specific behavior he was referring to didn't take place while he was at drill. But the disturbing pattern had been evident earlier to his Reserve colleagues, a fact that Mote alluded to when he said that unit members were concerned about Card's repeated reference to people calling him a pedophile.

That leads to the obvious conclusion that they witnessed this behavior while they were all at weekend drill. They clearly thought it was "concerning" behavior, as Mote indicated. Based on the JAG officer's explanation, were they derelict in their duties for not holding an inquiry?

The JAG officer went on to say that commanders *are required to refer soldiers for mental health evaluations or hospitalization per AR-600-20 and DoDI 6490.04. Soldiers would normally be placed on medical profile, which would restrict their ability to carry firearms and render them undeployable pending treatments.*

It's evident that didn't happen, and Card—whether he got the help that Mote said he and Captain Reamer would help him obtain or not—was allowed to attend training at West Point in early July. It wasn't until August, after training, that the Army Reserve restricted his access to military-issue firearms and declared him undeployable. That's because his attendance at annual training did result in his getting evaluated at a mental health facility. This fact exonerates the Army, the JAG officer points out, because it demonstrates that they actually executed a plan of action following proper protocol.

*"Having him attend the annual training gave the Army command authority over him, which resulted in him receiving mental health treatment. This would not have been possible without him having been on AT (active training)."*

That point will no doubt be argued strenuously by attorneys for the victim's families. They'll likely point out that allowing him to attend was due to negligence, not as part of a master plan. Plus, Card was demonstrating such irrational behavior by this point that Army Reserve personnel had virtually no other option other than seeking treatment for him.

The events that led to his twenty-day stay at a psychiatric hospital in Katonah, New York in late July and early August of 2023 were consistent with the behavior in Maine that had been the cause for concern—except for the fact that he assaulted a fellow soldier and locked himself in his barracks. This showed a pattern of escalating bizarre behavior.

Bravo Company's leadership now had clear and convincing evidence that he wasn't getting any better. Several senior enlisted men with extensive law enforcement experience had witnessed it themselves. His behavior had redlined the needle, moving from paranoid thoughts to abusive action. For the time being, he was secure. Surely, they would keep a very close eye on him after he got out. Wouldn't they?

# PEDOPHILE OBSESSION

By the time Bravo Company gathered again for their annual two-week training at West Point in July 2023, Staff Sgt. Card had spent the previous few months convinced that everyone around him—his family, his co-workers, the people he played cornhole with at Schemengees, as well as the employees at Just-In-Time, Gowell's Shop 'n Save in Litchfield, and Mixer's Nightclub & Lounge in Sabattus, and his fellow soldiers in the company—were calling him a pedophile.

This wasn't a sporadic thought he would blurt out from time to time. According to multiple people who were closest to him, he was absolutely obsessed with the notion that everyone in his vicinity, wherever he was, identified him as a child molester. It didn't seem to matter whether he was at home, with his son out shopping or getting something to eat, at Reserve drill, out with friends for a night at a local casino, bowling at Just-In-Time, or playing cornhole at Schemengees. In his eyes (and his ears), everyone spoke of him as a pedophile and talked openly amongst themselves about it in his presence.

His friends would notice that when he was out in public—at a restaurant, for example—he would lean in the direction of a nearby table and focus intently on what they were saying, hypervigilant for any reference to him "liking little girls or boys," or for "having a small dick." He referred to these alleged comments so often, and vowed retribution for them with such boiling rage, that his son became afraid to spend time with him, his fellow soldiers were afraid to attend weekend drill, and his family pleaded with law enforcement not to reveal they had spoken to them. He told his sister that four local businesses were broadcasting that he was a pedophile online. He eventually came to the determination that his own family—including his son—were involved in this mass conspiracy to slander and humiliate him.

Was there a specific event that led him to think that way? Was it related to his eventual TBI diagnosis? Was his hearing loss and his struggle with adjusting to the hearing aids contributing to this delusional fixation? Was the story he was telling himself the manifestation of a full-blown psychotic break? Was it a combination of some or all of these factors?

There was one episode that deviated from Card's relentless fixation on thinking he *heard* people calling him a pedophile, that. It happened at Just-In-Time Recreation Center and it might have been the catalyst for him deciding on the bowling alley as a target. Sometime in June of 2023 Card went with Staff Sgt. Hodgson to go bowling. They went to Just-In-Time, the only bowling alley in the region after the 2020 closing of Yankee Lanes in Brunswick.

The following day Card called Sgt. Daryl Reed who was supposed to have joined the two men for the night out but opted not to. Later, Reed's wife, who recounted this story in November on her social media feed, heard her husband telling Card on the phone, "No dude, that's crazy. I would trust you with my daughters."

When he hung up the phone he told his wife that Card said that he and his friend were bowling when a young girl approached him and flipped up her skirt and revealed her underpants. Card was incensed and convinced that someone in the bowling alley had sent her over to do that to taunt him and imply that he was a pedophile.

Later, in a March 2024 conversation, Hodgson confirmed this did happen, although the circumstances were slightly different. They were bowling when a girl between the ages of two and three came from the adjoining lane where her family was also bowling and laid down on the seats near their lane. Then she put her legs in the air and her dress bunched up around her waist, before her father came over and abruptly snatched her away. This immediately triggered Card, he said, and he turned to his friend and said, "See, they think I'm a pedophile."

Reed's wife, a mother of young girls, said in her Facebook post that this is nothing out of the ordinary. Young girls are not even aware that there's anything inappropriate about it. It's what young girls do, she said.

Interestingly, she also said that Card's interpretation of what happened in the bowling alley convinced her that the hearing aids *were not* the cause of his paranoia. His difficulty in adjusting to them might have contributed to it, but they weren't the root cause, she suggested, because what happened at Just-in-Time had nothing to do with hearing and everything to do with seeing and interpreting.

No one will ever know if this episode was what sent him over the edge. The answer went with him when he shot himself in a trailer full of empty cans and bottles sometime in the forty-eight hours between shooting eighteen people on the night of October 25th and when his body was found on the night of October 27th.

There is one tangible clue to the possible origin of the story he was telling himself, which can be found in the Maine Sex Offender Registry, an online database of all registered sex offenders in the state. Linked to the National Sex Offender Registry website, the registry is overseen by the Maine State Police, and has search functions that allow the public to search by name, town and zip code. At last count in 2023, there were 2864 registered sex offenders in Maine. Offenders are required to register if they are convicted of a sex crime of a victim under the age of eighteen, and in certain cases, crimes involving adult victims.

This could be relevant to determining the origin of Card's obsession with being called a pedophile, because there *is* a Robert Card listed on the Maine registry. In fact, there's been a Robert Card listed on the registry since 2017. But it's not the same man as Robert Card II of Bowdoin. This one was arrested in 2016 and charged with two counts of possession of sexually explicit material and two counts of dissemination of sexually explicit material of a child under the age of twelve. He's from the central Maine city of Waterville and was born on 4/3/84. Robert Card from Bowdoin was born on 4/4/83. Same name, same numbers in their birth dates, just in a slightly different order. Familiar with cards, Vegas bookmakers would surely lay long odds on the chances of this random happenstance.

The identities and life history of the two Robert Cards would be commingled in the chaotic aftermath of the shootings, when the guardrails of media responsibility were lowered to ground level. In the race to put out the news first, someone thought to either check the registry, or had received a tip about the listing, and incorporated the information into the lead paragraph.

Fact-checking be damned, some media outlets pasted this into their lead, and within minutes, people across the globe learned that the Maine shooter was a convicted sex offender. Meanwhile, the wrong Robert Card's photo started appearing on social media sites, and that image spread like an El Niño-fueled wildfire through the Internet. The twisted irony of this fact is that the Robert Card who committed the shootings did so because he thought people were calling him a pedophile. Which, for a short while after the shootings, they were.

From a layman's view, the mix-up is somewhat understandable. The *other* Robert Card has the same color hair, vaguely similar features, and is a white Caucasian around forty-years-old. His mugshot and the infamous video still of Robert Card near the front door of Just-in-Time with his rifle raised to his shoulder don't differ enough to make it obvious at a glance that they aren't the same person. Then, there's the fact that they share the same name. How common can that name be? More common than you would think, as it turns out. There's at least eleven other men named Robert Card living in the state of Maine. It's an English name, derived from the French word, *carde,* which means 'a ball of carded wool.' According to a surname origins website, the English adopted the name to identify men who worked as blacksmiths or tin workers.

So, the wrong Robert Card got swept up in the raging current of the biggest news story in Maine's history. Now that the flood waters have receded, it's time to ask a follow up question: if professional news reporters/producers got it wrong, isn't there a good chance that others got it wrong before them? Isn't it possible that the Robert Card who "imagined" that he heard people calling him a pedophile did hear people calling him a pedophile, because they thought that he was registered on the Maine Sex Offender Registry?

Isn't it possible that the new hearing aids he had just started using—the ones that gave him superhuman hearing, as described by Army Reserve colleagues—allowed him to hear muttered conversations or comments that actually did take place? He complained to several people that they would allow him to pick up distant conversations.

Could it be that his co-workers at Maine Recycling needled him about being a pedophile or talked behind his back because they had the mistaken belief that he was listed on the registry? How would they know? Because at least twelve of them are convicted sex offenders themselves, and their mugshots are up there along with the other 2,582 other registrants, including the *other* Robert Card.

Sean Hodgson said he's convinced they did, adding that Card overheard at least one employee referring to his alleged inclusion on the registry, and this was the kindling that started the fire. He worked there for a time with Card and heard him repeatedly complain about the other employees badmouthing him, Hodgson explained. At one point, Card unzipped his pants in the facility and showed his penis to prove he didn't have a "small dick" like they claimed he did, Hodgson said. Ultimately, this led to an altercation, and he ended up quitting before he would likely have been fired.

In a discussion with the author in early December, Card's sister, Nicole, said that he had complained to family members specifically about his co-workers at Maine Recycling and their alleged comments. She said she went online to the registry to check, but was unable to find a Robert Card.

It's odd that Nicole's search failed to produce a name. A search using his name produces his image and information right away. Unless she added "II" to her search to differentiate her brother from her father. If she did that, his name would not have appeared, as the author found out when he later attempted it. It's worth mentioning because Nicole told the author she thought her brother was confused and rambling when he angrily muttered something about Maine Recycling employees saying he was a sex offender. It's possible that her seeing the image of the other Robert Card might have helped her in convincing him that it was a simple misidentification that birthed the rumor. It's unlikely given his advanced psychosis at that point, but it remains a possibility.

Nicole was probably unaware of the possible danger of being listed on the registry, but veteran Maine lawmen would be very familiar with that prospect. In 2006, Stephen Marshall, a twenty-year-old from the Canadian province of Nova Scotia, went on the Maine Sex Offender Registry to select and then target two men in the small towns of Milo and Corinth before shooting and killing them in their homes. Marshall then boarded a bus to Boston, but it was surrounded by police near the city's South Station terminal, and he blew his brains out in front of the other horrified passengers. Later, authorities discovered that Marshall claimed to be the victim of childhood abuse himself.

Clearly Maine Recycling was about the worst place a man with an obsession about pedophilia could work. In taking a job there, Card was surrounded by the very people he despised—or despised being identified with. For a man mired in isolation, depression, and increasing paranoia, these coincidences and realities obviously created a toxic stew. As time went on, the pot boiled over.

Why was being called a pedophile the apparent motivating force in the deaths of eighteen innocent people? If people were alleging Card was a rapist, a murderer, or even a serial killer, would he have reacted the same way? No one knows the answer obviously, but his homicidal revulsion with being so labeled isn't out of the norm. Prison inmates consider "chomos" (their lingo for child molesters) the absolute lowest form of life in their world. In some of the more violent systems, it's a badge of honor for an inmate to stab or beat one to death.

In the outside world, TV shows like, *To Catch a Predator,* have popularized the practice of entrapping, then publicly shaming men who showed up with the intent of having sex with a minor before turning them over to law enforcement. That show was canceled in 2007 after a man who had exchanged sexually charged messages with an undercover officer posing as an underage child shot and killed himself while a police SWAT team stormed his house, a TV crew right behind them. The show ended in tragedy, but it also sparked a public lynch mob mentality, especially as social media platforms have spread their reach. A recent *Washington Post* article identifies more than 160 online 'predator hunting' groups, like the Facebook group, Truckers Against Predators, with its 150,000 followers.

Of course, the reach of social media has given child predators a far more effective way of finding their victims too, so these groups justify their existence by saying they're simply bringing a gun to a gunfight. And besides, the other gunfighter is the lowest of low, "the scum of the earth" as Marshall said of his prey. As his case demonstrates, it's not only societally shameful to be on the sex offender registry, but also potentially dangerous. But who could foresee the danger to the public from someone who wasn't on it, but believed that people thought he was?

As for why Card targeted Schemengees, his brother Ryan may have provided a Maine State Police detective a possible clue in the hours after the shootings, according to an affidavit submitted to a district court judge to obtain a warrant to search Card's Samsung Galaxy's S22 phone and cell records. Detective Blake Conrad wrote that when he interviewed Ryan that early Thursday morning at 3:00 a.m., Ryan told him that he used to go to Schemengees with Robert to play cornhole, and at some point Robert developed the idea that the people there were referring to him as a pedophile.

He told the detective that Robert had met a woman there at a cornhole event sometime in 2022 and the two began dating. She had two daughters who he ate with there. Ryan didn't say whether he would do this on his own, or together with his girlfriend. He did say that his brother claimed that people at Schemengees would look at him oddly when he was with the girls and start talking about him, and that's when he formed the opinion that they too were openly calling him a pedophile.

Card's sister and ex-wife also said that this girlfriend broke up with him in February 2023. But Hodgson claimed later that his friend was the one who broke it off with her because her two daughters insulted him, by saying his feet stunk while they were at a trampoline park. Card was very sensitive about his body image and hygiene, he added. In addition, she was $30,000 in debt and he had considered helping her pay it off, but the situation with her daughters made him reconsider and end the relationship, Hodgson claimed. Whatever the cause, law enforcement considered his ex-girlfriend an obvious target for revenge. Concerned for her safety, MSP tactical teams went to her house in Lisbon just after midnight—five hours after the shootings— on Thursday the 26th, but she had already fled to an undisclosed location in Auburn.

There's no evidence there's a correlation between Ryan's story, the breakup, and Card's decision to shoot people at Schemengees, nor is there any evidence that the episode at Just-In-Time involving the toddler lifting her dress prompted his decision to shoot people there. But to complete the puzzle, we need to see all the pieces and determine whether they fit.

In a final mind-bending twist of irony, there is also a Ryan Card listed on the Maine Sex Offender Registry. This Ryan Card is from the Aroostook County town of Limestone, which is in the far north of the state. He is not Robert's brother, and he has no connection to the horrific events in Lewiston.

# RIGHT UNDER THEIR NOSES

After being removed from his barracks room at Camp Smith, Card was brought to Keller Army Community Hospital on the West Point campus for a psychiatric evaluation. A full-service hospital staffed by Army doctors and clinicians, it's named after Colonel William Keller, who is referred to as "The Grand Old Man of Army Medicine."

Colonel Keller performed front line surgery in France in World War I, and subsequently was head of surgical services at the Army's flagship Walter Reed Medical Center in Maryland. Never fond of paperwork, Colonel Keller declined an appointment by President Herbert Hoover to be Surgeon General of the Army so he could continue working with patients.

His namesake hospital has limited mental health services though, and Card was deemed in need of more in-depth psychiatric help than they could provide. So, after an initial evaluation, he was transferred to Four Winds Westchester, a private psychiatric facility in Katonah, New York located about thirty miles away on the other side of the Hudson River. Situated on fifty-five wooded acres in a campus-like environment about an hour north of midtown Manhattan, Four Winds Westchester was established in 1978 by psychiatrist, Dr. Sam Klagsbrun. From day one, it's focused on providing child and adolescent psychiatric services. Seven of the eight separate units are dedicated to children and teens, while only one provides both inpatient and outpatient services for adults. The facility is an open campus concept. There's no security employed to keep patients in, according to Shannon Houlihan, a former mental health worker who was employed there for two years. That sounds like an invitation to walk right out, but that rarely happened when she worked there, she said in an interview in February 2024. Both juvenile and adult patients have a rigorously structured day, she explained, with private and group sessions, art and music classes, a gym to exercise in, and walking trails on the grounds.

Dr. Klagsbrun's daughter, Sarah, is now the Chief Medical Director of the 155-bed facility. She's a graduate of the prestigious college preparatory school, The Dalton School, in New York City. Known for famous alumni such as CNN's Anderson Cooper, Sean Lennon, son of the Beatles' John Lennon, actor Christian Slater and many more, it's now more infamously known as the school that notorious sex abuser Jeffrey Epstein taught at in the 1970s.

After finishing there, Dr. Klagsbrun then went on to get a BA in psychology at Princeton, and then her medical degree at Alfred Einstein College of Medicine in New York. In addition to her leadership post at Four Winds, she's also an adjunct professor of psychiatry at her alma mater. While that's an impressive pedigree and resume, Internet critics of the facility aren't very impressed. Out of forty-four reviews from former patients and parents of juvenile patients on Yelp, it has a 1.8 rating out of 5. It garnered a 2.2 rating from 334 reviewers on Birdseye, and a 2.3 rating from 265 reviewers on Google.

The scores are one thing, but the level of bitterness and hostility aimed at Four Winds Westchester and the length of the reviews are quite another. It's no secret that negative reviews on the Internet are not necessarily a fair and accurate barometer of the level of overall satisfaction of the business or product being reviewed. The reasons to doubt their veracity are lengthy; from unscrupulous competitors to fired employees to a myriad of other motivations, which are only compounded by the nature of Four Winds' business and the customers it attracts. Rightly or wrongly, the opinion of a person seeking or receiving psychiatric help is open to question. To be fair, there are some positive reviews from former patients, but they tend to be much shorter and lacking in substantive detail. Former employee Houlihan said her experience was that Four Winds provided a professional and caring environment to help patients stabilize before they could go on to longer-term care. She no longer works in the mental health field and is now a per-diem RN at hospitals in southwestern Maine.

Still, the sheer number and depth of the negative reviews make them hard to ignore. From, "This is nothing more than a daycare with a pharmacy," to "This place needs a lawsuit. Incredibly neglectful and abusive," to "If you weren't crazy when you checked in, I promise you will be when you check out," Four Winds Westchester's critics have elevated writing scathing reviews to an art form. From alleged filthy conditions to barely edible food, to barely trained, disinterested, and sometimes abusive staff, to an overemphasis on providing medications, these reviewers paint a picture of a facility that rivals the mental hospital in *One Flew Over the Cuckoo's Nest*. Once again, saying it doesn't make it true. None bother to mention the $1300 per day inpatient cost, presumably because insurance is picking up the tab.

A civil lawsuit filed against Four Winds in 2017 alleged that the plaintiff's daughter was sexually assaulted several times while she was a patient there. The plaintiff claims her daughter was housed in a boys' unit, with no locks on the bedroom doors. That suit was filed one day after the New York State Police arrested a male Four Winds employee on felony charges of sexual assault and sexual abuse. It's unclear if those two cases are related.

Judging from all the open position postings on Four Winds social media accounts, like most other health and service-based businesses, they are struggling to maintain staffing levels. Working in a psychiatric hospital can be demeaning and physically and mentally draining job, according to people who've done the work. At times it can become dangerous. Having to physically restrain people in the throes of mental distress who might identify you as the enemy is no cakewalk. With pay equivalent to entry level jobs at restaurants, retail stores and a whole host of other places, it's no wonder the turnover rate for the position is so high. Given all those factors, it's not a stretch to believe that the former Four Winds patients who complained about understaffing and poorly trained employees might have had valid complaints.

A more reliable barometer of its performance would be professional audits of the facility performed by a government oversight agency, either state or federal. But the New York State Office of Mental Health (OMH) does not require it, and neither does any other state agency. The OMH apparently doesn't care to discuss it either, because a spokesman initially said they would respond to specific questions about their oversight of private psychiatric facilities, but then failed to respond on multiple occasions when asked to provide answers.

Because it accepts Medicare and Medicaid services, Four Winds Westchester is required to submit CMS (Centers for Medicare and Medicaid Services) patient surveys and make them publicly available. However, despite receiving a reported $560,000 in Medicare payments in 2022, the facility has not provided any patient survey information. Those surveys are extensive and would certainly provide much deeper insight into how Four Winds patients feel about their care there.

The web-based American Hospital Directory does provide some nuts-and-bolts numbers about the privately-owned corporation, including that it took in over $71 million in revenue in 2022, but reported a net loss of nearly $5 million. It treated 3,434 patients during that year and registered 52,187 total patient days overall, the web site noted.

None of them was Robert Card II of course, because his twenty-day stay there didn't take place until July and into August of 2023. He obviously can't provide any insight into the level of care he received there, and Dr. Klagsbrun has also not responded to requests for comment. Card's treatment records likely won't see the light of day unless any future litigation manages to pry them loose. All we know for sure is that whatever treatment he received, it didn't seem to help.

When Bravo Company soldiers returned to Maine on July 23rd, he was still at Four Winds. We know he was released on August 4th and got home the same day, because Sgt. Reed texted his wife to tell her, adding that Card's "friend"—Staff Sgt. Hodgson—was on his way to go pick him up and bring him home. This text came after the couple learned from Hodgson that Card was set to go before a judge a couple of days earlier. They presumed at the time that meant he would be held over at the hospital, but it didn't turn out to be the case. A clerk at the Westchester County Mental Health Court confirmed that Card had some involvement with the court but said that the case records had been sealed by court order.

However, in an interview in mid-March 2024, Hodgson said that Card was scheduled to appear before a judge, but never did, and instead was released to him with little fanfare. In fact, he rolled up to the entrance of Four Winds to find Card waiting with his belongings in his hand and itching to get home. He offered to drive and Hodgson, tired after the six-and-a-half-hour trip there, gladly accepted.

Card was likely declared an emergency admission patient, as defined by New York's Mental Hygiene Law.

Under that definition, it would have been determined that he "engaged in a recent overt dangerous act," and presented a substantial risk of harm to himself or others. That would require that he be evaluated by a Four Winds staff psychiatrist within forty-eight hours. He could then be held for up to fifteen days. After that, if Four Winds wanted to continue his in-patient care two certifying physicians would have needed to conduct an examination and sign off for him to be transferred to involuntary admission status for an additional hold of up to sixty days. He would be entitled to a court hearing after that period.

Instead, Hodgson said Card told him that Four Winds staff asked him some questions, and he was able to answer them to their satisfaction, so they released him. But he added, on the way home Card told him that he almost messed up when he told Four Winds staff of his desire to punch a female patient he took a dislike to. He was able to talk his way out of it, he explained to Hodgson, and shortly after he was free and clear to leave. Dr. Klagsbrun did not respond to an inquiry about this allegation. Hodgson noted that his friend's knuckles were swollen and raw, and when he asked him about it, Card told him that he folded his bed mattress up in his room and used it as a punching bag. He had done the same thing with his mattress at home, Hodgson added.

Card was released on August 4th, 2023 and he and Hodgson came back to Maine. One day later, he was at an Auburn, Maine firearms store to pick up a suppressor he had ordered online. That was denied when he checked the box that asked whether he had been treated in a psychiatric facility.

How effective was his treatment at Four Winds? Obviously not very, because he was clearly fixated on his firearms as soon as he was out of the door. The fact that he was buying a suppressor does not necessarily mean he intended to use it on October 25th. But it's hard to ignore that possibility. It's also frightening to imagine how many more people might have died if he did.

So, how could the facility have released him if he were so evidently unfit? Shannon Houlihan says that he may have just presented himself as fit enough to be released. She witnessed patients there who were full-blown psychopaths who could appear perfectly normal for long stretches of time, then one little thing could set them off, and the mask would come off, she added.

If true, expressing a desire to punch a female patient was the moment when Card's mask slipped off. But apparently Four Winds staff didn't see it that way. Card was shrewd enough to convince them that he had improved and could go back out into the community. Maybe he learned to curtail the pedophile talk long enough to accomplish that. If that isn't the case, it means that the hospital was seemingly negligent. Or, as some have suggested, his insurance plan wouldn't authorize a longer visit. Either way, he was out and on his way home.

The news of Card's release from the hospital triggered a visceral text from Sgt. Reed's wife to her husband.

*"I'm super paranoid about this guy in your unit. If anything ever happens the #1 suspect is Robert Card—just always remember that name,"* she texted him.

She clearly didn't believe that a twenty-day stay at a psychiatric hospital did him any good. She was so upset about the news she told her husband that she didn't feel safe at home.

*"I'm trying not to, but every sound I hear in the woods or anytime Hazel starts freaking out I think it's him out there. He just got home yesterday. I don't even feel safe here."*

When her husband got home, she told him she wanted to move, to go into the witness protection program if possible, and that she feared he was out in the woods with his top-of-the-line thermal scope ready to pick off her and the kids. It took her hours to calm down, she said later in a Facebook post.

Considering he had been a friend of her husband for ten years and she had never personally witnessed any displays of his paranoia, it's pretty extraordinary that she was so spooked by Card and that she was so prescient about what he would do eleven weeks later. That's too easy to chalk it up to female intuition, but any other explanation seems just as unlikely, so that will have to do.

Had she known then what she learned in mid-September about his attempt to purchase a suppressor the day after his release, she would have grabbed the kids and the dog, jumped in the car, and put the pedal to the metal all the way down I-95 and not stopped until the gas tank was almost empty. Suppressors (also known as silencers) are more heavily regulated than firearms, and have been since 1934, when the National Firearms Act was signed into law in an effort to address mob violence and the use of machine guns and heavy weapons by the likes of gangsters such as "Machine Gun Kelly," "Pretty Boy Floyd," and John Dillinger. In addition to requiring a lengthy background check, the law created a national registry for suppressor owners and imposed a $200 tax for purchasing one.

When Card ordered it, he knew that the transaction would have been screened by the ATF. This process involves a thorough background search and can take up to nine months. He hadn't been committed to a psychiatric hospital then and had no other red flags that would prohibit the transaction, so the ATF gave it the green light. Once it was cleared by them, the suppressor was shipped by the manufacturer to an FFL dealer for him to collect after filling out a Form 4473 for an additional background check run through the NICS system. The dealer in this case was Coastal Defense Firearms in Auburn, just across the Androscoggin River from Lewiston.

The Form 4473 that he filled out includes this question: *Have you ever been adjudicated as mentally defective OR have you ever been committed to a mental institution?* Checking the box next to the question would be a disqualifying response and he wouldn't have been allowed to leave with the suppressor. Card checked the box. In April 2024 we learned from Hodgson that he told his friend that he ran the risk of being charged with a felony if he lied on the form and was caught. That warning apparently scared Card into complying.

We don't know if he intended to use it on October 25th for tactical reasons, or if he bought it to muffle the sound of the gunfire, which was undoubtedly amplified by his hearing aids. What we do know is he wasn't allowed to leave with it. Rick LaChappelle, the owner of the gun store, said Card was polite when he was told he couldn't take possession of the suppressor, and simply responded that he would return after talking to his lawyer. He never did.

La Chappelle, who is a Lewiston City Councilor who ran and lost in a state Senate bid in 2022, believes that if Card had used the suppressor after walking into Just-In-Time and Schemengees, many more people would have lost their lives. While suppressors only muffle the sound of a shot rather than silence it, those who survived wouldn't have heard the shots as easily and reacted as quickly.

When she learned about the suppressor in mid-September, just weeks before the shootings, Sgt. Reed's wife said she had two immediate responses. The first was to ask, *"Who gets out of a psychiatric hospital and the first thing they want to do is buy a silencer?"*

The second was the awful realization that something terrible was going to happen.

*"When I heard about this I knew right then that he was planning to do something very bad."*

Which once again begs the question: If a woman who never met the man had such premonitions, why didn't the trained law enforcement officers who were in his unit and personally witnessed his behavior recognize the warning signs and take the steps to ensure the safety of the public and try to get Robert Card long-term help?

After a long drive back from West Point, Card and Hodgson pulled into the Saco Reserve Center parking lot, where Card's Subaru wagon had been brought while he was in Four Winds. Hodgson noticed the rear seat was folded down, which enlarged the cargo space; he had never seen Card do that before. Before driving off, Card said to Hodgson, "Good thing they didn't search it." In hindsight, Hodgson is convinced that he had at least one of his rifles wrapped up and stored in the back.

Obtaining a silencer, concealing his firearms; this was not the mindset of a man who had benefitted from a three-week stay in a psychiatric hospital. But like the gun that sat in the parking lot of their Army Reserve center right under their noses, Bravo Company's leadership didn't bother to check.

# SEE NO EVIL: THE POLICEMEN OF BRAVO COMPANY

The primary responsibility for Bravo Company of the 3-304th was training West Point cadets in a variety of weapons, including the Army's standard issue M4A1 carbine rifle, machine guns, anti-tank guns, and grenades, so it's no surprise that so many of its members are law enforcement officers. After all, a familiarity with firearms was a prerequisite for both jobs.

Starting at the top, the unit's commanding officer, Jeremy Reamer, is a police officer with the Nashua, New Hampshire PD. Nashua is a city of 91,000 located in the southern part of the state. In addition to being New Hampshire's second-largest city behind Manchester, it's also northern New England's second-largest city. A native of upstate New York, Reamer, thirty-four, graduated from the police academy in 2016, and in August 2023, soon after returning from annual West Point training, he was named a master patrolman. This is the highest attainable rank for a patrol officer.

Oxford County (Maine) Sheriff, Christopher Wainwright, is another. First elected in 2018, Wainwright has spent his entire career of over thirty years with the sheriff's office and worked in almost every capacity as a deputy and then up through the ranks. Oxford County is a mostly rural county that borders Androscoggin County and Lewiston. Sheriff Wainwright is also an Iraq war veteran, and for a brief time, was assigned by the U.S. State Department to serve as a police officer in Kosovo. Since his election to the top post his career has done a complete 180 though. After several questionable decisions on his part, the Oxford County Commissioners took the drastic step of petitioning Governor Mills to remove Wainwright from his post. In February 2024 she appointed a retired judge to examine the issues they cited in their request. After a three-month investigation and a public hearing, Mills decided there wasn't enough to remove Wainwright from his elected position, saying that voters are the ones who should determine his future.

Those issues include selling dozens of seized guns from the department's evidence locker to an Auburn gun shop without maintaining any financial record of the transaction, allowing two school resource officers to carry weapons even though their law enforcement accreditation had expired, and urging a deputy to go easy on a woman who had received a traffic citation, and then bullying him after he reported it.

Wainwright's saga probably doesn't surprise many of the 57,000 residents of Oxford County. The sheriff's office has been the source of several salacious front-page stories in the *Lewiston Sun Journal* over the last decade. Most notably, the previous sheriff resigned in 2017 after it was revealed he had sent extremely lewd photos and texts to both a male officer directly under his command, and to a female officer in another law enforcement agency. Wainwright had been head of the office's criminal investigations squad then, and claimed to be working with the FBI in their own investigation into the office. After that sheriff's resignation, he was elected to the position.

Card's immediate enlisted superior, Kelvin Mote, is a corporal in the Ellsworth, Maine Police Department. Androscoggin County Deputy Sheriff, Matthew Noyes, is also a Bravo Company member. Both these men were at the convenience store along with Wainwright when Card attacked Sgt. Reed, and then rode with him in the car on the way back as he muttered vague threats "to take care of it," the "it" being his belief that people were publicly calling him a pedophile.

Mote was the point of contact between the 3-304th and the Sagadahoc County Sheriff's Office during their two responses to calls regarding Card. He told Deputy Carleton in their May 2023 phone conversations that they too were concerned about Card's behavior, and that he and Captain Reamer would try to work something out to get him help. In September, after Card failed to attend drill for two months, Mote wrote the email to the SCSO requesting they conduct a welfare check on him. It provided a summary of his decline, right up until a couple of nights before, when Card punched his friend Hodgson in the face and claimed he called him a pedophile as they returned from a night at the Oxford Casino. Attached to that email was the text he received early in the morning from Staff Sgt. Hodgson that expressed the fear that Card would commit a mass shooting.

Another Bravo Company member is Master Sgt. Ed Jurek, who has attained the highest enlisted rank possible in the Army. He's also a sergeant in the Brunswick, Maine Police Department, and a former member of the 75th Ranger Regiment, which is the Army's most decorated special forces unit. That's the same unit that Ryan Card, Robert's brother, served in, and there's reason to believe that Jurek and Ryan Card knew each other through that affiliation.

Master Sgt. Jurek's life in Maine is a little less hectic than his life as an Army Ranger—even considering the Lewiston shooting, believe it or not. He not only took part in the infamous 1993 firefight in Mogadishu, Somalia with members of a local warlord's militia, but he led a squad to try and rescue the pilots of the downed Black Hawk helicopters, which was memorialized in the gripping 1998 movie, *Black Hawk Down.* That operation cost the lives of eighteen American servicemen, which is morbidly ironic considering it's the same number of lives lost in the Lewiston shootings.

According to the texts that Sgt. Reed sent his wife, Master Sgt. Jurek was one of the senior enlisted 3-304th members who tried to get Card to open the door of his hotel room, where he had barricaded himself after returning from the beer run to the convenience store.

His connection to the Cards resurfaced on the fateful night of October 25th, when a frantic Ryan Card called Jurek and told him that the family were sure that Robert was the shooter seen in the Just-In-Time video footage. He also warned Jurek that he thought his brother might be traveling to the neighboring town of Harpswell to shoot Cara Lamb, his ex-wife. She had come to the same conclusion and had fled her home with her son Colby.

Command Sgt. Major Samuel Tlumac is the senior enlisted man in the 3-304th battalion. He's also a Maine State Police trooper who testified at an independent commission hearing that he was the one who recommended that the SCSO do a wellness check on Card in September after his threat to shoot up the Saco base.

Unlike Staff Sgt. Hodgson, a close friend who had lived with Card for a time in his trailer in Bowdoin, none of these law enforcement officers fraternized with Card outside of Army Reserve training and drill. Sgt. Reed, for example, also considered him a longtime friend, but he was too busy working and raising a family to hang out with Card off-duty.

It's important to note that no one in the Army Reserve could have required Card to turn over his personal weapons. First, because he was a Reserve member, they had no jurisdiction over him when he was off duty. That's one of the main differences between full-time active-duty status and Reserve status. The Reserves' authority over its personnel extends only to the time a soldier is engaged with his or her unit. In the case of active-duty soldiers, that authority extends to conduct on and off a military installation. For example, an active-duty soldier who engages in a barroom brawl off base and is arrested by local police, is under the federal jurisdiction of the Uniform Code of Military Justice (UCMJ) and would be subject to punishment in a military court. Asleep or awake, on base or off, an active-duty soldier is essentially government property, and the government is responsible for safeguarding and disciplining that property.

But for Reserve members, the government's responsibility mirrors their own. While they're on active duty, soldiers have to abide by Army regulations, and the Army, in turn, takes responsibility for the well-being of the soldier. When they're not, the two are free to ignore each other like feuding relatives. That means that the Army Reserve was responsible for Robert Card for one weekend a month when he attended battle assembly, and for two weeks a year during annual training. At any other time than that, he was on his own.

Additionally, the National Defense Authorization Act of 2011 prohibits the Dept. of Defense from infringing on the Second Amendment rights of armed services members to possess firearms for personal use.

Those restrictions certainly presented a hurdle for direct intervention, but they did not prevent any of Bravo Company's senior leadership and sworn law enforcement officers from recognizing that Card's increasingly erratic behavior should be a cause of concern and required mental health intervention and long-term monitoring, especially the ones who witnessed it at Camp Smith. At the very least, knowing that he was released from Four Winds, they could have paid attention to the frequent warnings from Staff Sgt. Hodgson that his behavior had moved the needle from bizarre to potentially dangerous. They all knew of their close friendship. Who would know better? Instead, once Staff Sgt. Card was out of their sight, he was out of their minds. This is consistent with the Reserves established part-time relationships with its soldiers, but this was hardly a standard case. Despite the behavior they personally witnessed, Bravo Company's leadership dismissed Hodgson, who admittedly suffers from PTSD and underlying mental health issues, as unreliable. None thought to check to see if Card had a mental health follow-up after his release. None thought to have a discussion with any SCSO officers to advise them about the situation either. All of these issues and many more would be addressed in an independent commission hearings throughout the spring of 2024.

As for Staff Sgt. Hodgson's repeated warnings to Bravo Company's commanding officer and NCOs over the summer, they culminated in a mid-September text he sent to First Sgt. Mote after he had gone to a casino with Card, and the night ended when Hodgson jumped from the car on the way home after his friend hauled off and punched him in the face. That prompted him to send the infamous text: *Change the passcode to the unit gate and be armed if SFC Card does arrive. Please. I believe he's messed up in the head... And yes he still has all his weapons...***I believe he's going to snap and do a mass shooting.**

# "ARMED AND DANGEROUS, BLA, BLA, BLA"

On September 15th, 2023, Sgt. Aaron Skolfield of the SCSO was requested to conduct a wellness check on a subject by the name of Robert Card II at his residence on West Road in Bowdoin.

It wasn't an unusual request. The SCSO conducted over 300 welfare checks in 2023. And it was a name he recognized. As a twenty-five-year veteran of the sheriff's office and a resident of the neighboring town of Bowdoinham, he was familiar with the Card family name. The entire extended family were highly regarded longtime residents who owned large tracts of land in the county he patrolled. Skolfield never had a negative interaction with any of them in all his years of service.

According to Skolfield's incident report, the wellness check was at the request of his Army Reserve unit in Saco, who reported that Card was hearing voices calling him a pedophile, had made threats to shoot up their Saco facility, and had been committed to a psychiatric hospital in New York earlier in the summer. The request had been sent via email by Ellsworth police officer, Corporal Kelvin Mote, to the SCSO accompanied by a screenshot of a text that Mote had received the night before. It was from a Bravo Company member, Staff Sgt. Hodgson, advising him to change the locks at the Saco Armory, and expressing his concern that Card would commit a mass shooting.

Skolfield also wrote in his report, *"It should be noted that Card is a firearms instructor in the Guard [sic] so utmost caution must be utilized."* Skolfield contacted dispatch and notified them he was headed to the West Road home. He gave the address, Card's name, and then added, "He's considered armed and dangerous, bla, bla, bla.*"* This is his verbatim quote in the audio recording of the call, which was first revealed in March 2024 by the *Boston Globe*. After going to the address and discovering that it was Card's old house next door, he made his way to the trailer and found no one home, and the driveway empty. He confirmed it was the correct address for Card by running a plate check on a motorcycle and a jet ski that were on the property, he wrote in his report. Skolfield finished the report by noting that he would ask the evening shift to check on him, and that he had requested that a File 6 be issued on Card. File 6's are a standard teletype way for law enforcement agencies to alert others that it is attempting to locate a particular person. The alert read:

*Robert has been suffering from psychotic episodes & hearing voices. He is a firearms instructor and made threats to shoot up the National Guard [sic] armory in Saco. He was committed over the summer for two weeks due to his altered mental health state, but then released... if located, use extreme caution.*

There's no report to indicate whether the night shift deputy tried to make contact with Card, but if they did they were unsuccessful, so Sgt. Skolfield went back to West Rd. the next morning. When he saw the white Subaru in the driveway, he made the decision to call for backup. While he waited forty-five minutes for a deputy from neighboring Kennebec County to arrive, he was parked on the side of the road within eyesight of Card's trailer. It was there that Maine State Police Sergeant, Thomas Pappas, rolled up on him by complete accident after exiting the Maine Turnpike, where he was assigned on patrol, and opting to use West Road to get to wherever he was going.

The interaction between the two isn't mentioned in Skolfield's report, but Pappas told the Independent Commission to Investigate the Facts About the Tragedy in Lewiston (the commission) in a February 2024 hearing that he saw the SCSO vehicle parked on the side of the road and stopped to see what was up. Skolfield told him about the welfare check and the fact that Card had threatened to shoot up the Saco Armory.

Pappas agreed with Skolfield's decision to call for backup rather than go to the door alone. He testified that he then advised Skolfield that they should set up a perimeter and call for a tactical team, but Skolfield curtly told him his opinion wasn't needed. On that sour note, Pappas said he left.

None of the commission members followed up with the obvious question: If you thought it was so potentially dangerous you advised calling in a SWAT team, why did you leave the scene? Where were you going? Were you responding to a situation more urgent than one that you thought required such drastic intervention?

Instead, commission chair, Daniel Wathen, the former Chief Justice of the Maine Supreme Judicial Court, jokingly told Pappas that he was a current member of the Maine Turnpike Authority, and he wondered why he would have left his patrol territory during his shift. After a round of laughter from those in attendance, they moved on to another subject.

Skolfield testified to the commission in a separate hearing a month before Pappas did, so there was no talk then of his failure to mention it in his incident report. The brief interaction between the two and the failure to mention it does invite some scrutiny though. Was it indicative of a turf battle or personal animosity between the two? Did this lead to Skolfield's rude dismissal of Pappas? Did that then trigger Pappas to leave the scene of what he clearly thought was a dangerous situation without even reporting it to anyone else?

At the end of the day, Pappas' advice ran counter to the SCSO's emphasis on de-escalating conflict. It's very likely that an armed and paranoid individual who had a history of answering the door with a gun in his hand would not act rationally when armed officers showed up at his house. It's also likely that any request for an MSP tactical team would have been denied because Card hadn't committed a crime or acted in any way that posed a danger to the public. He simply chose not to answer a knock on the door. Uncooperative? Yes. Unlawful? No.

The negative interaction with Pappas might well have affected Skolfield's attention though, because in the forty-five minutes he waited for his backup, he didn't bother to see if there was any available information on his patrol car's computer system about Robert Card. If he had, he would have found Deputy Carleton's extensive May report on his interaction with the Card family. It was available to him if he had bothered to look, he later told the commission when asked.

If he did, he would have learned about his deepening paranoia, about the family's fear of Card and how his son hadn't visited him in months because he was afraid to, about how his Army colleagues were concerned for him, about his extensive collection of firearms, and about the fact that he answered his brother and sister's knock on the door in May with a gun in his hand. There wasn't any particular reason he didn't look for Carleton's report then, Skolfield told the commission. He didn't know it existed, so he didn't look. Instead, when his backup showed up, he went to Card's door.

But it was for not. Card was in his trailer, and he wasn't planning on coming out. Skolfield said he knocked on the door, and for several minutes tried to talk him into coming out to talk to them. If he was going to initiate a protective custody hold, he would need to have face-to-face contact with him. He could hear Card moving around inside the small trailer, but he didn't respond at all. "Due to being in a very disadvantageous position we decided to back away," Skolfield wrote. Later, he told the independent commission that he was aware that he was in the line of fire if Card decided to fire at them. "He could have taken us out easily," he said.

In his defense, Skolfield knew that his options for taking Card into protective custody were limited to three: Card would have to come out voluntarily; SCSO would have to wait for him to come out, or they would have to initiate contact somewhere else. That's because there wasn't a Maine law that allowed law enforcement to obtain a warrant for the purpose of entering someone's home to place them into protective custody. To obtain a warrant to force entry into the trailer, Sgt. Skolfield would have had to show cause to a judge that Card committed a crime. Didn't his threats to shoot up the Saco Army Reserve center rise to the statutory definition of terrorizing, a commission member asked Skolfield at a hearing. Maybe, but the jurisdiction would have been Saco, not Bowdoin, he replied. So instead of persisting, Skolfield released his backup, and went back to his car to make some phone calls.

He first had a brief conversation with a member of the Saco Police Department, who told him that, based on Card's threats to shoot up the reserve center, they had deployed four officers that morning near the building in case Card showed up for weekend drill. Their reaction was in stark contrast to the wait-and-see approach that Bravo Company leadership had taken, and far more proactive than the SCSO's deployment of one officer sitting in a cruiser outside his house. Despite having far less information than the SCSO had about Card's state of mind and access to firearms, they responded in a way that seemed appropriately vigilant.

"I can't speak for Saco's decision to respond that way," Skolfield told the commission. "They probably have more manpower than we do." A valid point, in that while he was sitting outside Card's trailer for the next three-plus hours, Skolfield asked his supervisor to call in another deputy to patrol his territory while he dealt with the situation.

Skolfield then had a conversation with Ellsworth police officer Corporal Mote, Card's platoon leader in Bravo Company. He had written the email asking for the welfare check after consulting with company commander, Captain Jeremy Reamer. In that email, he wrote, *"I'd rather err on the side of caution with regards to Card since he is a capable marksman and, if he should set his mind to carry out the threats made to Hodgson, he would be able to do it."*

They had a brief conversation, and then Skolfield spoke to Captain Reamer. This call was recorded on his cruiser's videocam. Skolfield opened by telling Reamer that based on what he had learned about Card, he was concerned about his threat to do a mass shooting, about the fact he was having auditory hallucinations, that he had recently been in a psychiatric facility, and that it was clear to him that his condition would not improve on its own.

Reamer, on the other hand, seemed more inclined to downplay the gravity of the situation. He said he had spoken with Card the day before, and that he expressed anger about being involuntarily committed to Four Winds Hospital in July. But Card didn't make any specific threats against anyone, he said. Plus, the Card family and Hodgson had a verbal agreement that the family would take his firearms away and store them somewhere safe where he couldn't access them, Reamer claimed. That however, was an aspiration, not a concrete agreement.

As for Staff Sgt. Hodgson's alarming late-night text to Mote expressing the fear that Card would do a mass shooting, Reamer told Skolfield that Hodgson was an unreliable source and prone to being an alarmist, an opinion seconded by Mote in a separate conversation.

*"How did you square that in your mind?,"* a commission member asked Skolfield. "On one hand, Sgt. Mote wrote that Card was a capable marksman and could carry out the threat he made to Hodgson, and on the other hand, you have Reamer saying Hodgson was an alarmist."

The pause was so long before Skolfield answered, it appeared the Zoom recording had glitched.

*"It seemed to me like a game of hot potato. They throw it and go, 'here, you catch.'"*

*"You mean like they were throwing it over to you?"*

*"Yes."*

When asked whether Captain Reamer's description of Hodgson as an alarmist diminished the urgency of his situation that day with Card, Skolfield said, "When his own command staff says the man has credibility issues, it makes a difference, yeah." In the months after the shootings, Skolfield would lean on this argument to justify his decision to close the case without a resolution.

Nearly five months later, Hodgson said in a conversation that his decision to report his best friend was a difficult one for him. He didn't want to damage Card's twenty-year Reserve career, but at this point, he didn't know what else to do. Card had just punched him in the face that night as they were driving back from an Oxford casino, forcing Hodgson to demand that Card stop the car so he could get out.

Card's anger came from the belief that his best friend was posting that he was a pedophile on social media. Hodgson tried to reason with him, which resulted in Card banging on the steering wheel and almost plowing the car into some trees on the roadside. Then he hauled off and hit Hodgson square in the face. He had bought a heavy punching bag and a speed bag in July and had been using them to channel his aggression. The punch hurt like hell, Hodgson said.

He acknowledges that he's struggled with his mental health and alcohol abuse since he returned from a deployment to Afghanistan in 2021, and he understands why his colleagues would question his judgment about some things. He wasn't a squared away soldier by any means. But they were aware how increasingly detached Card had become from reality. They heard it all spring and summer. They saw it at West Point. Mote and Reamer had fears for their own safety because they command-directed him to Four Winds. Everyone walked on eggshells around him. Yet, they were willing to ignore all those facts and focus on Hodgson's "reliability" instead.

Card called Hodgson twice after he reported him. He answered the first call, Hodgson said, to hear his friend yelling about betrayal and pedophiles and traitors.

Reamer had let slip to Card that Hodgson had alerted Mote about his fear that his friend was ready to snap. Given Card's documented physical aggression against both Hodgson and Reed, that "slip" could have proven deadly to Hodgson. By this time, he was asking his supervisor at the trucking company they both worked for to schedule their routes to clock-in at different times so he wouldn't encounter his friend. It wasn't always possible, however, and Hodgson would keep his eyes averted and his mouth closed when he saw Card in the yard. Card did the same, but it was a nerve-wracking few weeks, he said.

He didn't answer the second call from Card. They never spoke again. With that, his alienation from family and friends was now complete. Hodgson was the last person in his universe he had a history with. He was also the last who was actively trying to help him. For the final six weeks of his life, Card was trapped alone with his paranoia.

As a fellow police officer, Reamer told Skolfield in their phone conversation on September 16th that he thought trying to force contact with Card would be like throwing a stick of dynamite into a pool of gasoline. He didn't want to see any SCSO personnel get hurt. Card's MO in New York was locking himself in the room, just like he was doing now in his trailer. Better to let him simmer down, and give him a little space, Reamer advised. Skolfield agreed, then called his supervisor, Lt. Brian Quinn. When he explained the situation and his conversation with Reamer, Quinn also agreed it was best to let him calm down, give him some space, and visit it later.

*"I had done what I could do. I couldn't stake out his house for days and wait for him to come out."*

*"Did you ever consider going to visit Robert Card some other time at his place of work instead?"* a commission member asked him.

*"No."*

Once Card was outside his house, Skolfield or any other law enforcement officer could have placed him in protective custody, and they would have been within their rights to use force if necessary if he resisted. There was no reason to force a potentially deadly confrontation at his trailer with this option available. But Skolfield didn't consider it. Neither apparently did his boss, Lt. Quinn. Nor did Skolfield think to ask Reamer where Card worked. If Reamer couldn't tell him, Hodgson certainly could. He obviously knew, because he worked with him at the same Auburn trucking company delivering bakery products.

In a conversation in late March, Hodgson said if asked, he would have advised officers to stay away from Card when he was in his car because he had taken to carrying a handgun under the front seat. Instead, he would have advised them to pull him over at work after he had unhitched the truck cab from the trailer. He never carried a firearm in the cab, Hodgson said. But no one ever called him to ask.

Skolfield pulled away from his vantage point on the road near Card's trailer and drove five miles to see Robert Card Sr. at the family farm on Meadow Road. When he began asking about a plan to take his son's guns away, the father suggested he talk to Ryan, his oldest son. Skolfield eventually contacted Ryan the next day, who assured him that he and his father would make sure the guns were removed from the safe at the family farm, and that "he would try to work with Robert to make sure he doesn't have any other firearms."

At this point during the commission hearing, member Attorney Toby Dilworth, a former federal prosecutor who had been questioning him, asked abruptly as Skolfield was looking at a document, "Is that the Cunniff review you're looking at?"

He was referring to the ninety-three-page review that the SCSO had commissioned that exonerated Carleton, Skolfield, and the rest of the agency for their handling of the Card responses. This came after Dilworth asked for clarification: Did Skolfield say his understanding was the guns were already secured *or* did he say they would be secured? They would be secured, Skolfield answered defensively.

"Had you determined what kind of firearms he possessed?"

"No, I hadn't."

"You never thought to ask what kind of firearms? Long guns, handguns?"

"I didn't. To me, a gun is a gun is a gun. I figured there would be some handguns, some hunting rifles because they're a farm family."

Skolfield concluded the call with Ryan by saying that he didn't want Robert to hurt himself or others, and if he thought his brother needed to be evaluated at any point, he should contact the SCSO for help to facilitate it.

With that, the SCSO's contact with the Card family was over. Skolfield went home to make a sandwich and had hardly got two slices of bread out when he received a call to handle a domestic violence assault in his hometown of

Bowdoinham. He spent the rest of his shift handling that case and then went on vacation for the next week.

When asked by Dilworth whether he asked anyone in the SCSO to follow up with the Cards while he was gone, he said, no, he considered the case closed. They couldn't contact Card, the family had made assurances that his guns would be secured, and the Army had suggested leaving him alone, he added.

"So, you were relying on the family to protect the community?"

"It was a lot of weight to put on the family, but I couldn't get through that door legally, so that's what I did."

"But they were intimidated by him, weren't they?"

"I didn't get that impression."

The SCSO had teamed up with other local law enforcement agencies to work with a mental health liaison who was available to ride with officers and respond to mental health crises. The September 15th request for a wellness check on Card would have been a clear-cut case for utilizing this new resource. Unfortunately, the start date for the liaison was October 1st.

"Did you consider consulting with the liaison about Card when they came on board?"

"I did not. The case was resolved at that point," Skolfield responded.

On October 18th, Skolfield received an automated notification requesting the status of Card's File 6 classification. An alert to other law enforcement agencies to use extreme caution if they located Card, it had been in the system since Skolfield had entered it before the attempted wellness check. He responded to the notification by pulling it out of the system.

"Did you speak to Ryan Card before doing that to see if he had followed through on the plan to secure his brother's guns?"

"I did not."

The commission members never brought up the transcript of the recorded call between Skolfield and dispatch when he first called it in that he was headed to Card's house, and concluded by saying, "He's considered armed and dangerous, bla, bla, bla." It's a curious omission. A logical follow-up question would have been to ask Skolfield why he would be so dismissive of an 'armed and dangerous' warning.

Perhaps they might have asked: *In hindsight, would you agree that your cavalier comment about the danger that Mr. Card could have presented is indicative of the approach you took to handling this call? Isn't it fair to say that you dismissed the possible danger to the public outright without establishing any factual basis for doing so?*

The next time the SCSO would have contact with the Card family was the night of October 25th, when they were called to protect the family at a house in Bowdoinham where they had gathered because of the fear that Robbie was on his way to the family farm. By this time, he had been identified, and the overwhelming realization that one of their own had just committed the worst atrocity in Maine history would be starting to sink in. No one had any idea what he would do next. Sgt. Skolfield responded to the call. He saw Ryan there. They spoke a little to each other, but Ryan was very upset, visibly shaken. No one spoke much, he explained to the commission. If he recognizes the tragic irony of the fact that he was providing protection for the family of a mass shooter whose case he considered closed, he's kept it to himself.

*Arthur Barnard, the father of shooting victim, Artie Strout, playing pool at Schemengees on the night of October 25, 2023. Artie took this photo of his father just minutes before he was shot and killed by Robert Card Jr. while he played at the same table. (Photo courtesy of Arthur Barnard)*

# THE LIGHTS WENT OUT AT SCHEMENGEES

Destiny Johnson was most likely the first person in Schemengees to see Robert Card II enter. She was seated with her three golfing friends at a high-top table closest to the door, her chair oriented so that she was facing the entrance. The four had finished nine holes at a golf course in Auburn earlier and decided at the last minute to go Schemengees rather than a restaurant they normally went to which was closer to the golf course.

He had no expression on his face at all when he came in. He fired the rifle once in the air, made an adjustment, then repeated that two more times, she said. The mother of a ten-year-old daughter, Johnson dove to the floor and started crawling toward the kitchen, her ears ringing from the shooting.

Jennifer Zanca was seated across from Johnson, her back to the door. She had never been to Schemengees before, and she was surprised to see how crowded it was on a Wednesday night. As soon as she heard the incredibly loud noise, she immediately dove to the floor and started crawling to a nearby half-wall.

As she approached the wall, a high-caliber bullet tore into her left shoulder with such an impact that she felt like her arm had been severed from her body. A former nurse, Zanca found herself somehow upright in the kitchen, her other hand clamped over the entry hole to try and stem the bleeding. As she staggered to an exit door out the back, the sound of gunfire continued unabated.

A neighbor across the street saw her stumble into the road, and immediately put her in the back of his car and raced to the nearest hospital. He ran red lights at speeds approaching 100 m.p.h. In a fog of pain, Jennifer recalls seeing one driver give them the middle finger as they flew past. She was the first victim to make it to a hospital that night.

Sherry Stanton was also at a table facing the door when she heard a loud noise that she thought was a beer keg exploding. She heard Schemengees' Manager, Joe Walker, yell "What's that?!" and then looked to see Card shoot two friends who were sitting a few feet away. She watched him walk around the table, then take aim at the cornhole players who were up at the boards adjacent to a wall with nowhere to go. She and a friend ran into a small utility room when Card's Ruger SFAR-10 jammed, and then found their way to a rear exit.

As they huddled under a lifted pickup truck in the parking lot, her friend's husband came running out. He had a big hole in his jeans with fragments of debris hanging from where a bullet had struck his wallet. His leg was penetrated by fragments of the bullet and debris, but the wallet probably saved his life. Mike Roderick and his eighteen-year-old son, Jackson, were playing in the Wednesday night cornhole league. They had started seven weeks earlier, and in that brief time, had made a new bunch of friends, which was not an easy thing for an introvert like Jackson. That night was also opening night for the Boston Celtics, and the two had put on their green jerseys with the iconic leprechaun logo and taken and posted a selfie on social media and tagged Schemengees. Their network of family and friends now knew exactly where they were.

The two were playing on separate boards exactly twenty-seven-feet apart when the first shots rang out. Everyone around him froze for a few seconds, the elder Roderick recalls, and then they ran into a nearby utility room. The shots continued, and then he yelled out loud, "Where the fuck is my son?!" As the bullets tore through the long, rectangular building, he ran back out, and looked across the room to make eye contact with his son as he crouched behind a half wall, a look of stark terror etched on his face.

The forty-nine-year-old father ran back into the utility room, and as he pushed up against the wall, he saw an electrical panel, instinctively reached over, and pushed down the main circuit breaker handle. The building plunged into darkness. Roderick didn't know it at the time, but Card had walked his way towards the back of the cornhole room and was nearly face-to-face with his son. He had just emptied a magazine and was reloading when the lights went out.

Jason Barnett had been playing nearby on Court Five. A career Navy machinist's mate, he had been in thirteen active shooter training drills in his Navy career and as a civilian employee for the Department of Defense at Bath Iron Works. He didn't have either a fight or flight response when the shots rang out, he told the independent commission in an early March hearing. Instead, he "melted" to the floor along with just about everyone else.

That's where he was, in the process of crawling towards safety of any kind, when Card approached, the green laser dot trained on him. If he recognized him, he didn't say so. The two had played as cornhole partners at Schemengees and other area venues, and Card was the one who had recommended Barnett come to the Lewiston sports bar to play. He had just reloaded another magazine, Barnett said, when the lights went out. Then the flight mode kicked in, and he sprang up and ran for the back door. He's fairly sure Card fired at him twice in the near darkness as he sprinted for the door.

Steve Richards-Kretlow, Kyle Curtis, Chris Dyndiuk, and Richard Morlock are all deaf, and members of a tight-knit Deaf cornhole league that would gather every Wednesday at Schemengees. There were ten of them playing that night. As much as it's a social gathering for all cornhole players, their group at the Lewiston club was especially meaningful for them, because it's difficult for members of the Deaf community to get together and socialize in such a large and sparsely populated state with long driving distances.

They were just finishing up their first game when the firing started. Instead of hearing the shots, they felt the vibrations made by bullets striking objects, and they saw glass shattering and wood splintering. Like virtually everyone else, they dove to the floor, desperately looking for cover under tables, pulling chairs and cornhole boards over themselves—flimsy protection against ammunition used to hunt big game animals.

Richards-Kretlow had started running, but he was shot in the leg, and he collapsed to the floor under a table and pretended he was dead. A friend that he was playing with dove to the floor next to him and pulled a chair over himself. Card shot him several times. He was one of ten men who drew their last breath there that night.

Kyle Curtis felt the vibrations, saw glasses at the bar shatter, then looked to see muzzle flashes from the rifle and people falling to the ground. He got down under a table, and then he spotted a door and crawled towards it. A friend was crawling behind him, but he was shot and killed, as fragments of bullets peppered Curtis' arm as he made his way to the door.

Chris Dyndiuk had only been in Schemengees once before. He took cover behind a cornhole board, and as he did, he saw Card shoot and kill two friends who had been army-crawling across the floor. When his gun jammed, Dyndiuk ran as fast as he could for the exit as bullets tore through the room. He instinctively jumped in his car and tore out of the parking lot, but then thought of his friends and turned around and went back.

Richard Morlock saw bullets strike a wood counter in front of him and shards of wood exploded and penetrated his arms and side. He dove to the floor and played dead. As he lay there with his eyes squeezed shut to black out the scene of horror around him, he faintly heard Card change a magazine and then a click as the gun jammed momentarily. Then the lights went out, and he opened his eyes. Illuminated by the parking lot lights, he saw Card exit out the building through the rear door of the arcade room.

Andrew Chessie was a diehard Schemengees cornhole player—at least twice a week, sometimes three times, over six years. He was on court four, the farthest from the front door, when he heard the shots. He dove to the floor, and looked up to see Card walking towards him, so he grabbed the cornhole board and pulled it over him and his partner. As he lay there thinking this was how it would end for them, the lights went out. He saw the green laser dot bouncing around, then looked to see the forty-year-old career soldier headed out the arcade door. Later, he remembered that he knew Card from other cornhole venues and thinks he even partnered with him at blind draw tournaments.

Tori Patterson had been a four-year Schemengees employee who worked her way up to assistant manager. She loved the job, loved the people and the community they had built there. She was serving the cornhole players when she heard an unbelievably loud bang and stood there, completely frozen, looking directly at him. Patterson was thinking that perhaps he came to rob them when she saw him shoot someone. Still, she was frozen to the spot, and then a co-worker grabbed her, and they ran out the back door. As they were sprinting outside the building, shots were still ringing out, and she was both desperate for the people she left behind in there, and terrified that the shooter would come out to hunt them down like prey.

Ben Dyer wasn't usually at Schemengee's on Wednesday nights. Joe Walker had texted him that morning asking him to substitute for another player. He ducked behind a half-wall when he heard the first shots, but Card shot him through the wall four times in his legs and arm, then came around the wall and shot him in the hand, shredding a finger, looking straight at him when he fired the final shot. Then the lights went out and Dyer lay bleeding on the floor as Card walked calmly out the arcade door.

Ryan Dallesandro told the *Lewiston Sun Journal* that he was sitting at a table near the cornhole boards looking at his phone when he heard an explosion. He looked towards the kitchen and then heard Joe Walker yell, "What's that!?" as he turned to face the shooter. A volley of gunshots rang out and Dallesandro dove to the floor and then crawled to take cover under a pool table. He found Joe Walker next to him, struggling to breathe and moaning. Dallesandro held his wrist as the gunfire reverberated through the building.

Then there was silence and a pause in the shooting as Card stopped to reload. Dallesandro whispered Walker's name, but he didn't respond. His mind was scrambling with options of what to do next when the lights went out. He saw the green laser dot bouncing around, and then there was a pause. He could tell that Card was deliberating what to do next, Dallesandro said. Then he walked out of the exit door in the arcade area.

Robert Card II had been inside Schemengees for seventy-eight seconds. In that time, he fired thirty-six rounds. When the door shut behind him, the air in the popular sports bar was thick with the smell of gunpowder and the moans of the dying and wounded. When Dallesandro realized Card was gone, he called 9-1-1 from his wristwatch phone and told them he was with a wounded man. They told him to try and apply pressure to the wound, and Dallesandro reached for a cornhole bag to stuff into the holes in Walker's stomach. At 7:10 p.m. the police and paramedics arrived and took over.

*Schemengees shooting victim, Artie Strout, with four of his five children. (Photo courtesy of Arthur Barnard)*

Arthur Barnard had been shooting pool with his son, Artie Strout, helping prepare him for an upcoming tournament. He left shortly before 7:00 p.m. and was driving down Lisbon St. in front of Governor's Restaurant, a local landmark, when his ex-wife called and told him there had just been a mass shooting at Schemengees. By that time, he had already heard about a shooting at the bowling alley.

"No, it was at Sparetime [sic]," he told her as the sounds of sirens pierced the air and blue lights lit up the night sky. "No, Schemengees too!" she cried to him.

Artie was playing at the table closest to the door. Arthur knew at that moment that his son would be a victim. He found out later from his son's friend, Justin Karcher, that the two of them dove under the table as Card opened fire. Justin was hit multiple times, and as they lay there, Artie said to him, "You'll be okay." His friend watched as seconds later Card pumped four to five rounds into Artie, killing him instantly.

As survivor after survivor of the Schemengees shooting recounted the horror of that night to the independent commission in a March hearing, almost everyone had the same story line: Moments of horrifying, incomprehensible carnage that only stopped when the lights went out right after Card had emptied a clip and put a new one in.

THE LIGHTS WENT OUT. A spiritual person would see Mike Roderick's quick-thinking reflex as the hand of God at work. An atheist might start believing. Jason Barnett, the career Navy man, turned to face Roderick as he gave his searing testimony. "Mike Roderick, you're my hero," he said.

Barnett had fled out of the darkened building and was outside when Card came out. He watched him dump a clip out of the rifle and reload. He looked disappointed that there was no one outside to engage in a firefight, the ex-Navy man said. Instead, he jumped into his white Subaru Outback and turned right out of the parking lot. He was headed south in the direction of Lisbon. Behind him, ten men lay dead or dying, others were wounded, and scores of stunned people were left to try to make sense of the unimaginable horror they had just witnessed.

# THE SHERIFF'S OFFICE LAWYERS UP

Can a review commissioned and paid for by the subject of said review truly be considered an unbiased, independent, third-party examination of the facts?

Your answer to that question is a good litmus test about your belief system. Answer yes without any caveats and you demonstrate a strong belief in the honesty of your fellow human beings. Answer an unequivocal no and you demonstrate a strong distrust in your fellow human beings, whether it's arrived at through experience, genetically inherited, or both. Answer it depends and you're the proverbial fence-sitter, occupying the gray space where much of life plays out between the lines of black and white.

Whatever your answer, the facts are as follows: In response to a FOAA (Maine Freedom of Access Act) request, Sheriff Merry provided the legal agreement between his agency and a lawyer from a Portland law firm commissioned to conduct the review.

On November 3rd, 2023, the SCSO and the firm of McCloskey, Mina, Cunniff & Frawley, and most specifically attorney Michael Cunniff, signed an agreement to "produce an *objective* [italics in the agreement] review of the Sagadahoc County Sheriff's Office response to concerns about the well-being of Robert Card." Per the agreement, the law firm's rate was $300 per hour, with billable rates of $95 per hour for additional paralegal work and $125 per hour for senior paralegal work, billed entirely to the SCSO.

In the agreement, Attorney Cunniff emphasized the approach he intended to take: "McCloskey, Mina, Cunniff & Frawley offers no promises or guarantees concerning the outcome of its findings, which shall, of course, be the product of a totally *objective* [italics included in agreement] process." The law firm also noted that it had conducted "internal checks pursuant to its conflict systems, and has determined there are no known conflicts of interest in this matter." At the very bottom of the last page on a line marked "Authorized Representative of the Sagadahoc County Sheriff's Office" is Sheriff Merry's signature.

While it appears on paper that Sheriff Merry was fully involved in commissioning Attorney Cunniff to produce the review, that wasn't exactly the case, according to the county's attorney. Instead, the sheriff contacted Bernstein Schur, a major Maine law firm that Sagadahoc County retains to do legal work on its behalf, and spoke to attorney Matt Tarasevich, a partner in the firm's Municipal & Regulatory Practice Group.

In an email response to questions about his involvement in the production of the review, Tarasevich said that Sheriff Merry determined shortly after the shootings that a review "would be in order," so he advised the sheriff to contact Attorney Cunniff, "who was known to me as a well-respected Maine attorney experienced in law enforcement and public sector investigative matters."

On November 1st, 2023, two days before the agreement was signed, a somber Maine Governor, Janet Mills, stood at a podium in the State House in Augusta and announced that she was ordering the formation of an independent commission of experts "to determine the facts and circumstances of the October 25th shootings in Lewiston, including the months preceding the shootings and the police response to it."

*It is important to recognize that, from what we know thus far, on multiple occasions over the last ten months, concerns about Mr. Card's mental health and his behavior were brought to the attention of his Army National Reserve Unit, as well as law enforcement agencies here in Maine and in New York. This raises crucial questions about actions taken and what more could have been done to prevent this tragedy from occurring.*

Among the seven members of the commission, she appointed the former U.S. Attorney for the District of Maine, the former Chief Justice of the Maine Supreme Judicial Court (SJC), and the former Associate Justice of the SJC. The former head of the FBI field office in Maine and the former longtime head of criminal investigations for the Maine Attorney General's Office were chosen to be the commission's chief investigators.

When asked if he had advised Sheriff Merry as to whether he should commission his own review independent from the state's own, Tarasevich said he could not divulge the conversations he had with Sheriff Merry because they involved attorney-client confidences.

He also didn't respond to the question of whether he felt Attorney Cunniff could provide a more thorough review of the SCSO's involvement in the case than the team of heavyweight law enforcement and judicial officials on the newly appointed commission. In addition to being invested with subpoena power to obtain documents and testimony that wouldn't be available to Attorney Cunniff, the Governor's commission was also prepared to spend at least six months, likely more, to produce its findings. In contrast, Attorney Cunniff completed his review on November 21st, a mere eighteen days after the agreement was signed. It was released by the SCSO on December 8th, 2023.

Despite not having the cumulative experience of the commission members, Attorney Cunniff does possess some impressive credentials. If any single person was to be tasked with such a complex review, he is a worthy candidate. The son of a former Boston police officer, Cunniff spent twenty-seven years in the Drug Enforcement Administration (DEA), working in supervisory roles in Boston, New York City, and Portland. He also served as lead financial crimes investigator for the Iran-Contra investigation, and DEA liaison to the FBI's New York Joint Terrorism Task Force. If that's not impressive enough, he was also the coordinator of the DEA's international training program in Africa, South America, Asia, and Australia, and later, served as Director of Investigations for the Major League Baseball's Commissioner's Office.

Among his many roles in the DEA, he was the lead investigator for the Maine task force that was formed in the late 1990s to investigate the illegal diversion and distribution of the opiate, Oxycontin, in Washington County, a sprawling, thinly populated coastal region of small fishing and logging towns and Passamaquoddy reservation land that borders the Canadian province of New Brunswick. Working with the United States Attorney for the District of Maine, the DEA and other law enforcement agencies struggled to keep up with the exploding OxyContin abuse epidemic, which was first observed in Maine, and later in rural regions in Ohio, West Virginia, Kentucky and elsewhere.

The drug's manufacturer was Purdue Pharma, a company that's since become synonymous with corporate greed. The United States Attorney was Jay McCloskey, who was the first ranking law enforcement official in the country to sound the alarm about the OxyContin problem and the marketing tactics used by Purdue Pharma to put the highly addictive opiate in the hands of virtually anyone who claimed to be experiencing pain. After he left office in 2001, McCloskey started a private law firm and went to work as a paid consultant for Purdue Pharma, even going as far as to defend the same marketing practices he sounded the alarm about in a Senate hearing in Washington DC in 2007. He's since defended his decision to switch hats like that over the years, but his reputation has taken a hit in the court of public opinion; close to 2,500 Mainers have died of pharmaceutical opioid-related overdoses since OxyContin was first introduced in 1997.

Meanwhile, Cunniff went on to law school after retiring from the DEA and has since built an impressive and eclectic legal resume—from serving as a judicial advisor to governments in Kosovo, Serbia, and Ethiopia, to criminal defense work in high profile cases, to serving as a member of the University of Maine Law School faculty, to providing pro bono services to juvenile and mentally ill offenders. He was also a founding partner in McCloskey, Cunniff, Mina & Frawley, reuniting with Jay McCloskey, his former law enforcement colleague on the front lines of the OxyContin battle. The law firm has deep connections to law enforcement, judicial, and political power brokers in Maine. Two other members of the independent commission put together by Governor Mills work with the firm. They are former U.S. Attorney Paula Silsby, a senior lawyer for the firm who succeeded McCloskey as lead law enforcement agent in the state, and former lead FBI agent in Maine, James Osterreider, who works as the senior case manager of investigations for The McCloskey Resource Group, an internal investigations and consulting group consisting of former DEA, FBI, and IRS agents. Cunniff was also a principal in that business.

As if he wasn't busy enough, Cunniff also worked as an adjunct instructor for an Auburn-based public safety training company called Dirigo Safety, which was selected in 2020 to manage the Maine Law Enforcement Accreditation Program by the Maine Chiefs of Police Association (MCPA). Before he left the company in 2021, he spent four years there providing instruction to police departments all over the state about the use of deadly force, police accountability, oversight and leadership issues, and court testimony by law enforcement officers. Brian McMaster, the former Maine Attorney General's Office Chief Investigator, is currently the Chief Law Enforcement Consultant for Dirigo Safety. He's also on the executive committee of the MCPA, and he was appointed to be the lead investigator for the Lewiston independent commission.

The privately-owned Dirigo Safety has overseen the accreditation of dozens of Maine police departments through its work with MCPA. It's also the primary lesson plan writer for the Maine Criminal Justice Academy, and it offers a wide variety of individualized training classes to law enforcement and public safety agencies, as well as school districts and other institutions. In fact, on October 6th, 2023, just nineteen days before the Lewiston shootings, the company provided an Active Shooter and De-Escalation training session for the 575 employees of School Administrative District 75 in Topsham, which includes Mt. Ararat High School, where Card graduated in 2001.

The SCSO is also one of its clients. Dirigo Safety has provided yellow flag law training to at least twenty SCSO personnel, including Sheriff Merry, Chief Deputy Strout, and Patrol Supervisor, Lt. Brian Quinn, who is Deputy Carleton's and Sgt. Skolfield's immediate supervisor. For the yellow flag training Dirigo provided, as well as work they did on its standard operating procedures manual, the SCSO paid the company $7,120, according to documentation provided by Sheriff Merry.

In a state as thinly populated as Maine—1.36 million at last U.S. Census count—there's bound to be some overlap between public officials and private enterprise. It's pretty much unavoidable. However, it is worth noting that a company that Attorney Cunniff served as a law enforcement instructor for is the same company that trained the SCSO's personnel in the use of the yellow flag law. His review of the agency's response to calls about the man who shot and killed eighteen people largely revolves around whether its officers should have initiated the yellow flag process to take Card into protective custody and remove his firearms. It's also worth noting that Dirigo Safety's current chief law enforcement consultant is the lead investigator for the independent commission.

Cunniff declined to comment when asked whether he personally trained any law enforcement personnel in the use of the yellow flag law. He also declined to comment when asked whether he interviewed any other parties mentioned in the review or relied solely on the testimony of SCSO personnel to arrive at his findings. His firm was paid $27,800 by Sagadahoc County to produce the review.

With these facts and tangential connections established, this would be a good place to re-ask the question posed at the beginning of the chapter: Can a review commissioned and paid for by the subject of said review *truly* be considered an unbiased, independent, third-party examination of the case?

*The Frost Hill Road boat launch in Lisbon. Card's Subaru hatchback was found abandoned on the ramp less than three hours after the shootings. (Photo by Robert Conlin)*

# MANHUNT PART I: ON THE RUN

Having just committed the most heinous crime in the 203-year history of the state of Maine, Robert Card was on the run. The carnage he left behind at Just-in-Time and Schemengees was unspeakable. The phrase, "there are no words to describe it," is as just as inadequate as any single word used to describe recurring scenes of horrible bloodshed and acts of incomprehensible inhumanity.

"Horrific," "gruesome," "senseless"—it doesn't matter, they're inadequate. By now, as common as mass shootings in America have become, these words ring as hollow as an urn emptied of the ashen remains of what once was a human being. Like "thoughts and prayers," they've been used so much to describe these shootings, they lost their meaning.

What did Card do after he committed these indescribable acts? Unless the Maine State Police (MSP) release any possible video footage or credible eyewitness testimony, his actions from the time he got in his white 2013 Subaru Outback bearing Maine license plate # 9246PD and drove out of Schemengees parking lot until the time his body was found nine miles away over forty-eight hours later are unknown. We may eventually fill in the blanks for that time span, but we'll never know what he was thinking. Did he feel gratification, relief, rage, remorse? Or was he numb to the gravity of what he had just done? Should we even be asking those questions? Does his mindset deserve our attention?

There are plenty of people who would answer no. Emphatically! Some of the Lewiston victims' family members feel that way, just as family members of the victims of other notable mass shootings feel about the person who murdered their loved ones. So too must some of the families of the victims of the 4,011 other mass shootings (four or more victims, non-gang or terrorist-related) in the United States from 2014-2022.[3]

It's hard to argue with their logic. In this attention-seeking society, it's thought that killers beget killers, and there's plenty of evidence of copycat killings and failed plots to support that. Mark Follman, one of America's leading experts on mass shootings, finds proof of that in case after case as he works to decipher the motivations for these heinous acts.

In a 2015 investigative report for *Mother Jones* magazine, Follman outlined seventy-four plots or actual attacks in thirty states that were inspired by the infamous 1999 mass shooting at Columbine High School in Colorado. In ten of those cases, the attackers or suspects specifically referred to the name of the two Columbine shooters. Fourteen of them were meant to happen on the anniversary of the attack. In three of them, the perpetrators made a pilgrimage to the school from distant states. In 2019, city officials submitted a plan to tear it down and build another in its place to reduce the stream of copycats and social media selfie-takers, but eventually dropped the idea.

Social policy impact aside, the pure visceral response to deny shooters their day of infamy is understandable. There's been a groundswell of public support calling for that approach. After an anti-immigration zealot murdered fifty-one Muslims in their houses of worship in New Zealand in 2019, Jacinda Ahearn, the country's former prime minister,

---

3. Characteristics of Mass Shootings By States, 2014-2022, *Journal of American Medical Association Network Open*, 7/26/23

vowed never to speak the man's name. "He is a criminal. He is an extremist. But he will, when I speak, be nameless."

Like every complex issue, there's a flip side, and on that side are believers just as committed to their viewpoint. Like the authors of the 2021 book, *The Violence Project: How to Stop a Mass Shooting Epidemic[4],* who argue that to find some semblance of a solution, we need to form an evidence-based understanding of what causes these perpetrators to decide to commit these horrendous acts.

Of course, it's much simpler to come down on the side of information gathering if you've never lost a loved one or were present at a mass shooting. You simply can't walk in their shoes. Until you dive under a table and watch a man execute your friends as they crawl on the floor in a desperate attempt to flee. Or you watch your youngest children go down to the basement every night to kiss a flickering lightbulb which they think of as their dad now that he's been inexplicably taken from them. Until you've looked into the eyes of a man that are as blank and cold as a corpse while he points a Ruger SFAR A-10 semi-automatic rifle fitted out with a thermal scope and green laser directly at you.

Then there's the middle ground, where your heart says yes, if there's any chance to stop this we need to understand; and your head says no, these cowards who shoot innocent people aren't worthy of any more attention. For the purposes of trying to understand what drove Robert Card II to do what he did we have to examine all the factors that may have contributed, all the while never forgetting the pain and suffering so many people are living through because of what this man did.

Without access to any possible video feed from area businesses with security systems, as far as we know, the

---

4. *The Violence Project: How to Stop a Mass Shooting Epidemic,* James Densley, Jillian Peterson, Abrams Press, 2021

next time Card's Subaru was spotted was in the nearby town of Lisbon just after 10:00 p.m. on October 25th, some three hours after law enforcement had been alerted to the shootings. Lisbon and Lewiston are connected by Rt. 196, which is the major road between the town of Brunswick and the city of Lewiston, a stretch of twenty miles that cuts southeast roughly parallel to the Androscoggin River—which, easily forgotten now—was the lifeblood of the area for centuries and the reason all the towns along its banks came into existence.

The river's name is thought to be a mashup combining the native Eastern Abenaki term meaning "river of rock shelters" with the name of Sir Edward Andros, the British colonial administrator of New England in the late 1600s. Like so many place names on maps of the globe, the cities and towns sprouted along the riverbanks because water is not only a life source; it's an energy source that fueled industry and was a key means of transport before the advent of trucks and automobiles.

All along its 178-mile length, from Umbagog Lake in northern New Hampshire to Merrymeeting Bay in the Gulf of Maine, paper and textile mills and other industries took root and grew. With an average vertical drop of eight feet per mile, the river generated abundant natural power for the massive brick mill complexes that employed thousands of workers in Berlin, New Hampshire, and Bethel, Rumford, Mexico, Livermore Falls, Lewiston, Brunswick, and other Maine towns and cities along its banks.

Lured by the jobs that those mills provided, immigrants flooded into the region; first waves of Irish, followed by French-Canadians from Quebec, who comprised over half the population of Lewiston by 1900, and essentially transformed the city into a bifurcated border crossing between the U.S. and Canada. The closest border is a three-hour drive away at the Coburn Gore crossing into Quebec, but in Lewiston, a few blocks downtown around the enormous Bates Mill complex—"Little Canada," it was known as—was the French-speaking outpost.

The closing of the mills, the migratory pattern of new generations, and a wave of Somali immigrants in the last two decades has diluted the Franco-American influence in the city somewhat, but it's still recognizable most anywhere you go. From the venerable FX Marcotte furniture store to Lepage bakeries to the Colisee, home of the Maine Nordiques NAHL professional hockey team, to the "In Memoriam" pages of the church bulletin at the Basilica of Saints Peter and Paul, Lewiston still waves its Franco-American flag proudly.

At the other end of Rt. 196 lies Brunswick, a town that was home to a succession of mills built on the site of a late 1600's British colonial fort named after the British administrator, Andros. Those mills churned out millions of yards of textile goods for over 150 years, but the town never did become the immigrant magnet of its upstream neighbor. Known primarily as the home of Bowdoin College, a liberal arts school that's been churning out graduates for over 225 years, Brunswick is the tonier bookend to Lewiston's grittier urban environment. Many of those Bowdoin grads became household names—poet Henry Wadsworth Longfellow, author Nathaniel Hawthorne, U.S. President Franklin Pierce, North Pole explorer Robert Peary—while contemporaries like Netflix founder Reed Hastings, and journalist Evan Gershkovich, the *Wall Street Times* reporter currently held in a Russian jail as a pawn in the current geopolitical war with Vladimir Putin, get a mention in the current news cycle.

The town was also once home to the Brunswick Naval Air Station, its squadrons of P3 Orion maritime patrol aircraft and over 10,000 personnel at its height, but the base closed in 2010, and Brunswick's population now numbers 22,000. That's a small town by many state's measures, but it cracks the top ten in the list of the most populated municipalities in Maine. In fact, its population exceeds that of the state capitol of Augusta, thirty miles as the crow flies to the north.

The towns of Topsham and Lisbon straddle Rt. 196 between Brunswick and Lewiston. Like so many places that lie in between two bigger destinations, they're a pass-through for much of the daily traffic that travels Rt.196. Topsham does boast the Topsham Mall, the region's largest shopping center, and its home to Mt. Ararat High School, which serves the towns of Topsham, Bowdoinham, Harpswell, and Bowdoin, Card's hometown. His boyhood home is located six undulating miles of woods and farmland away from the school he left in 2001.

Lisbon, the town where he ended his life, butts up against Lewiston's city limits to the south. Yes, it was named after the capital city of Portugal. Apparently, the town's residents decided its original name of Thompsonborough was too long, so they changed it in the early 1800s. Why they chose to name it after a European city 4500 miles away is a mystery. But then, Maine has towns named Rome, Paris, Dresden, Bremen, Frankfort, Stockholm, Madrid, Moscow, Naples, Athens, Vienna, and a whole bunch named after English cities, so the shoe fits.

A town of 9,000 inhabitants, Lisbon is known primarily as the place where famed horror author Stephen King graduated from high school, and then took on his first writing job as a sports reporter for the local newspaper, the *Weekly Enterprise.* For fans of Americana pop culture, it's also known as the former home of the Moxie Museum. It's unlikely too many people outside of New England know about Moxie—either one of the most delicious or one of the vilest soft drinks ever made, depending on personal taste—but they might have heard it used to describe a person's character. As in, "That kid's got a lot of moxie asking for extra Halloween candy."

The town is made up of three villages—Lisbon Falls, Lisbon Center, and Lisbon proper. Lisbon Falls, on the Topsham end of Rt.196, is home to the remains of the old Worumbo Mill, a faded white concrete building at the base of the falls that gives the village its name. Abandoned and beaten hard by 140 years of mercurial Maine weather, it's all that's left of the original woolen mill after a 1987 fire. It's not completely forgotten though; King gave it a mention in his time travel novel, *11/22/63*.

With its one-street downtown and a cluster of storefronts, strip malls, and weather-beaten houses along Rt. 196, Lisbon Falls has a scuffed, down-on-its-heels look to it, but it's a proud working-class section of a proud working-class town, where residents line the impressive Lisbon High School football field to watch the Greyhounds in action, and host and attend spaghetti suppers to support their neighbors— like the two families displaced by a fire in early 2023 who received $4000 to help with housing.

This is the town Robert Card decided would be his destination after he shot and killed eighteen unarmed people and wounded thirteen others with a high-powered rifle. Whether he mapped it out and stuck to a plan, or fled there spontaneously, is anyone's guess. Given the location where his body was ultimately found, and his familiarity with the area and the roads as a truck driver for decades, the better guess is he was following a master plan.

Which makes it more likely that he took the back roads from Schemengees to the boat launch. Had he used the direct Rt. 196 route, he could have easily driven south out of the parking lot onto Lincoln, taken an almost immediate left onto South St., gone less than a quarter mile or so down that street, and then taken a right onto the main road.

He would have a straight shot for the next eight miles, but he'd be on one of the most heavily traveled roads in the area, driving a car he knew would be the subject of an intense manhunt. He'd have to travel through brightly lit sections of the roadway, past a major printing company, a large liquor and beer distribution center, and, inexplicably for a state that only has three, occasionally four, months of summer, four swimming pool stores. After that, he'd have to stop at a traffic light at a busy intersection in front of a mill converted to condos, and then go past a long stretch of small strip malls and businesses, where local police who normally might be sitting there in a speed trap could be on high alert for a white Subaru Outback with a distinctive black bumper.

If he was parked in the Home Depot lot at the Topsham Mall, the Subaru might not stand out. There were 53,000 of them on Maine roads ten years ago, and Maine is second only to Vermont for Subaru sales in the U.S. With its all-wheel drive, ample cargo space, and fairly low sticker price, it's a ubiquitous car in Maine. It screams Yankee practical, which makes them well-suited for the roads, the weather conditions, and the people who drive them.

So, chances are he didn't take that route. Instead, he might have fled from Schemengees, traveled a short distance up Lincoln St. onto River Rd., then went left on Goddard St. and skirted behind a Wal-Mart distribution center. From there, he could have navigated a series of connecting country roads for the next six or seven miles. Most are sparsely populated, skirted by thick woods interrupted by farms and fields, and would have had little traffic on them in the pitch-black evening hour. It would be a challenge under the circumstances, but he was a professional truck driver with an encyclopedic knowledge of local roads.

Maybe all this speculation is a waste of time. There's always the possibility that his descent into paranoia had reached rock-bottom at this point, and he didn't even plan his getaway and didn't care about what would happen next. The only problem with that theory is that it isn't well-supported by the evidence of his behavior leading up to October 25th. Despite his well-documented paranoia, he clearly had moments of lucidity. He had laid out the breadcrumb trail for anyone to follow. Of the five W's pillars of journalism—who, what, when, where, and why—he had already provided two.

He told multiple people what: "I'll take care of it" and "I'm capable." And there was no question as to why: he thought everyone was calling him a pedophile. By 7:10 p.m. on October 25th, we learned the who, the where, and the when. But was his mission complete? That was the question on everyone's mind when his Subaru was discovered at the Miller Park boat launch ramp off Rt. 196 three hours later.

# A FATHER'S PLEA

The argument about the freedom to own guns and the determination to control them will rage on in Maine and the rest of the country for the near future, just as it has in the past. Except here it will now be fueled by the previously unthinkable: A mass shooting with a semi-automatic weapon that killed and injured scores of innocent people while they bowled, shot pool, and played cornhole in a central Maine city.

The shootings have created new gun control advocates out of the unlikeliest of people. Arthur Barnard, the father of a Schemengees victim, for example, says he won't stop pushing for new laws until there's a law requiring that gun owners register their weapons. He's a convicted felon (decades ago he sold some cocaine to a "friend" who turned out to be a police informant), so he can't own a gun. He never gave much thought to how he felt about others doing so. He's got plenty else to think about. Barnard is a busy guy with a big extended family he supports. The whole argument about gun control isn't something he could have ever imagined getting involved in until he lost his son.

"People should just stop and think. Right now, you have to register your car, your boat, canoe, snowmobile, ATV, even your friggin' dog," he told the author on a snowy January afternoon in his apartment in Topsham. The sixty-two-year-old takes off his glasses and rubs his eyes. He looks drained of energy, but his voice is laced with the indignation he feels as a new gun control advocate who wasn't aware of the complexity of the issues until he was forced to be.

The three teenage grandkids he's raised from an early age because of another son's drug addiction watched TV upstairs. Terry, an adult relative with some cognitive impairments who he also adopted, came down the stairs occasionally to listen to the conversation. A photo of his forty-two-year-old son, Artie Strout Jr., stood on a nearby desktop. Artie had been shooting pool with him just minutes before Robert Card walked in and pumped multiple large-caliber rounds into his body. It makes no sense to Barnard why so many gun owners are so resistant to change.

*What's the big deal about registering your gun? Did they take away your car or your dog after you registered them? As long as you're responsible and follow the laws, no they didn't. So don't just scream and yell that they'll take away your guns and think that's a good argument.*

He knows he's in for a long and tough fight, but he doesn't care. His son's death has hardened his resolve. How will his argument play in Maine towns like Princeton, Van Buren, Caribou, or Columbia Falls, all of which declared themselves Second Amendment sanctuary cities in recent years? He'll get sympathy for the loss of his son, and probably a grudging respect from some for his tenacity, but little in the way of agreement.

Same goes for Byron, a town with a population of 140 people located up in the foothills of the Western Maine Mountains along the Swift River. The town got national attention in 2013 when residents voted on a resolution to demand that everyone in the town be *forced to own a gun.* It was a gimmick to call attention to state and national legislator's attempts to regulate gun ownership, they acknowledged, and they all voted it down, even the guy who submitted it.

Meanwhile, at the State House in Augusta, the shootings have energized gun control advocates, while putting gun owner's supporters on the back heel. Arguments for and against new legislation have been flying since the new session started in January 2024. As Maine House Majority Leader Rep. Maureen Terry (D-Gorham) told a local TV news crew, "We're having conversations about red flag laws, we're having conversations about doing everything and about doing nothing," she said. "The table is clear for anybody to be able to share what they feel are priorities."

As those conversations go on in fits and starts, gun sales surged in Maine after the Lewiston shooting. It's a common phenomenon after mass shootings across the country. They incite a primal need in humans to protect themselves and their families, especially if the shooter is on the loose, as Card was for over forty-eight hours. In fact, while virtually every business in Lewiston and the outlying area complied with lockdown orders over that period, many of the gun stores stayed open. Some of those store owners told the *Washington Post* they arrived at work the day after the shooting to a parking lot jammed with cars. One store owner in nearby Turner said his daily average of twenty firearms sold shot up to over one hundred in the week after the shooting. Over one-third of those were AR-15 models, similar to what Card used on his rampage.

Some of these customers were first-time gun owners. But many of those purchases were made by gun owners who already have more than enough firepower to defend themselves. The National Shooting Sports Foundation (NSSF), the firearms manufacturer's industry trade group, estimates that only 30% of firearms purchases are made by first-time buyers. That means that some 10 million of the 15.9 million guns purchased by Americans in 2023 were destined for a household that already owns firearms. Gun owner's advocates point to renewed efforts by lawmakers to introduce gun control legislation as a driving force behind these purchases. Fearing that lawmakers will succeed in efforts to restrict access to certain weapons, gun owners are simply stocking up before that happens, they say.

The twin factors of the increase in mass shootings and the subsequent calls for new legislation make the surge in gun sales in recent years, especially since the pandemic year of 2020, easier to understand. The NSSF has a simpler explanation, though.

"Santa and his reindeer apparently got an extra workout delivering presents under the tree this Christmas," the group said in an early January 2024 press release. "They were carrying the extra weight of new firearms to millions of Americans thirsty to exercise their Second Amendment rights."

One must wonder whether Santa and his hard-working team violated any laws for transporting those firearms across state lines in an unlicensed sleigh. One thing Mainers can be sure of is that few, if any, of the gift-wrapped guns they received were made in the state. Not since the announced closing of Windham Weaponry, the state's last gun manufacturer, earlier in 2023. Its best-selling items were AR-15-style rifles.

Windham Weaponry was the reincarnation of Bushmaster Firearms, the manufacturer credited with being one of the first to develop the AR-15 for private citizens. Bushmaster was launched in 1976 in the northern Maine city of Bangor, then was relocated to the suburban Portland town of Windham by the man who bought it, a flamboyant Maine resident named Richard Dyke. An astute businessman who had a knack for buying failing businesses at a discount, then turning them around and reselling for substantial profits, Dyke was a native Mainer, born in the north central mill town of Wilton. Despite not knowing anything about guns (he didn't even like to hunt, a rare aversion for a man brought up in rural Maine) he bought Bushmaster for $276,000. Within a few years, it became the largest AR-15 manufacturer in the country and remained in that position for nearly a decade. In 1999, for example, Bushmaster sold 65,000 semi-automatic AR-15s, which was more than its ten largest competitors combined.

Along the way, Dyke became a friend and confidante to powerful Maine legislators, including former Senator and U.S. Defense Secretary, William Cohen, and current Senator, Susan Collins. He even counted the Bush family as friends and became Maine campaign chairman for George W. Bush in his run for the presidency. But Bushmaster's notoriety as the maker of AR-15s proved too toxic for the Bush campaign, and Dyke subsequently resigned.

While serving in the Senate, Senator Cohen assisted Dyke's company in navigating loopholes preceding President Clinton's ten—year assault rifle ban in 1994, according to news reports, which helped lead to a record sales year for AR-15s in the civilian market.

Prior to her running for Cohen's seat as senator after he was appointed Secretary of Defense in the Clinton Administration, Dyke chose Collins to be the executive director of the Richard Dyke Center for Family Business at Bangor's Husson College after her unsuccessful bid to become Maine governor. Dyke had first met Collins when she served on Cohen's staff. When she won election for Cohen's old seat in the U.S. Senate, Collins also voted on legislation favorable to Bushmaster several times, including on a bill that prohibited lawsuits against gun manufacturers resulting from the misuse of their weapons. That didn't help Remington, the company that eventually bought Bushmaster, however. Plaintiff's lawyers found enough loopholes in the law to force the company to agree to a $73 million settlement with the families of the Sandy Hook Elementary School victims in 2022, ten years after a seriously deranged young man killed twenty-two students and four adults there with a Bushmaster AR-15.

Bushmaster's brand has become intrinsically tied to mass shootings. In 2002, a pair of snipers using a Bushmaster AR-15 gunned down ten victims in the Washington D.C. area in what became known as the Beltway shootings. Then came Sandy Hook, followed ten years later by a mass shooting in a Buffalo supermarket, where a white supremacist shot and killed ten African Americans. On the stock of his Bushmaster AR-15 the shooter had painted the words, "Here's your reparations." But as the evidence has borne out, the sales of Bushmaster weapons increased after these shootings. Dyke and his executives were well aware of that phenomenon. According to the authors of the 2023 book, *American Gun: The True Story of the AR-15,* they maintained a chart that showed a link between spikes in sales and events like mass shootings, political elections, the 9/11 terrorist attacks, and calamitous predictions of doom, like the 2000 Y2K scare. This chart would help them in deciding when to ramp up production to meet an expected surge in demand.

Dyke eventually sold Bushmaster to a venture capital company in 2006 for a reported $70 million. The new company then decided to move its entire operation out of state in 2011. His five-year non-compete clause just expired, Dyke rehired several Bushmaster employees and took over the old Windham manufacturing plant to start Windham Weaponry. By the end of 2021, it was making 22,000 weapons annually.

Dyke died in the spring of 2023. Soon after, Windham Weaponry announced it was stopping production. By October 16th, 2023, just nine days before the Lewiston shooting, an auctioneer had closed the bidding for the company's $1.5 million in weapons inventory. Windham Weaponry later announced on its social media pages that it had sold to a new group of investors and would be continuing operations. As of February 2024, it's only selling parts and accessories on its website. Unless and until it resumes making weapons, Maine is no longer a gun manufacturing state.

*Card walks into Just-In-Time Recreation Center just before 7:00 p.m. on October 25, 2023. He killed eight people there and ten others at a sports bar four miles away.(Photo from Androscoggin County Sheriff's Office Facebook page)*

# MANHUNT PART II: THE FACE HAD A NAME

Where was the shooter? It wasn't only law enforcement asking that question. Virtually everyone in the state was asking the same thing the moment the infamous video still image of him inside Just-In-Time was first released on the Androscoggin County Sheriff's Office's social media feed at 8:00 p.m. One of the first things Samantha Juray was asked to do when the police arrived at Just-in-Time was to retrieve the business' security camera footage. The image that was flashed around the world in mere minutes came from a camera pointed at the front entrance door.

One person didn't need to see the image to know exactly who it was. Sean Hodgson, his longtime friend, had been warning his Army Reserve colleagues for months that he feared that Card was a ticking time bomb, but those warnings were widely dismissed as the workings of a troubled mind. He was sick to his stomach to be proven right. As his friend of nearly twenty years was fulfilling his gruesome prophecy, Hodgson was sitting in the cab of his Fleet First trailer truck on the evening of October 25th, 2023. Six hundred racks of bread were stacked in the trailer behind him. He was headed south on Rt. 196 in Lisbon, making his way to his destination in West Bridgewater, Massachusetts, when he heard the news. As he drove on in a state of stunned disbelief, police car after police car raced north towards Lewiston, their blue lights blinding him as they sped past.

Card's name was still unknown to most everyone at that point. The only ones who had very strong suspicions of who it was were Hodgson, Card's family and his ex-wife, who came to the awful realization that the most wanted man in America on the night of October 25th and for the next forty-eight hours was her ex-husband and her son's father.

She recalled that tragic memory in a March 2024 conversation. That night, she and Colby were in the house they shared with her boyfriend in a coastal town not far from Brunswick when she saw a Facebook post with the image from the bowling alley. It was a grainy image, so it was difficult to pick out distinguishing features. And the man had a beard, which is not a familiar look for her ex-husband. Still…it did look like him: his profile, his height, his stance.

As she was processing the image, her knowledge of his paranoid behavior was churning in the background. She was the one who initiated the family's first contact with law enforcement when she spoke to the Topsham Police Department's school resource officer with Colby back in early May. That conversation led to another with a Sagadahoc County Sheriff's (SCSO) deputy. She knew that Colby was afraid to spend time with his father, and she was equally afraid to let him. She knew that a second encounter with the SCSO in September when he wouldn't answer their knock on the door led to a round robin of conversations between Card's family, the Army Reserve, and the SCSO about removing his weapons. She knew that virtually everyone in her ex-husband's life had been walking on eggshells around him. And she knew that he had cut contact with his family in the previous months, and that the paranoia he was experiencing before surely wouldn't be helped by his isolation.

With all this knowledge bubbling to the surface, she strongly suspected as she sat on her bed and stared long and hard at the image on her phone that it was Robert Card II.

She swallowed hard, then called Colby to come look at the photo.

"It was so friggin' hard to ask him. I mean, it's his father, and I'm asking if he thinks it's him that shot and killed all those poor people," she explained later. He looked gut-punched as he nodded and handed the phone back to her. "It looks like him."

So, she made a call to her former sister-in-law, Katie Card, the wife of Robbie's brother, Ryan. Had she seen the photo? What did she think? She had had a close relationship with him and was aware of his condition, and also at a complete loss as to how to help him. She had tried. She'd had endless conversations with her husband and family about how they could get him help. But he was alternately resistant or evasive. Everyone was calling him a pedophile in his mind. No doctor or medicine could change that fact. By summer, he completely cut ties with his family after accusing them of doing the same.

Katie agreed with Cara and Colby. It looked like Robbie. As she stared at the photo and took in Katie's observation, the odds that the three of them were all wrong seemed very slim. She ended the call with her former sister-in-law, and at 8:57 p.m. she dialed 9-1-1. Cumberland County Regional Communications Center picked up.

\*\*\*

**8:57**:

9-1-1. *What's the address of your emergency?*

*Uh, it is not an emergency. Um, it's about the shooting in Lewiston and we're a little concerned. We might know who the photo is.*

9-1-1: *Okay. Um, do you have—*

*Um, not that we're in contact with this person, but, um, we're a little concerned that maybe we might know who this person is.*

9-1-1: *All right. Hang on one second.*

*And we just don't know what to do.*

9-1-1: *Well, do you have his name?*

*Robert Card. He's from—uh, he lives on West Road in Bowdoin.*

9-1-1: *Can you spell his last name?*

*Um, C-A-R-D.*

9-1-1: *Do you know his date of birth?*

*It's, uh, 4—4-4-83, I think, or 4-3-83.*

9-1-1: *And he's, uh, Bowdoin?*

*He—yup, up on West Road.*

9-1-1: *Guessing you saw the picture?*

*Uh, we saw the picture online.*

9-1-1: *Okay.*

*And we've been very concerned about his—we know he has firearms in his house. He lives alone. He shut his family out recently. We've just been really concerned about his mental health lately.*

*Okay.*

*And, um, it's just the photo, it's blurry. It's hard to tell. But what—you know, and we're just—we're pretty concerned.*

9-1-1: *When was the last time you talked to him?*

*Uh, when was the last time you talked to him?* [speaking to another person] *Like on the phone or anything? Like he kicked his family out of his house recently. A month ago, Um, you know, they're basically estranged and he's just not been well. He's in the military. We've already dealt with the sheriff's department.*

9-1-1: *Okay. Can I get your name and number and I'll pass this along.*

\*\*\*

Nicole Herling, Robert Card's sister, then made a separate call to the Lewiston Police Dept. Chief, David St. Pierre, at 9:26 p.m. to report that the man identified as a suspect was her brother. Michael Sauschuck, the head of the Maine Dept. of Public Safety, said later that three separate Card family members called that night to identify Robert. "They were incredibly cooperative," he added.

Just over an hour after the shootings began, police had a name to check. They also had a security camera image of a white Subaru Outback in the Just-In-Time parking lot. The driver's door was open wide, but the vehicle was empty. Whoever owned the vehicle was somewhere else at the time the image was recorded, and they either forgot to shut the door, or they left it open on purpose. It appeared that both its headlights and rear running lights were on too, which indicates that whoever owned it also forgot to shut the engine off—or they left it running on purpose. The latter was obviously the more likely of the two. Investigators cross-referenced Card's name and vehicle registration. A white 2013 Subaru Outback was registered in his name. At 9:20 p.m. Maine State Police formally identified Robert Card II as a suspect. Now the face had a name. They also broadcast the vehicle's description and plate numbers to first responders and incoming law enforcement agencies, which at that point were swelling by the moment.

The number of law enforcement officers already involved had ballooned from the Lewiston P.D. and Androscoggin County Sheriff's Office's initial response to about 350 by midnight. It was like throwing a rock into the water and watching the ripples spread further away from the center. First, they reached out to local department's—Auburn, Lisbon, Sabattus, Topsham, Brunswick initially, more as time went on. Right on their heels were deputies from Sagadahoc, Oxford, and Cumberland Counties. Eventually, specialized teams came in from local departments in Massachusetts and New Hampshire as well. The ripples reached out further and landed on distant shores. Agents from the FBI, ATF, Border Patrol, U.S. Marshals Service, and later the Coast Guard swarmed in with their robust resources and commanding presence.

No matter how large the initials on the back of their jackets were, they all deferred to the Maine State Police (MSP) though. Because in Maine, the MSP are charged with being the lead law enforcement agency in any homicide investigation outside of the two largest cities of Portland and Bangor. This was Maine's largest murder investigation ever, and its largest law enforcement agency would be in charge.

The MSP has a sprawling jurisdiction of over 35,000 square-miles. It covers it with a complement of 341 sworn troopers assigned to patrol state roads and take part in investigations. The agency, which celebrates its one-hundredth anniversary in 2025, also has a number of specialized teams, providing everything from crisis negotiation to canine patrol, air support, underwater recovery team, executive protection for the Governor, and more. It also operates the Incident Management Assistance Team (IMAT), a mobile unit that was formed to coordinate the response to large or complex incidents. At 7:20 p.m.—

twenty-four minutes after the first call to 9-1-1 came in from Just-In-Time—IMAT got the call to get to Lewiston on the double. By 8:20 p.m. they had set up in the parking lot at the Colisee, Lewiston's 4,000-seat multi-purpose facility. Surrounded by densely settled neighborhoods, the sixty-five-year-old building has seen better days, but it did offer a parking lot large enough to accommodate the arrival of tactical teams in armored vehicles and swarms of other law enforcement agencies.

Just ten minutes before the IMAT team arrived at the Colisee, the emergency communications system fielded multiple calls reporting an active shooter at the massive 810,000-square-foot Wal-Mart distribution Center on Alfred Plourde Parkway, about two miles east from Schemengees. IMAT sent a tactical team to respond, but as post-incident reviews of the law enforcement response to the shootings pointed out, the haze of battle/fog of war had already set in. Someone else from another agency had heard the call and sent in their team, which then accessed a separate entry point to the sprawling facility. As the two teams searched for signs of an active shooter, they converged together, and for a brief, very tense moment, ended up challenging each other.

Later that evening, 9-1-1 emergency responders would also get a call about an active shooter at Davinci's Eatery, a popular downtown Lewiston Italian restaurant. Both reports proved to be false. The MSP would acknowledge later that with so many agencies involved in the manhunt, there were numerous cases of "self-dispatching" by some officers. That led to some harrowing moments in the hours to come as the search area widened and the number of law enforcement officers increased. Those were just two of the 800 tips and leads that law enforcement would follow up on in the next forty-eight hours.

One important piece of evidence the MSP could substantiate and follow up on was Card's home address on

West Rd. in the town of Bowdoin, about fifteen miles east of the bowling alley. At 10:01 p.m., forty minutes after he had been named as the suspect, MSP tactical teams surrounded his trailer and set up a perimeter. They had barely enough time to do that and work up a plan to gain entry into the trailer before the call came out on the radio at 10:08 that a white Subaru matching the description of Card's was discovered at a boat launch parking lot in Lisbon, about five miles from his home.

The boat launch is located directly off Rt. 196 on the east side of the road. It lies just off and under the road overpass and is in plain view of any passing vehicle traveling in either direction. Situated in what's known as Miller Park, it consists of a small, paved area perhaps twenty-five yards deep and fifty yards wide, and a concrete boat ramp that slopes down into the outlet where the Sabattus River empties into the Androscoggin River. A four-mile-long paved walking and biking trail transects the parking area.

Lisbon Police officers were the first to spot the car. It wasn't exactly hard to miss out in the open like that. If forensic psychologists had already started on a character profile of Card to be able to predict his next move, it's unlikely any of them would have envisioned that. Later, as the manhunt intensified, the so-called "experts" popped up by the dozen on media outlets to weigh in on Card's extensive Army training, marksmanship, and rural upbringing. Then there was Maine's vast forest, countless waterways and proximity to Canada. Those factors, they predicted, would make the manhunt exceedingly difficult and dangerous for law enforcement. It might take weeks, months even, before they found him. Few mentioned the fact that he left his vehicle out in the open to be found or pondered why he would have done that.

Nor did they mention the significance of him leaving the Ruger SFAR used in the killings, along with six magazines containing seventy-seven rounds of ammunition on the passenger seat. There were documents with his name on them on the seat as well. Even as some were predicting that he had left a jet ski or small boat at the launch to escape via the river, there was little public discussion about why he didn't do anything to hide his identity, and in fact, made it easy to identify him and narrow down a search area.

One expert who did think long and hard on it was MSP Sgt. Gregory Roy, who headed up the agencies' tactical team—more commonly known as the SWAT team. Ironically, Sgt. Roy grew up in Lisbon. Even more ironically, he spent countless weekends and summer days at Miller Park messing around as a kid. When he learned that Card had abandoned his Subaru at Miller Park, he undoubtedly asked the same questions in his head over and over: Why here? What's the significance of this place to him?

Sgt. Roy knew from his boyhood that it's a popular spot for kayakers, canoers, and fishermen to launch, so a water escape couldn't be ruled out. There's also plenty of hikers and bicyclists who use the four-mile Papermill Trail, which starts upstream along the Sabattus and winds through open fields, farmland, and woods as it approaches, then transects, the Miller Park launch. The smoothly-paved path then continues another two miles along the Androscoggin before ending behind the Lisbon High School football field. Was the trail important to him? Did it lead to somewhere he wanted to go? Even as he probed these questions, Sgt. Roy was thinking of another: *Is this a setup to ambush us?*

In fact, others in MSP command were thinking the same thing. They were especially mindful of the 1997 case in Colebrook, New Hampshire, when a local man named Carl Drega shot and killed two New Hampshire State Police troopers after a traffic stop. Drega had been engaged in a longtime dispute with town officials over code enforcement violations involving his home. He then stole the trooper's patrol car and drove to the nearby courthouse and shot and killed the local judge and a newspaper editor who tried to disarm him. After burning down his own house on the banks of the Connecticut River, he shot and wounded a New Hampshire Fish & Game warden, then fled across the state line into Vermont, parked the car on the side of a dirt road and took position to ambush responding law enforcement officers. By the time the Korean War veteran was eventually killed in an intense gun battle, three more officers lay wounded in the woods. That case is seared into the memory of northern New England law enforcement officials. On the night of October 25th, 2023, it was front and center in their minds.

When MSP tactical teams responded to the boat launch fifteen minutes after the call came in, upwards of forty police officers surrounded the Subaru, and the small parking lot was jammed with law enforcement vehicles. By now, they were aware that their suspect was a career soldier with extensive firearms training. They knew from video footage and witness testimony that he had fitted out the Ruger with a thermal scope, so they had to consider the fact that he might have another rifle with a similar setup, which would give Card night vision capabilities.

So Major Lucas Hare, MSP Director of Operations, Sgt. Roy and others weighed two options: Have a K-9 team pick up the scent at Card's vehicle and begin tracking immediately? A fresher scent would likely produce a better outcome, although there's documented evidence that some breeds can track months-old human scent. Or, given what they knew about his capabilities and the potential weapons he might be carrying, back away from the vehicle and call in a helicopter with thermal imaging equipment to fly over the area?

They opted for the helicopter. Thinking back on the Drega ambush, they decided that the risk of sending a K-9 team was too high. Armed with a high-powered rifle and thermal scope, Card could pick them off like sitting ducks. So, they ordered all officers to back away from the vehicle and secure the site as a crime scene. The car would sit there the entire night under the glare of spotlights like a single Rembrandt painting behind glass in an otherwise empty museum. The K-9 team wouldn't start tracking until 8:00 a.m. on Thursday, the morning after the shootings.

Hare acknowledged later in the independent commission inquiry that it was a controversial decision. In fact, it was openly questioned by some in law enforcement, including in a scathing social media post by an Androscoggin County Sheriff's Office sergeant a week after the manhunt had ended:

*"The upper echelon of the MSP Major Crimes Unit are utter clowns and I wouldn't hire them to manage the morning rush at Dunkin Donuts let alone an investigation of this size."*

"We wanted to find him and take him into custody," Hare told the commission. "But the first responders had done a fantastic job to make sure the killing stopped. Once we found the vehicle, our approach had to become more deliberate. Knowing what I know now, I would make the same decision."

While Miller Park was lit up like midtown Manhattan that night, the rest of the region was dark and deathly silent. The official declared shelter-in-place order covered Lewiston, Lisbon, Bowdoinham, Bowdoin—a 700-square-mile area with close to 55,000 residents. For anyone who harbored doubts, this stark message on the MSP social media feed early on spelled it out:

*"There is an active shooter in Lewiston. We ask people to shelter in place. Please stay inside your home with the doors locked. Law enforcement is currently investigating at multiple locations. If you see any suspicious activity or individuals, please call 9-1-1. Updates to follow."*

Many residents in towns and cities further away weren't taking any chances. The streets in Auburn, Brunswick, Topsham, Bath, and dozens of small towns in Androscoggin, Sagadahoc, Oxford, Cumberland, and Lincoln Counties were all noticeably quieter that night. A mass shooting wasn't supposed to happen in Maine. A mass shooting with a killer on the loose was even harder to comprehend.

By most standards, Maine is not a lively place at night. Especially after Labor Day when summer tourists head home, and the mostly older fall foliage tourists who follow tend to lay their heads on a pillow early to rest up for a full day of leaf peeping the next day. But there are usually some gas stations and convenience stores open, an occasional fast food restaurant or two, and bars and clubs in the larger towns and cities. Not the night of October 25th. Most closed early and sent their employees home. The most noticeable signs of life in southern and central Maine were the flicker of TV screens and the reassuring sight of local law enforcement vehicles patrolling the empty streets.

A more reassuring sight would be to see the shooter in custody. But it was just the beginning of the longest forty-eight hours in Maine history. As the horrible day of October 25th ended in Maine, and a new one began, Robert Card II had vanished like a ghost.

# REVIEWING THE REVIEW

Two days after Governor Mills announced the formation of an independent commission to examine all the facts of the Lewiston shootings, the SCSO and the law firm of McCloskey, Cunniff, Mina, and Frawley agreed that attorney Michael Cunniff would conduct his own review of the agency's response to calls it received about Card in May and September.

Cunniff made it clear in the opening of his review that it was written "using the lens that focused on the circumstances known to SCSO personnel *at the time that relevant events were occurring.*" It's a phrase he repeats again to stress that yes, hindsight is indeed 20/20, and the SCSO officers didn't have the benefit of knowing then what we know now. In other words, how could Deputy Sheriff Chad Carleton and Sgt. Aaron Skolfield know that the elusive Card, who they never laid eyes on or spoke to directly, would murder eighteen innocent people later? On the flip side, that lack of foresight can't stand on its own to absolve them and the department of any culpability in the tragic events that occurred only six weeks after their last encounter with him. But like a glossary in a quantum physics textbook, it's a good thing to refer to from time to time.

In addressing the May 3rd interaction Deputy Carleton had with the Card family and Army Reserve personnel, Cunniff summarized his findings as follows:

*It was not feasible under the totality of the circumstances for Deputy Carleton to facilitate a voluntary psychiatric evaluation of Mr. Card's mental health status, but Deputy Carleton acted diligently to obtain assurances from third parties (i.e., family members and Army Reserve personnel) that Mr. Card would be guided toward a psychiatric evaluation and treatment.*

*The factual findings establish that after a diligent effort to assess the circumstances surrounding the concerns about Mr. Card's mental health status, Deputy Carleton reasonably concluded that he did not have the discretion to take Mr. Card into protective custody due to insufficient grounds for a conclusion that Mr. Card posed an imminent risk of self-harm or harm to others, which foreclosed his discretion to initiate the process for confiscation of Mr. Card's firearms.*

*However, to promote public safety and Mr. Card's safety, Deputy Carleton requested that involved third parties notify the Sheriff's Office of any future concerns about Mr. Card, including concerns that Mr. Card would pose a risk of harm to himself or to others. Until September 15, 2023, no such concerns were communicated to the Sheriff's Office.*

September 15th is the date when Sgt. Skolfield responded to a request from Army Reserve personnel to conduct a welfare check on Card. Cunniff issued separate findings for that interaction. At ninety-three pages, the review goes into great detail to describe the legal options available to the SCSO law enforcement officers when they responded to the calls about Card. It then assesses each option and explains why they weren't used.

After concluding the Mt. Ararat meeting and multiple phone calls he had with members of the Card family and the Army Reserve, Deputy Carleton had four statutory options available to him. He would be familiar with those options because he was one of sixteen SCSO personnel who had completed forty hours of CIT mental health screening training. According to training records supplied by the SCSO in response to a FOAA request, he had also completed a three-hour in-person training on weapons restriction and yellow flag training from Dirigo Safety on April 3rd, 2023, exactly one month before the call from Mt. Ararat High School to meet with Colby Card and his mother, Cara Lamb. Sgt. Skolfield attended that same training, which for him, was a follow-up to a two-hour training he had in 2020. Their boss, Sheriff Merry, was one of twenty SCSO personnel to receive yellow flag training from Dirigo Safety from April to December 2023. His last training session came on December 20th, days after Cunniff's report was issued. In addition to the Dirigo Safety training, the SCSO had adopted the minimum standard policy entitled, *Response to Mental Illness, Involuntary Commitment and Protection from Substantial Threats Policy,* which was issued by the Maine Criminal Justice Academy in 2022.

Despite all that training, the SCSO had never taken a subject into protective custody and initiated the yellow flag process. They had taken people into protective custody, however. Just a couple of weeks before his attempted wellness check on Card, Sgt. Skolfield had assisted in taking a Bath man into protective custody after he challenged law enforcement officers to a fight and lunged at them with a knife while he was in clear mental distress. Skolfield and the Bath police officers were lauded at the time for their restraint in using a stun gun on the man and disarming him rather than shooting him with their service weapons.

As Cunniff points out in his review, law enforcement officers are increasingly forced to act as behavioral health practitioners. Given the limited training they receive in a field that requires at least six years of education for professional practitioners, this is a heavy burden to place on officers when dealing with a combination of mentally ill people and oftentimes alcohol and drugs. Nothing spells that out more than the fact that nearly three-quarters of cases involving officer- involved shootings in the last five years in Maine involve people in a mental health crisis, according to a 2023 report by the Maine Deadly Force Review Panel.

When assessing his options on how to respond to what he had learned about Card's condition, Deputy Carleton was weighing the fact that the man was clearly in a full blown mental health crisis, had made vague threats to shoot someone, possessed ten to fifteen firearms, and answered his front door with a weapon in is hand and a belief that non-existent people were casing his house. All this information came from reliable family sources. On the other hand, he had a number of concerned family members and Army Reserve soldiers, some of who are also active-duty police officers, assuring him that they would get him to a doctor, and that they would contact the SCSO if they had any concerns about him hurting himself or others in the future. The proactive options that were available to Carleton under Maine law are the following:

- *Ask him to submit to a voluntary psychiatric evaluation.*
  Card's family had suggested on multiple occasions that any law enforcement intervention would only escalate the situation Plus, both the Card family and Army Reserve personnel had assured him they would work to get him into treatment, and, in fact, he had told his siblings he would go to a doctor.

- *Invoke an emergency involuntary commitment.*
  This option requires a psychiatric evaluation, court approval, and a determination that there is a likelihood of him causing serious harm to himself or others.

- *Place Card in protective custody.*
  This option would have required Deputy Carleton to determine that Card did pose a likelihood of serious harm to himself or others and would have required him to deliver him immediately to a medical practitioner for an evaluation.

Carleton could not arrive at that determination unless he laid eyes on him and was convinced of the need.

We know what option he chose. It was none of the above. Was it the right choice? When answering that question, we should keep in mind Attorney Cunniff's reminder that he made that choice "at the time that relevant events were occurring."

There's a common thread in the three potential options Deputy Carleton could have chosen: They all required him to conclude there was a likelihood that Robert Card posed serious harm to himself or others. Attorney Cunniff points out that "in the context of protective custody situations," Maine law defines "likelihood of serious harm" as follows: (paraphrased)

1. A person poses a substantial risk to others based on recent violent or homicidal behavior.
2. A person poses a substantial risk to themselves based on recent suicidal behavior or ideation.
3. Based on recent behavior, there's a reasonable certainty that the person will suffer physical harm and is unable to avoid the risks on their own.
4. Considering recent behavior and an inability to make informed decisions, there's a likelihood that the person's mental health will deteriorate and there's a good chance they'll harm themselves or others.

The language is legalese and makes every attempt to cover all the bases, but it's still open to interpretation. For example, you might be a cautious parent and define it as a "reasonable risk" if little Billy wanted to go fishing when the forecast predicted a 50% chance of thunderstorms, while another parent may scoff at your caution and say a "reasonable risk" would be if Billy wanted to wear his metal fireman's helmet while he fished. It's hair-splitting, of course, but interpretation is vitally important in the context of assessing the SCSO's handling of its interactions with Robert Card. It's important because of the options that Deputy Carleton had to choose from, "protective custody" was the only one he could have used to trigger Maine's yellow flag law and take possession of the ten to fifteen weapons he was known to have, including the ones he took with him on that October night six-and-a-half months later.

There's a familiar saying that you don't know what someone else has experienced until you walk a mile in their shoes. Put yourself in Deputy Carleton's shoes back on May 3rd, 2023. Knowing all the facts he knew about Card's condition, his access to firearms, and his proficiency with them, did he pose a risk to himself or others? Was his mental health deteriorating to the point that he couldn't make informed decisions for himself? Should Carleton have tried to track down Card and decide on his own?

Or was the fact that his brother, a former U.S. Army Ranger, his sister, a nurse, his sister-in-law, also a nurse, and his Army Reserve colleagues, some police officers themselves, assured Carleton that they would get him help and would call the SCSO if they thought he posed a risk of serious harm to others or himself enough to outweigh those other factors? That's the call that Deputy Carleton had to make. We know that he chose to rely on the family. The independent commission agreed with Cunniff and didn't assign any blame to Deputy Carleton in its March 2024 interim report.

Sergeant Skolfield's involvement with Card came more than five months later when he was called out on September 15th to do a wellness check on Card at the request of Bravo Company commander, Captain Jeremy Reamer. This is what Attorney Cunniff concluded about his handling of the case:

*The factual findings establish that it was not feasible under the circumstances for Sergeant Skolfield to facilitate a voluntary psychiatric evaluation of Mr. Card's mental health status, but he acted diligently when encouraging Ryan Card, Mr. Card's brother, to do so and when offering the assistance of the Sagadahoc County Sheriff's Office in that regard.*

*The factual findings also establish that Sergeant Skolfield did not have sufficient grounds to take Mr. Card into protective custody, which also foreclosed his discretion to initiate the process for confiscation of Mr. Card's firearms. After Sergeant Skolfield completed his response to the concerns about Mr. Card's mental health on September 17, 2023, the Sagadahoc County Sheriff's Office did not have any contact with Mr. Card. Similarly, no member of the Card family and no member of the Army Reserve contacted the Sheriff's Office after September 17, 2023, to report new concerns about Mr. Card's mental health, which would have prompted an additional response from the Sheriff's Office.*

Sgt. Skolfield had the same exact options available to him as Deputy Carleton did. However, he had a whole new set of facts to work with, given all the events that occurred in the four-plus months from the time Deputy Carleton met with Colby Card and his mother, Cara Lamb. He also had all the facts that Carleton had recorded in his 1300-word incident report in May to consult as well. What else did Sgt. Skolfield learn after he answered the call?

- He knew that Card's Army Reserve colleagues were concerned enough to ask the SCSO to do a wellness check.
- He learned that the Saco Police were concerned enough about Card's threat to shoot up the armory that they posted four officers there on the day he was supposed to show up for weekend drill.
- He learned that Card's closest friend had written a text to a Bravo Company senior NCO two nights

before expressing the fear that he would do a mass shooting.

- He learned that Card's senior NCO believed Card was a proficient marksman and more than capable of carrying out a mass shooting if he chose to.
- He also learned that Card had spent nearly three weeks in a psychiatric hospital that summer, that he possessed ten to fifteen firearms, that his family members were fearful of him, and that his paranoia had increased to the point that Skolfield had already concluded that he would not get better on his own.

Put yourself in Sgt. Skolfield's shoes. Was the assurance from family members that they would ensure that his guns would be secured and that they would contact the SCSO if they thought he needed to be evaluated enough to outweigh those factors? We know that he ultimately chose to rely on the family. We also know that he never followed up after making that decision, and he considered the case closed after his last phone call with Ryan Card. The next time the SCSO would respond to a call about Card, it was to protect his family from him after he shot and killed eighteen innocent people.

During the Maine State Police's hearing with the independent commission, a member asked Sgt. Thomas Pappas, who randomly drove up on Skolfield outside of Card's trailer, whether Attorney Cunniff spoke with him about his presence there that day. "No, he did not," Pappas replied. After the hearing concluded, the author emailed Attorney Cunniff and asked whether he had interviewed anyone other than SCSO personnel to inform his review. Because frankly, how could a review be called independent if it only relied on the testimony of the agency that solicited and paid for it?

"Thanks for your inquiry. I have no comment other than what was stated in the review," he wrote back.

*Card took this path from his abandoned car to the Maine Recycling overflow lot on the night of October 25th. The path runs parallel to the Androscoggin River and is largely out of sight for most of his 1.1 mile trip. (Photo by Robert Conlin)*

# MANHUNT PART III: "MAYBE YOU'LL BE THE ONE I SNAP ON"

Robert Card II had vanished into thin air. As tens of thousands of Mainers in the Lewiston region locked their doors and stayed glued to news outlets, hundreds of heavily armed local, state and federal law enforcement officers scoured the area for the forty-year-old career soldier. As the massive manhunt unfolded into the daylight hours of October 26th, the initial euphoria of discovering Card's vehicle at the Lisbon boat launch faded as it became evident, he wasn't going to be easy to find.

Officers who searched his Bowdoin trailer in the pre-dawn darkness found a note he left to his teenage son Colby indicating that he didn't intend to be alive when the final chapter was written. He was a well-equipped, highly-trained career soldier with buckets of blood on his hands and absolutely nothing to lose The Maine State Police command staff directing the search for Card recognized the potential for a bloody shootout if they encountered him. So they opted to proceed slowly and methodically instead. Any of the officers involved in the manhunt privately hoping for a dramatic showdown would ultimately be disappointed. Instead of a gunfight at the O.K. Corral, they got an exhausting two-day tour of central Maine.

A half hour after discovering Card's car at Miller Park at 10:08 p.m., MSP command staff called on a New Hampshire State Police helicopter with a thermal imaging camera to overfly the area. The helicopter crew reported it had acquired a heat signature on the trail to the north of the boat launch, but the initial adrenaline rush fueled by that find died off when tactical teams deployed to the area determined it was a false positive. Just ten minutes later, reports of a loud, suspicious noise from inside the greenhouse of Springworks Farm, New England's largest aquaponic lettuce farm, triggered another tactical team response. The farm is located just a mile from the boat launch. An employee reported that the unusual noise came from inside the sprawling greenhouse and growing facility, which produces one million heads of lettuce and 150,000 pounds of tilapia annually. After a thorough seventy-five-minute search, the team returned to the command post empty-handed.

It would be the first of hundreds of tips that law enforcement authorities would receive over the next two days. Some were hoaxes: one man who called a suicide prevention hotline claimed to be Robert Card, for example. Most involved the tipster knowing or seeing someone with a likeness to Card. None amounted to anything, but they all had to be checked out. The most notable involved a man in Rumford, a paper mill town fifty miles northwest of Lisbon on the Androscoggin River. This man apparently bore such a strong resemblance to Card that he was stopped and confronted by police officers, before he was eventually cleared.

Before the week was out, there would be more excitement in the town of 6,000 residents. A few days later, two Oxford County Sheriff's Office deputies shot and killed a local man who inexplicably confronted them in front of the Rumford police station with a rifle. It was the second officer-involved fatality impacting the town in a month. In September, a Rumford man was shot and killed by Maine State Police in an adjacent town after he stepped out of a van wearing a bulletproof vest and holding two rifles. He was wanted on a warrant for illegally possessing firearms.

MSP Detective, Blake Conrad, who interviewed Ryan Card the night of the Lewiston shootings, was involved in tracking down the man.

By 8:00 a.m. on October 26th, criminal intelligence analysts from the Maine Department of Public Safety had set up a system to disseminate leads and tips to investigators. Soon after, officers responded to an early morning tip about a property owned by a Card family member in Lisbon and searched a house in Monmouth and an apartment in Lewiston, but came up empty. At one point early on, the MSP received information that there might have been other people involved in the shooting, the agency's head told the independent commission inquiry later. "Once that comes into play, this thing really starts to go in a lot of different directions. And those things we had to track down," he said.

Short of a tip that aliens from outer space were involved, nothing could be ruled out. The Massachusetts State Police, for example, were notified early on the morning of the 26th by New Hampshire authorities that a woman saw a vehicle with a man who resembled Card crossing the state line into Massachusetts. They put out a BOLO (be on the lookout) alert, but soon withdrew it after determining it was a false lead.

One tip did prove to be very credible and revealing. Police in the town of Hudson, New Hampshire went on high alert after they discovered that Card had made a delivery to a local bakery outlet in the town on October 19th and had a chilling altercation with employees while he was there. The town is located outside Nashua, about 140 miles from the Lisbon boat launch.

After leaving Maine Recycling in April 2023, Card had signed on as a truck driver with the Auburn-based branch of First Fleet Trucking, a nationwide freight hauling company with 3,700 employees in 140 cities. The company is contracted to deliver bakery products throughout New England. His best friend Hodgson also left Maine Recycling and signed on with Fleet First at Card's urging, despite his awareness of his friend's worsening paranoia. Within a few months, he was doing his best to avoid Card, and he had to ask his new employer to schedule his routes for a time when he wouldn't cross paths with him.

He did accompany Card on his route initially, Hodgson explained to the author in a March 2024 conversation, as he learned the ropes and prepared for his own route. His friend's route was supposed to take eleven hours, Hodgson said, but Card drove fast, pushed hard, and backed the truck in more quickly and more precisely into the tightest spaces than any driver Hodgson had ever seen. He was usually done in eight hours. Most of the stops on his route were Market Basket supermarkets, but one exception was the Country Kitchen bakery outlet in Hudson. One of a half dozen in New England, the outlet sold the brand's short-dated bakery products at steep discounts to the public. The Country Kitchen brand was owned by Lepage Bakeries, one of Lewiston-Auburn region's most successful locally grown businesses. It was sold to a Georgia-based food company for $370 million in 2012, but Lepage still bakes the Country Kitchen and Barowsky baked goods brands in its Lewiston bakery. Eager to distance itself from anything to do with the Lewiston shootings, Lepage Bakeries issued a statement afterwards stating that Card did not and never had worked for them.

But he did make a delivery at the outlet in Hudson on the 19th, and according to the Hudson Police Chief, he told the startled employees, "I'm not gay or a pedophile. Just show me where the bread goes." He then chillingly added, "Maybe you'll be the ones I snap on."

Card came back to the Hudson outlet to make another delivery on October 24th, the day before he went on his murderous rampage, but apparently that stop was free of conflict. The outlet's employees didn't report their October 19th encounter with him to authorities until they learned of the shootings and came to the horrifying realization that it was the same man, and he did snap as promised.

As the manhunt continued, the 9,700 residents of Lisbon were especially edgy, even with all seventeen members of the police department called in for duty and swarms of heavily armed law enforcement officers on the ground, helicopters in the air, and patrol boats on the water. By the late morning of October 26th, police boats and divers scoured the Androscoggin River, and a Coast Guard boat patrolled the Kennebec River, which connects with the Androscoggin. Brookfield Renewable Partners, the operators of two dams on the river, lowered the water levels behind the downstream dam to assist divers and air and water patrols. The Subaru's final destination at the boat ramp, and the discovery that Card owned and had registered a jet ski and used to own a fifteen-foot Bayliner boat sparked speculation that he might have slipped the noose by using the river to make his getaway. Internet sleuths speculated that he may have tried to make a run for the Atlantic Ocean, by following the river downstream for a few miles to Merrymeeting Bay, where the Androscoggin joins the Kennebec before emptying into the Gulf of Maine. From there, the feverish speculation went, he could make way for any one of hundreds of small ports and inlets strung along the mid coast. There was only one problem with that theory: he and his jet ski would pay the price for trying to drop over the dam just downstream and wouldn't get any further.

As the manhunt came to the twenty-four-hour mark, the roads in the region were virtually empty. Schools had closed throughout Androscoggin, Sagadahoc, Lincoln, and Oxford counties, and even as far away as Portland, Cape Elizabeth and Scarborough. Any cars approaching the twenty-four Maine border crossings into Canada were scrutinized with extra caution. Several area colleges called off classes. The 1,800 students at Bates College, which is roughly two miles from Just-In-Time, went into lockdown, huddling in their dorms for over forty-eight hours by the time it was over. The University of Maine's Orono and Machias campus— some 200 miles away—canceled classes as well. With one of their own on the loose and quite possibly harboring a grudge, the Army Reserves shut down all its facilities within a hundred-mile radius of Saco. All throughout the region, mail delivery stopped, and courts and government offices closed. Sporting and cultural events statewide were canceled. So too were numerous Halloween-related festivals, and the inauguration of Bates College's first black president in its 169-year history.

With virtually every restaurant in the region closed, MSP command had to deal with the mundane detail of how to feed and house hundreds of officers who arrived en masse within hours of the shootings. Most of the region's supermarkets, drug stores, convenience stores, and gas stations were closed, compounding the problem. The only retail stores that stayed open in the Lewiston region were area gun stores. After all, was there any safer place in Maine than a gun store?

While the lights were dimmed virtually everywhere else, the Central Maine Medical Center (CMMC) in downtown Lewiston blazed with frantic activity. Situated almost epicenter at a distance of two miles from both Just-In-Time and Schemengees, the hospital was flooded with fourteen victims within minutes of the shootings. They were triaged by a staff that swelled with the arrival of off-duty doctors and nurses who heard news of the shootings and raced to the hospital, despite the possibility of encountering a mass shooter on the run. Minutes later, family and friends of victims began congregating outside, so desperate for any information about loved ones that they also ignored the danger. Inside, hospital staff had just ten minutes from the time they were alerted to the shootings to the arrival of their first patients. For a medical facility not used to mass casualty events, they performed remarkably well. A charge nurse, who was ex-military, and the team moved fifty patients out of their rooms into the hallways to make room for the incoming wounded.

The hospital's medical staff spent up to eight hours in surgery to treat the catastrophic injuries caused by the large-caliber bullets Card loaded into his weapon. While gunshot injuries at CMMC weren't unusual, mass casualties were for most of the staff, except its chief of anesthesiology, who had been training at a Boston hospital in 2013 when the Boston Marathon bombing sent 264 wounded victims—many of those with limbs blown off—to area hospitals.

Sadly, three of the Lewiston victims would pass away in the hospital. Three more would survive emergency surgeries and be listed in critical condition by the following day. One was transferred to Maine Medical Center in Portland. The rest were treated and released over the course of the next few days.

Fifteen miles away, the eerie stillness of the apocalyptic landscape was shattered in Bowdoin the next night, when heavily armored tactical vehicles rolled up outside of the weathered Card family farmhouse on Meadow Road. While a helicopter hovered above with its blinding searchlight trained on the property, a voice blared repeatedly over a loudspeaker for anyone in the house to exit with their hands in the air. Television crews filmed the dramatic scene from a distance. After twenty-four hours on the hunt, it appeared there might be a breakthrough. At one point, the loudspeaker assured any occupants that they would guarantee their safety if they exited with their hands held high. After a fruitless hour of this, and then a forced entry into the house that turned out to be empty, everyone packed up and left.

When asked why authorities had sent tactical teams in force and used a loudspeaker to call out occupants who didn't exist, Maine Department of Public Safety Commissioner, Michael Sauschuck explained that it was a common practice when serving a search warrant. This explanation was met with an eye roll by the gathered media.

Sauschuck became the face of the investigation with his highly detailed media briefings. An owlish-looking ex-Marine and career law enforcement officer, he had served as Portland's chief of police before his appointment by Governor Mills in 2019. The morning after the raid on the house on Meadow Road, he acknowledged that the longer the manhunt went on, the more concerned he became that authorities could not locate or apprehend Card. With hundreds of law enforcement officers scouring the region—200 FBI agents alone by that Friday, October 27th—they were no closer to finding him.

As Friday dragged on and the manhunt stretched into its second full day, the forty-year-old career Army Reserve soldier was inheriting the near mythical status some Americans like to attach to criminals and killers who are able to elude massive dragnets. Whether he wanted it or not, he had achieved worldwide notoriety.

While news of the shootings and manhunt crisscrossed the globe, and speculation about Card's whereabouts clogged social media feeds, one guy was convinced he knew where Sgt. Card had gone, and he had been since he first heard about the shootings. He wasn't a random tip line caller eager to involve himself in the investigation either. He had known him for nearly twenty years, and at the time, he was the person who knew him the best. In fact, he was convinced just a short while after hearing news of the shootings that Card had methodically planned his attack and targeted Just-In-Time and Schemengees, and that his next destination would close the loop in his paranoid plan for revenge.

On the night of October 25th and the early morning of October 26th, Sgt. Sean Hodgson told multiple law enforcement personnel where he thought Card would go next. He also told Card's brother Ryan the same thing that night, and Ryan passed that information to a MSP detective a couple of hours later. Hodgson expected that the authorities would pay close attention. Eventually though, he came to the realization that it was like playing the telephone game around a campfire; the story he was telling them got lost in translation by the time it got passed along.

Instead, Hodgson's warnings were once again brushed aside, just like his text warning on September 15th that he was afraid his friend would commit a mass shooting. Despite the vow to follow every tip, investigators never acted on the one that made the most sense by far. They followed up on random tips from strangers, but somehow missed doing the same on the same tip from Card's best friend and his brother.

Their failure to do so could have almost surely resulted in the deaths of some of Card's former co-workers, and it extended the manhunt by at least forty hours. Had they acted on it, there well could have been a shootout and even more loss of life. Thankfully, we'll never know. But the fact that it happened—and then was only mentioned briefly by investigators and commission members—offers a lesson plan for law enforcement if they choose to acknowledge it. As of this writing in June of 2024, they haven't.

# "I SHOULD HAVE DONE MORE"

In late April of 2024 the independent commission held its eighth public hearing. All were live streamed on Zoom and shown on a split screen with ASL interpreters. The interpreters switched off every hour or so, an indication of how mentally and physically exhausting it is for them to bridge the gap between the hearing and the deaf. The Lewiston shootings haven't spun too many silver lining stories, but one just may be a new awareness of the challenges that Maine's estimated 70,000 hearing-impaired face in participating in many aspects of life the rest of us take for granted, including civic affairs. If it continues, these interpreters are going to be in high demand.

The hearings began with a bang with the testimony of the Sagadahoc County Sheriff's Office (SCSO) in late January, and they concluded as of this writing in late April 2024 with the testimony of members of the Army Reserve's Bravo Company of the 3-304th, 104th Training Division, based in Saco, Maine (later hearings involving Bravo Company soldiers and the Card family were held in May). The soldiers were the first witnesses to be served with a subpoena compelling them to testify under oath. Some would have agreed to do so voluntarily, the commission chairman pointed out, but they would have needed the Army Reserve's permission. They wouldn't provide it, apparently, though they did provide three high-ranking Army Judge Advocate General officers to sit in person in the cramped hearing room at an Augusta state government building. Their presence underscored the gravity of the stakes for the Army Reserve—the Pentagon really, but ultimately American taxpayers. They no doubt were aware of the presence of lawyers for the victims' families and survivors.

The Army's legal team pulled a tried-and-true play out of the litigation playbook by providing the commission with a large tranche of subpoenaed documents the night before the first hearing involving Bravo Company soldiers. Commission members were unable to review all the documents, which meant the need for another hearing and new witnesses. The JAG team would have also been aware of the Card family's authorization to release the findings of a study done of Robert's brain by a team at Boston University's CTE Center the day before the first hearing involving soldiers in early March. It would have been hard to miss because it was front-page news on media platforms worldwide. Robert Card had significant traumatic brain injury consistent with long-term exposure to blast pressure produced by grenades, the study team concluded. They determined that this injury was most likely a contributing factor in his drastic personality change and lack of impulse control that led to the shootings.

None of this was ever mentioned during the first eight-hour hearing, but this information provided new context for questions both asked and neglected. Instead, the general tenor of the questions posed to deposed soldiers addressed whether they had failed Card and endangered the public by not proactively working to get him help. In essence, commission members wanted to know:

- Were his Army Reserve commanding NCOs and officers negligent in not ensuring he received follow up mental health help after his release from Four Winds in July?

- Were they negligent in not engaging pro-actively with local law enforcement to make sure that his firearms were removed from his home and secured?
- Did they downplay the severity of his erratic and worrying behavior and their knowledge of his possession of an extensive collection of firearms?
- Given that many of them were civilian law enforcement officers and had working knowledge of the dangers of mental health distress and firearms, should more have been expected of them than an average Army Reserve "weekend warrior"?

Judging from the testimony of Sgt. Jordan Jandreau, Sgt. Matthew Noyes, Master Sgt. Samuel Tlumac, First Sgt. Kelvin Mote, and Captain Jeremy Reamer, the collective answers were, *No, No, No,* and, *I guess, but we did what we could.*

At the time, none of these soldiers knew their colleague had a diagnosed traumatic brain injury, so, like Attorney Cunniff's reminder in his review that we could only judge the SCSO officer's interactions with the Cards based on what they knew at the time, not what we know now, we should keep that in mind. But they were all aware to a varying degree of his increased paranoia, his involuntary hospitalization, his threats to "take care of things," his physical assaults on junior members, and his extensive collection of firearms. In summary, they were aware of the symptoms, but not the diagnosis.

The inclusion of Sgt. Jandreau on the witness list was baffling. A five-year veteran of the Rockland Police Department, he transferred to the 3-304's HQ company and hadn't spoken with Card in five years. He was aware that Card was discharged from the Four Winds psychiatric hospital in early August but had little other knowledge of events other than that.

The highest-ranked enlisted soldier in the 3-304th, the bald, stern-faced Command Master Sgt. Tlumac brought along his own lawyer to sit by his side as he faced the commission's panel. A longtime Maine State Police trooper, Tlumac testified that he was aware that Card was command-directed to the psychiatric hospital in July but didn't hear anything about his condition in the months following and believed "he was all good." He also was the one who suggested that the SCSO do a welfare check on Card in September, which led to Sgt. Skolfield's aborted attempt to establish contact with him at his trailer.

Given how little these two witnesses had to offer and the fact that they had to be subpoenaed to testify, the complaints of Attorney Benjamin Gideon, who is helping to represent the families of victims and survivors of the shootings, after the first hearing seem to have some merit. Gideon later publicly accused the commission's panel of being ill-prepared to question the witnesses. He didn't mention the selection of witnesses, but the absences of Sgt. Daryl Reed and Sgt. Sean Hodgson from the witness list was truly puzzling at the time. Reed had been a close friend with Card for ten years, while Hodgson was his best friend. In addition to serving in the same unit with Card for years, he also lived with him in his trailer for a time and worked with him as a delivery driver. Both men witnessed his downward spiral from the beginning of 2023, and both were assaulted by Card over the summer of 2023. Bravo Company's command had suggested that Hodgson take charge of removing the firearms from Card's home, and both men had issued prescient warnings to their families and to superior NCOs in Bravo Company about Card's mental state and what he might do. "I'm afraid he'll snap and do a mass shooting," Hodgson wrote to First Sgt. Mote in a late-night text in September. Based on her husband's accounts of Card's behavior, Reed's wife was texting him throughout the summer of 2023 stating that she was terrified of Card and what he might do.

A spokesman for the independent commission did not respond to messages from the author at the time asking why Reed and Hodgson weren't called to testify at either the first hearing involving Bravo Company soldiers in early March or the second hearing in mid-April. Instead, the two showed up on the calendar for an unscheduled hearing in late April - after the commission had issued an interim report.

Third to testify at the March hearing, Sgt. Noyes, an Androscoggin County Sheriff's deputy, provided some more context of the circumstances surrounding Card's involuntary admission to a West Point Army hospital, where he was seen by a staff psychiatrist who was called in on his day off that Sunday afternoon. After examining Card, he recommended a transfer to Four Winds, which had many more available mental health resources. Noyes had been with Card and two other unit members, Sgt. Wainwright, and Sgt. Reed, when Card assaulted Reed in a convenience store parking lot, and then later threatened he "would take care of it" in reference to his allegation that his fellow soldiers were calling him a pedophile. He later cleaned out Card's room and discovered he had brought a set of bowling balls with him.

Noyes testified to the "surreal position" he found himself in on October 25th as he responded as a sheriff's deputy to the shooting and then took part in the manhunt for his Army Reserve colleague. He arrived at the Lisbon boat launch soon after the discovery of Card's car, and roughly thirty-six hours later, went to the overflow parking lot of Maine Recycling in Lisbon with the understanding that the dozens of fifty-five-foot trailers there had been searched and cleared. Inexplicably, that was not the case.

Looking for some respite from the chaos of the manhunt, Noyes sat in the lot in his patrol car and talked to another cop a short distance from where Card's body was found in a tractor-trailer twelve hours later. He has no idea whether his former Bravo Company colleague was alive and in the trailer at the time. If he was, he was armed with an assault rifle, a handgun, and over 200 rounds of ammunition. Given the coroner's estimate that he died eight to twelve hours before his body was discovered at 7:45 p.m. later that evening, he might have just taken his own life. Any way you slice it, Noyes and the other officer came closer to Card than anyone else during the manhunt.

Ultimately, Noyes told the panel, he believed that his interaction with Card in July at West Point was beyond reproach. He last saw him when they dropped him at Keller Army hospital, he said, and was only aware that it was an unsuccessful intervention when he heard of his September threat to shoot up the Saco facility from Sgt. Wainwright, the Oxford County Sheriff. "I felt good that we had done the right thing. He was command directed to get mental health treatment, which is something you don't see in the Army Reserve."

The two remaining witnesses received the brunt of the panel's attention that day. First up was First Sgt. Kelvin Mote, an Ellsworth Police Department officer for twenty-three years and an Army Reserve soldier for eighteen years after a stint as an active-duty Army soldier. Of all the Bravo Company members involved with Card, he was the most familiar with the cumulative details over the seven months from April to October of 2023. In fact, like the character in Woody Allen's movie, *Zelig,* he was in the middle of almost every pivotal event over that period. Mote had been notified of Card's allegations that other soldiers were calling him a pedophile in April, he engaged with SCSO Deputy Carleton in May when Card's son and ex-wife voiced their concerns, he had been at Camp Smith in July when Card was committed to a hospital and had searched his room for a weapon prior to his committal, he had received the text from Staff Sgt. Hodgson warning of a mass shooting threat, and had actively engaged with the SCSO and Saco PD in mid-

September about a welfare check and the threats to shoot up the Reserve center.

A balding, seemingly genial, soft-spoken man in his fifties, Mote appeared with his own lawyer by his side. He maintained his cool in the face of a staccato drumbeat of questioning from Paula Silsby, a former United States Attorney for Maine, but by the end he looked like a man who had undergone a full blood transfusion during his two hours of questioning. Mote did appear forthright and unscripted, and some of his testimony was frank and unfiltered. Describing his reaction when he heard Card tell NYSP troopers that "he was capable of doing something," he said,

"I've been a cop for twenty-four years and the hair stood up on the back of my neck when he said that. That's when I knew we had to get him to a hospital."

When asked whether he expressed his deep concern to the SCSO about their failure to have face-to-face contact with Card in September to determine whether he needed to be put into protective custody, he said. "In the law enforcement community, if you tell someone in another jurisdiction how to do their job, they hang up on you. It was their jurisdiction and their responsibility."

When asked whether he was familiar with Army Reserve regulations requiring mental health evaluations in an emergency, he told Silsby, yes, he was, he had done annual training at the battalion level every year for the past nineteen years on the subject. Yes, he responded matter of factly to a Silsby line of questioning, he was familiar with the Army Reserves' Psychological Health Program, which provides clinical assessment, counseling services, and case management for soldiers, and tools and resources for commanding officers to determine the best course of action for their soldiers in need of mental health help. On its website, the Psychological Health Program urges Reserve unit commanders to contact the program anytime they have a question about referring a soldier for mental health assistance. In fact, they provide the name and contact information for the point person in each of the four Readiness divisions of the Reserve. Bravo Company is in the 99th Readiness Division, based in Fort Dix, New Jersey.

Mote also agreed that, as the training officer for the Ellsworth PD, he had also trained on communicating with people in mental distress and identifying schizophrenia and had completed yellow flag training in April 2023. In fact, he had sought and obtained a yellow flag order in September 2023—the same month he was resisting the urge to stress the need for the SCSO to obtain one for Card—for a forty-year-old man who had threatened his family with a firearm. In that case, he had gone to the door, despite knowing the man was armed, and convinced the man to give up his guns.

All these questions about Mote's extensive training in the field of mental health intervention on both the civilian and military side proved to be a setup for the next series of questions:

*"After you informed Deputy Carleton in May that you and Captain Reamer would sit down with Sgt. Card and work on a plan to get him some help, did you follow through on that?"* No, he replied, he did not. He didn't speak to Card again until July when Card refused to open the door to his Camp Smith barracks room.

*"Were you aware that an Army psychiatrist at Keller had declared Sgt. Card psychologically unfit for duty and that he suggested his access to firearms be restricted?"*

*"No, I was not."*

*"Were you aware that this psychiatrist's 2283 report, 'Report of Mental Health Evaluation' determined that Card suffered from an 'unspecified psychosis' and recommended that he be separated from the military?"*

*"I was not."*

The three JAG officers weren't in view on the Zoom screen, but it didn't take much of an imagination to picture their expressions at that moment. After a few more questions, Silsby mercifully finished up with him by asking how he felt when he found out Sgt. Card had committed the shooting.

*"It broke my heart. We gave him the opportunity for treatment, but he wouldn't take it...Those people were innocent. We're soldiers. We protect and defend."*

*"It broke your heart!? More than the families of the victims? Did you feel sad for Robert Card that the help his family was seeking wasn't available to him?"* Mote looked stricken as he stared down at the table mutely.

Captain Jeremy Reamer took the hot seat next. If he was hoping it would cool down some, he would be disappointed. Rather than lower the flame, George 'Toby' Dilworth, a former Assistant U.S. Attorney, slowly twisted the dial to the right. A short, trim, bald man in his mid-thirties, Reamer saw combat in Afghanistan in 2013 as an active-duty Army officer. He became a full-time Nashua, New Hampshire police officer in 2016, joined the Army Reserve in 2020, and assumed command of Bravo Company in 2021.

Reamer acknowledged that he never did have the sit down with Card in May as Mote had assured Deputy Carleton they would do. In fact, he didn't attend April, May, or June weekend drill due to "personal and medical reasons," and initially wasn't at West Point in July when some Bravo Company soldiers, Sgt. Card included, showed up for their two-week annual training. That changed when he received a phone call from Mote and Jurek explaining the circumstances that led Card to lock himself in the barracks. Reamer drove four-and-a-half hours to West Point and arrived at Keller Army Community Hospital for a consultation with the Army staff psychiatrist who first evaluated Card.

He was glad that Card had been brought to the hospital, the doctor told Reamer. His behavior, mannerisms, and anger were concerning, as was his reference to, and personal possession of, firearms. For these reasons, he referred Card to Four Winds. He and Reamer talked further, and then the Bravo Company commander signed the authorization form and hopped in his car for the long drive back to Nashua.

On the 28th of July, the same psychiatrist filled out the 2283 Status of Mental Evaluation form to summarize his evaluation and recommendations. Referring to records that the commission must have subpoenaed, Dilworth went through the summary and checklist.

*"It says here that the Army psychiatrist discussed with you at Keller the medical board process for Sgt. Card to be separated from the Army for psychiatric reasons. Do you recall that?"*

*"No, I do not."*

*"Do you recall him discussing with you the need for any firearms to be removed from his home to ensure safety?"*

*"No, but I understood from Staff Sgt. Hodgson [Card's best friend] that the family would remove his weapons."*

*"Do you agree that it was important to remove weapons from his home?"*

*"Yes, I agree."*

Dilworth then referred to a section of the report entitled "Recommendations and Comments for Commander." The boxes were checked for the following:

*"Did you ensure that the service member attend all follow-up appointments?"*

*"No, I didn't have any idea that he had follow-up appointments."*

*"Did you speak with Sgt. First Class Card afterward about his treatment plan and follow-up appointments?"*

*"No, I did not."*

*"Did you speak to First Sgt. Mote about this?"*

*"No, I did not."*

*"Did you have a plan to restrict his access to military weapons at the Reserve Center."*

*"Not a specific plan, no."*

*"Did you follow this recommendation for you to follow up on Sgt. First Class Card's treatment upon his discharge and share that at the brigade level?"*

*"No, I didn't."*

*"Did you initiate the medical board process to facilitate his discharge from the Army?"*

*"No, that's handled at a higher level."*

*"But you didn't notify anyone in your chain of command about this recommendation?"*

*"No."*

*"Did you take measures to remove his firearms from his HOR [home of residence]"?*

*"No, according to the evaluation he posed a low risk of harm to himself and others."*

*"But you agree he posed a danger?"*

*"Yes, but a low risk. That's what it says."*

*"But you didn't follow up with the family?"*

*"No, because that was a civil matter between Sgt. Card and his family. We had no authority to remove his firearms."*

*"Were you aware that Sgt. Card had completely cut off communication with his family for months before this?"*

*"No, but I thought the fact that he was released from the hospital meant he was better off than he was."*

Unlike the previous two witnesses, Captain Reamer did not bring a private attorney to the hearing. He looked like a man shipwrecked alone on an island there at the table, face to face at a distance of ten feet from the former Chief Justice of the Maine Supreme Judicial Court (SJC), a former associate judge of the SJC, a former U.S. Attorney for Maine, a former Asst U.S. Attorney for Maine, and a former Maine District Court judge and county district attorney.

*"Did you get a phone call from a caseworker at Four Winds, who noted that he told you that he recommended that Sgt. Card have no access to firearms when he got home?"*

*"No, I don't recall that."*

Reamer told the commission he had no contact with Card until September 15th, when he and Mote reached out to the SCSO to do a wellness check. It was precipitated by Card's threat to shoot up the Saco armory and Hodgson's warning that he might snap and commit a mass shooting.

*"So, you hadn't spoken with him all summer?"*

*"No, I was relying on Staff Sgt. Hodgson to provide me information about him and his family."*

*"And you weren't aware that by that time he had cut off contact with his family?"*

*"No."*

*"Was it a good plan to rely on the family to secure his firearms?"*

*"I didn't know the family dynamic. In my experience as a law enforcement officer families are capable of doing that, and they can reach out if they have any concerns."*

*"Did it occur to you to ask Sgt. Wainwright, who's the Oxford County Sheriff and a soldier under your command, to speak with Sheriff Merry about all this?"*

*"No, I didn't think to. First Sgt. Mote is my right-hand man and I trust his judgment and knowledge."*

*"Do you think Sheriff Merry would want to know that a man in his jurisdiction was suffering from psychosis, having auditory hallucinations, had recently been committed to a psychiatric hospital, possessed multiple firearms and had made threats to use them?"*

*"Yes, I suppose he would."*

*"As a Nashua policeman, wouldn't you want to know if someone like this had threatened to shoot up Nashua High School?"*

*"Yes, it would be beneficial."*

*"Did you consider having Sgt. Card charged with criminal terrorizing?"*

*"No, I did not."*

*"Would you choose to charge someone with criminal terrorizing if they threatened to shoot up Nashua High School?"*

*"We would have to do our due diligence."*

*"Did you ever check with the Sagadahoc County Sheriff's Office to see whether they had face to face contact with Sgt. Card?"*

*"No, I did not."*

*"When you spoke to Sgt. Card on September 15th, did you ask him whether he was getting any treatment?"*

*"No, I did not."*

*"Did you ask him whether he still had his guns?"*

*"No, I did not."*

He looked exhausted as he rose, but the commission wasn't done with Reamer. If he harbored any hopes that his personal nightmare was over, they would soon be dashed. A month later, he was called back to Augusta to testify for another two hours. Wathen and the rest of the panel might have been chastened by the public criticism from Attorney Gideon that they had been ill-prepared at the first hearing.

Armed with several documents compelled by a subpoena, they put Reamer through the wringer, getting him to acknowledge that he ignored guidelines that required him to make sure Card attended additional mental health appointments. He was also forced to acknowledge that the Army psychiatrist at Keller had informed him Card suffered from psychosis and should not have access to firearms, and despite that warning, he failed to make sure that law enforcement in Sagadahoc County were aware after Card was released from Four Winds.

The panel methodically wore him down with emails, texts, and Army Reserve medical forms. By the end, his attempts at deflecting any responsibility were reminiscent of a beaten boxer on the ropes praying for the bell to ring.

*"I should have done more,"* he concluded

*The view of the trailers in the overflow lot of Maine Recycling in Lisbon as seen from the Papermill path. Card's body was found in one of the trailers 48 hours after the shooting. A former employee there, he harbored a bitter resentment of employees at the facility. Armed with an AR-15 and 200 rounds of ammunition, it was very likely he went there to kill them, but the region-wide shutdown after the shootings kept the business closed and employees away. (Photo by Robert Conlin)*

# MANHUNT PART IV: THE END OF THE TRAIL

By sunup on Friday, October 27th, the manhunt for Robert Card was beginning to resemble a military operation that started out full of decisive optimism, but soon bogged down into a siege mentality.

As the hours ground on, the thought that he had managed to evade the dragnet and escape somewhere deep into the woods of the most heavily-forested state in the country was taking root. If Vegas bookies had decided to put it in play, the safe bet would probably have favored that he had slipped the noose. After all, the Maine State Police had sixteen different tactical teams from fourteen different agencies flooding the area looking for him for the previous thirty-six hours. That's not discounting the eyes and ears of hundreds of other law enforcement officers, and countless citizen lookouts keeping watch around property lines from Berwick to Van Buren, Wiscasset to Wilson's Mills.

Still, they pressed on, turning over every stone they could, even as their own concern grew that he had high-tailed it out of the area. The tips kept coming in, and they were assessed and responded to when appropriate. For example, at 2:45 a.m. on Friday a tactical team acted on a tip and searched an apartment in Lewiston, while another team followed a separate tip and conducted surveillance of a gravel pit in Lisbon. At the Friday 8 a.m. briefing, tactical teams were assigned to search the woods around a residence in Bowdoin, search two residences in Monmouth, and follow up on reports of gunshots in three different areas in Lisbon. Non-tactical teams were assigned to search a sand pit in Lisbon Falls, a vacant house in Bowdoin, and do grid searches around the two crime scenes at Just-In-Time and Schemengees. At the same time, MSP and Maine Warden Service teams were assigned to scan and dive the river near the Lisbon boat launch where the Subaru was found and to sweep the riverbank for evidence. Meanwhile, over at the Maine Forest Service in Augusta, a team began working on Geographic Information Systems to assess mapping and capabilities data for an overhead macro approach to determine where Card might have gone.

As morning slipped into afternoon, tactical teams followed up on reports of a man running in the woods in Monmouth, searched and cleared hunting blinds in Bowdoin, and deployed to the Card family farm on Meadow Road after there was an unfounded report of a 9-1-1 hangup call made from the residence. All this activity might seem reactive and scattershot, but it wasn't entirely off the cuff. Investigators were paying some attention to the threads that were tied to Card. That certainly included his family, which up until the beginning of the year, had been an important constant in his life. Given that his whole life had centered around the sleepy little town of Bowdoin, that's where they allocated a lot of resources. His favorite stomping grounds were surveilled and searched. Of course, the Meadow Road farm was being watched carefully, even though the family had gathered in another house in Bowdoinham and were being protected by law enforcement.

They had also tracked down Card's ex-girlfriend, the one who he met at Schemengees and had broken up with in February. More than one Card family member believed that she would be a likely target of his anger, and investigators agreed. They went to her Lisbon home just after midnight, five hours after the shootings, and eventually found her at a location in Auburn.

Cara Lamb, his ex-wife, and Colby had made the decision to leave their Harpswell house and go to the Topsham Police Department after making the call to 9-1-1 on Wednesday night to report their belief that it was Rob (as she called him) who was the man in the Just-In-Time surveillance video. Cara was worried that he would come to do her harm, and she stressed that in a conversation in February. He had never let go of the anger he felt at her for ending their marriage sixteen years before, she said. His sister, Nicole, remarked in a phone conversation in December 2023 that Cara was the one true love of his life, a sentiment that his friend Sean Hodgson repeated later. Whether she believed that or not, she wasn't about to stick around and find out whether that bought her any mercy.

When she and Colby got to the Topsham Police Department building and identified themselves, officers told them they should go somewhere else if they didn't feel safe at home. Then the call came that his car had been found at the Lisbon boat launch, and they dismissed them without any further instruction and raced to the scene, she claims. She had told the officers about her and Colby's connection to Card, and assumed they would hustle them to a safe place until he was found. Instead, a female Topsham officer told her in so many words that they were on their own. Adding this treatment to that experienced by Ryan Card and Sean Hodgson, an inexplicable pattern emerged over the two-day manhunt of law enforcement dismissing the people closest to their suspect, and therefore, the ones who would have the most potential knowledge of his whereabouts and what he might do next.

Months later, MSP officials would say that their past experience had taught them to not believe everything family members of suspects told them and to treat their information with a grain of salt. In the case of the Card family, it's an interesting paradox, because the state's lead law enforcement officer, Michal Sauschuck, singled out the family for their pro-active cooperation in a press conference days after the shootings.

Left to their own devices by police officers, the shaken Cara Lamb and her son called the owners of the restaurant where she worked, and they swung into action, bringing them to a private rental house they owned, and stocking them with food and other supplies for the duration of the manhunt. They could not have been more supportive, Cara stressed in a conversation months later.

Even as they tugged on the familial threads with the hope of finding him on the other end, investigators overlooked a key clue that was handed to them on multiple occasions in the early hours after the shooting by Ryan Card and Sean Hodgson. Despite these two men being the closest people to Card of any in his satellite, they didn't pay any attention to their assessment of where he might have fled to.

When MSP decided to stand down with the K-9 team on Wednesday night after the discovery of the Subaru, it seemed like a prudent decision, although it's been roundly criticized since. Fearful of an ambush, they opted to wait for the light of day. At 8:00 that Thursday morning, they were back out with the dogs to search the woods north of the launch, and at 12:30 they followed the Papermill Trail south in the direction of Lisbon Falls.

We don't know how far south they went, and we don't know if that search was conducted by the K-9 team. But we'd have to assume investigators—especially MSP Sgt. Roy, the Lisbon native—would track the entire four-mile trail in both directions from Miller Park. Headed southwest twenty-five yards from the ramp where the car was found, they'd pass under the Rt. 196 overpass, and then up around the corner headed south, they'd see a building on the left along the road about 150 yards up. That's the home of Daniel Buck Auctions and Buck's Guns, Lisbon's largest gun retailer, and a certified Ruger dealer. The trail runs within spitting distance of the back of the building.

From that point on, Rt. 196 curves slightly to the east and both the road and the traffic noise disappear. It's difficult to see anyone on the trail unless you're in a boat on the 200 to 300-hundred-yard-wide river, or in the tree line on the other side. At night it'd be nearly impossible. Searchers would see the east bank of the Androscoggin on one side of the trail and thickets of trees and brush on the other and surely recognize how easily anyone who didn't want to be seen could vanish in the night. It's a scenic and peaceful place to meander, or stretch out and run, or ride on the smooth pavement. It's also a quiet and secluded corridor to move from one location to another in Lisbon without being spotted.

About three-quarters of a mile from the boat ramp the woods along the trail give way to a small grass clearing, where a granite bench near the riverbank is engraved with the names of three Lisbon High teenagers who died in a 1973 car crash. A little further on, the trees thin out again, and the trail loops east over some train tracks and then straightens out behind a large lot in an industrial park surrounded by a five-foot high chain link fence.

There, dozens of fifty-five-foot tractor trailers are lined up in rows in the lot. Some, but not all of them, bear the name of a company called Maine Recycling. Robert Card II used to work here as a driver. He quit in April 2023 after confronting his co-workers, who he accused repeatedly of calling him a pedophile. His body was found in one of those trailers at 7:45 p.m. on Friday, October 27th, just over forty-eight hours after he took the lives of eighteen innocent people. The largest manhunt in Maine's history was over. After thousands of man hours scouring the landscape by hundreds of law enforcement officers, after helicopter searches, dive teams and Coast Guard patrols, Card was found a mile away from his abandoned car in a trailer full of empty bottles and cans. The man who had once volunteered to be the suicide prevention officer in Bravo Company had taken his own life.

He had shot himself in the head with a Smith & Wesson MP .40 handgun. Medical examiners would later estimate that he'd been dead for eight to twelve hours. Near his body investigators also found a Smith & Wesson MP 15 semi-automatic rifle, forty rounds of ammunition for the handgun and 211 rounds for the rifle. He was wearing the same clothing seen on the Just-In-Time video two days before. For all those who predicted that Card had gone deep into the woods and would hold out for an interminable length of time, the news that he was so close by all that time came as a shock. It shouldn't have been. Had they shared key information known to some of them early on, the MSP could have ended that speculation before it even started. Because when asked by MSP Detective, Blake Conrad, in an interview at 3:00 a.m. on October 26th where he thought his brother might go after leaving Schemengees, *Ryan Card specifically told him that he thought he'd go to Maine Recycling.* He had an issue with some employees there, he added.

Ryan had called Lieutenant Ed Yurek of the Brunswick PD four hours before that interview and warned him that he thought his brother would be headed to Harpswell to shoot his ex-wife. Both Ryan and Yurek had served in the 75th Ranger Regiment, and Yurek was currently a Master Sergeant in Bravo Company who also knew Robert and was familiar with his mental health struggles

It's not clear what Conrad, a detective with the MSP for eleven years, did with the information Ryan provided to him. He wasn't called before the commission and asked. The MSP finally released 3,000 heavily-redacted pages of investigatory materials in June of 2024, but there was no mention of it. The only thing we know for sure is no one acted on that information.

In a March 2024 conversation Sean Hodgson said he was convinced within seconds of the shootings and the news that the shooter was on the run, that it was his friend and he would be on his way to Maine Recycling next. He was dead sure after hearing his Subaru was discovered at the boat launch, located one mile away and connected by a well-concealed trail. Hodgson first told Ryan his belief that his brother would go to his former workplace in a phone conversation from a highway truck stop that night. He claims he then called the Lewiston Police and told the person answering the phone that Card would be headed to Maine Recycling, being sure to mention his longtime relationship with him. Then he says he called Detective Nick Bagley of the Ellsworth PD, who served with the two of them in Bravo Company and repeated that. Bagley has not responded to inquiries asking for confirmation of that conversation

The MSP didn't conduct their first search of Maine Recycling until the afternoon of the 26th, at least ten to twelve hours after Conrad had been advised by Ryan Card that if he could think of anywhere his brother might go next, it would be there. Even then, the tactical team only searched the main building and the grounds of the sprawling property. They wouldn't be aware of an overflow lot until the night the manhunt ended, when the state's chief law enforcement official said in a press conference that the manhunt for Maine's most prolific killer was over. Nobody had any idea that across the street from the main facility there's an overflow parking lot for Maine Recycling, DPS Commissioner Sauschuck claimed. Their only indication was when the Lisbon PD received a call on October 27th from a former Maine Recycling employee urging them to check there, he added.

Putting aside the fact that the author or anyone else driving on the road next to the main facility can clearly see the lot and the marked Maine Recycling trailers, that's not accurate. Three officers from the Lisbon Police Dept. did search the lot at 2:00 a.m. on the 26th, just seven hours after the shootings. They shone their flashlights into the trailers that had their rear doors opened but decided that it wouldn't be tactically smart—or safe—to open the ones that were shut to search, given that the shooter they were looking for was military-trained and had just cold-bloodedly murdered eighteen people. After reporting it all clear, they were notified that the MSP was assuming command of the overall search. Ryan McGee, the Lisbon Police Chief, did tell the independent commission later that he also notified the MSP about Card's connection to Maine Recycling sometime in the night hours after the shootings. But, he added, there was no specific evidence that pointed to him being there.

There was no hard evidence, but there was Ryan Card's warning to MSP Detective Conrad just an hour after the Lisbon PD initial search of the lot that he thought his brother might go there. There was also the fact that the trail connected the boat launch and the business where he had worked until six months before. When you're in the business of connecting the dots, these two should have stood out.

Testifying later at the independent commission, MSP leaders acknowledged there were communication difficulties and a myriad of unexpected tactical challenges during the manhunt. With two separate crime scenes, so many different agencies involved, and so many officers from those agencies "self-dispatching," the conditions were set for organized chaos. To expect a flawless operation with those conditions would be the same as expecting an F5 tornado to tear through a back yard and leave the clothes hanging on the clothesline. Maine has never experienced an F5 tornado, and its law enforcement agencies have never conducted such a massive and challenging operation. There's no doubt they put forth maximum effort to capture or kill Robert Card II.

But one undeniable fact is that simple police work would have led officers to Card's hideout. In the middle of all that chaos of helicopters, armored cars, SWAT teams, Coast Guard cutters, and alphabet soup of federal agencies, all it would have taken is for someone to confirm Card's work history, follow the breadcrumbs from the Subaru to the Papermill Path to Maine Recycling, and pay attention to the people who knew him best. The guy they were looking for had a plan. The authorities had the blueprint for that plan spread out in front of them. They just needed to glance at it.

Everything Card did that night sprang from a well of deeply rooted paranoia, but it appeared methodically planned and designed to punish the people he was convinced were leading the perceived smear campaign against him. His buddy, Sean Hodgson, is one hundred percent convinced he had a plan, and he almost succeeded in fully executing it.

"We were trained in the Army to crawl, walk, run. You make a plan, practice the plan, and then execute it. That's what he was doing that night," he explained.

In the leadup to October 25th, Card warned multiple people he intended to do something violent, he bought the Ruger SFAR in July, he tried to purchase a silencer the day after being released from a psychiatric hospital, he identified area businesses—including Just-In-Time, Schemengees, and Maine Recycling—as the source of misinformation about him, and he ominously warned employees of a bakery in New Hampshire that he was "going to snap" less than a week before the shootings.

On the night of the shootings, he left a note in his trailer with the passcode to his cell phone and a message on the phone that appeared intended for law enforcement, he carried three firearms and hundreds of rounds of ammunition, and he left his car door open and his engine running at the bowling alley to facilitate a quick exit to Schemengees. Once he got there, he left the car's engine running again. After shooting his victims, he left the sports bar and made a right on Lincoln Street towards Lisbon. He then abandoned his car at a spot that would allow him to travel to Maine Recycling without being seen by anyone.

Why was he so laser-focused on his former employer? Because he loathed Maine Recycling employees. He told both his brother, his sister Nicole, and Hodgson that they were calling him a pedophile, which was clearly the red line for him. He also told his brother that he had to quit the job because of it, which was confirmed by Hodgson. There's also the possibility that he discovered that at least a dozen of those employees were themselves listed on the Maine Sex Offender Registry. To a man driven to a homicidal rage by the thought of being identified as a deviant sex offender, this would have been more than enough reason to seek revenge.

Maine Recycling employees didn't come to work on Thursday or Friday because the area was in lockdown. Was his plan to lay in wait in the trailer, then walk across the street to the main facility when everyone arrived for work Thursday morning, October 26th and open fire? He was prepared; in the trailer with him was his Smith & Wesson semi-automatic rifle and over 200 rounds of ammunition. His friend of eighteen years is convinced that's exactly what he intended to do. "He went there to shoot them the next morning. I don't have any question about that," he said forcefully in a March conversation.

When no one showed up for work on Thursday, did he continue to wait through Friday, thinking they might eventually clock in? If that's the case, there was a major flaw in his plan: He overlooked the possibility that his rampage would result in a lockdown on both days. Was it the only reason he didn't kill far more than eighteen people? It's very likely.

With the coroner's autopsy estimating that Card died eight to twelve hours before his body was discovered, it meant that he spent at least thirty-six hours in the trailer before he shot himself. By then, he'd know that Maine Recycling employees hadn't shown up for work two days in a row, and he would know that the chances of them showing up on the weekend were slim to none. If he wanted to kill more people, he could have easily ambushed law enforcement officers on a number of occasions, but apparently, they were not the target and that wasn't in his plan.

He didn't have a cell phone. He was cut off from the world, literally and figuratively. He was a man alone with his twisted, irrational thoughts and he was armed and prepared to die. This is how it ended for Robert Card II, father, son, brother, soldier, and at the end of it all, a mass murderer.

# SOURCE OF THE PSYCHOSIS

The ground was thick with mud, the ice turned to slush on the lakes and ponds as the spring of 2024 rolled in. The last of what little snow central Maine received in the winter had already melted away, and the news surrounding Robert Card II was starting to do the same. But the Lewiston shootings were a cataclysmic event in Maine, so months later related news events still do flare up from time to time. Card's name was back on the front page again in March with the testimony of his Army Reserve colleagues before the independent commission, which came a day after the release of the findings of Boston University's CTE Center's study of his brain.

After all the speculation that his hearing aids might have been a major contributor to his paranoid delusions and auditory hallucinations, the findings that he had significant evidence of a traumatic brain injury consistent with repeated exposure to explosive blasts painted a clearer—and more sympathetic—picture of what could have led a man who appeared perfectly normal for virtually all of his forty years to suddenly turn into a psychotic killer.

Researchers at the lab, which is considered a pioneer in the study of traumatic brain injury and chronic traumatic encephalopathy (CTE), determined that the white matter that forms the wiring deep in the brain had "moderately severe" damage, and in some areas was completely missing. The tissue that protects the brain's circuitry lay in "disorganized clumps," and there was scarring and inflammation in his brain that was indicative of repeated trauma.

*"While it is unclear whether these pathological findings are responsible for Mr. Card's behavioral changes in the last 10 months of life, based on our previous studies it is likely that brain injury played a role in his symptoms,"* the report concluded.

A BU professor of neurology who analyzed Card's brain tissue with an electron microscope told the *New York Times* that the connecting threads called axons that pass messages from one part of the brain to another were severely damaged.

*The damage was just tremendous, I'm seeing cables that have lost their protective wrapping, cables that are just missing, cables that are inflamed and sick, cables that are essentially filled with cellular garbage bags,"* he said. *"These cables control how one part of the brain communicates with another. If they are damaged, you can't function right.*

Could it have been caused by the thousands of grenade explosions he had been exposed to at West Point? He didn't play contact sports and didn't work at a job that could lead to brain injury. He did fall off the roof of the house he was building and break his neck in 2008, his sister Nicole said in an interview in December, which his ex-wife Cara confirmed later. But he didn't have any symptoms consistent with brain trauma then, and his behavior was perfectly normal for the next fifteen years of his life.

Card's friend and Bravo Company colleague, Sgt. Sean Hodgson, said in a phone conversation in mid-March that safety was paramount at the West Point range, and the grenade exercises were well-controlled. There would be the occasional errant throw, with one landing just two feet away from the pit they threw from, he recalled, but they were protected behind concrete in the pit. That was about the worst in the seven or eight years he and Card trained cadets there. Most of the throws went as planned: Cadet pulls the pin, throws the grenade at a sand-filled marked area about fifteen-feet away, which releases the safety lever and lights the fuse, then hits the deck, and waits four to five seconds for the explosion. This is monitored by an NCO trainer in the throw pit and an NCO up in a tower looking over the range. As soon as a cadet releases the grenade, the pit NCO puts their hand on the cadet's shoulder and they both drop behind the concrete pit wall.

The volume of the explosion was noticeable through the ear protection they wore, but not overpowering, Hodgson explained. Same with the blast pressure. When asked whether he thought that the cumulative effect of thousands of those explosions could have caused the amount of damage seen in Card's brain, he hesitated, then said he didn't know, but he was planning on getting his own brain MRI soon. Card never complained of feeling any effects during or afterwards, Hodgson said. But something had caused significant damage to his brain over a long period of time. If not that, then what?

The Army has been aware of a possible link between repeated exposure to grenade explosions and brain injury for nearly a decade, if not longer. As far back as 2015 its research teams have investigated reports of instructors on grenade training ranges in Georgia and South Carolina complaining of headaches, fatigue, memory issues and confusion. Researchers took blood samples of the soldiers who conducted the training, but funding for the studies dried up, and the samples went into a freezer with no further follow up. In 2020, grenade trainers at Fort Leonard Wood in Missouri voiced similar complaints. A study funded by the Army examined the brains of new grenade and explosives instructors there using positron emission tomography scans. Researchers found that instructor's brains looked healthy before they began, but in follow-up scans five months later, their brains were riddled with a protein associated with Alzheimer's disease.

Researchers couldn't say for sure that Card's brain injury and his exposure to grenades is linked. Nor could they say that his injury caused Card to do what he did. There's mixed opinion in the medical community about whether TBI in and of itself leads to violent behavior. The possible existence of other factors, including an undiagnosed mental illness, make pointing the finger solely at TBI misplaced, some say. For the time being, the Army is acknowledging the possibility of a connection. They issued this statement the day of the study's release:

*The Army is committed to understanding, mitigating, accurately diagnosing and promptly treating blast overpressure and its effects in all forms,"* the statement said. *While prolonged blast exposures can be potentially hazardous, even if encountered on the training range and not the battlefield, there is still a lot to learn.*

Is that a sincere statement or is it a smokescreen? The catastrophic damage caused by IED explosions in Iraq and Afghanistan led to a concerted effort then to find mitigation and treatment solutions. But that was combat-related, and if a link is established, this case is not. If an Army Reserve "weekend warrior" who's never seen combat can suffer such devastating effects from training exercises, it creates a big problem for the military. But maybe not an insurmountable one; researchers in the field have said that a new helmet designed specifically to mitigate the effects of overpressure blasts could cut damaging effects by up to 80%.

The Card family is hoping that the study's findings will lead to solutions. They authorized its release to the public and issued their own statement to accompany it. "While we cannot go back, we are releasing the findings of Robert's brain study with the goal of supporting ongoing efforts to learn from this tragedy to ensure it never happens again."

In a subsequent email exchange with the author, his sister, Nicole Herling, said the study's findings have given the family a chance to forgive her brother, and an opportunity to find some silver lining in the tragedy.

"I do know my brother's life was used to prove the damage happening. Now we know we must do something to stop it. He would want that for the men and women he served beside."

As his adult-age next of kin, Colby has granted the Boston University researchers permission to continue with their study of his father's brain. They've expressed a very keen interest in finding out the extent of the causal link between his brain injuries and long-term exposure to grenade blasts, Cara Lamb said later in a conversation.

Aside from the statement that they'll continue to look at ways to combat blast overpressure, the Army has said little else. That reticence extends to the Card family, which hasn't had any communication with them at all, not even after the TBI findings, Nicole Herling said. She's hoping they're sincere in their pledge to find a solution.

Will the Army ever address the failure of Sgt. First Class Card's senior NCOs and commanding officers at the company and battalion level to make sure he got the help that Keller Army Community Hospital's staff psychiatrist said he desperately needed? The Inspector General of the Army is doing its own investigation. Until it's released, that question remains unanswered. If they do take any disciplinary action, it will likely be internal and sealed from public view, because doing that would be tantamount to admitting there was negligence involved. That wouldn't be of much help in mounting a defense against pending lawsuits.

Another question that will go unanswered for the time being is why Four Winds Hospital released him and who authorized that? His family doesn't know the answer, as they haven't seen the medical records, Nicole Herling told the author. Unless the independent commission subpoenas them and then includes the findings in its final report, they likely won't see them for years because ongoing litigation will keep them from doing so.

She did say that Robbie initially indicated to his family that he would be at Four Winds for a few weeks, but to their surprise, he was released to his friend Hodgson after just twenty days. Hodgson said Card had told him he was supposed to see a judge, but that didn't happen, and he was released instead. They're not sure why that happened, but speculate it had something to do with insurance and the maximum allowable stay at a mental health facility. An inpatient stay at Four Winds costs $1300 per day.

Her brother was clinically assessed to be suffering from psychosis. Is it acceptable for a mental health facility to send someone with that diagnosis back out into the world, especially if they're aware of the patient's access to firearms? Four Winds did not respond to requests for comment, so we won't get an explanation from them. Whatever their answer might be, it's worth remembering that the first thing Card did when he got back to Maine after his release from the psychiatric hospital was to try and purchase a suppressor for the Ruger SFAR that he used to kill eighteen people.

These questions and more were also put to the New York Office of Mental Health, which oversees facilities like Four Winds. They initially proved responsive, but then later clammed up and didn't provide any answers when they heard it had to do with the man who committed the mass shooting in Maine.

Card was given a prescription by Four Winds for lithium, but he complained to his mother from the hospital that it hurt his stomach and made him feel weird. The only treatment plan—which was conveyed to the family by a Four Winds team in a conference call with the family— called for Mrs. Card to monitor her son's behavior and for

Robbie to continue taking his medication, Nicole Herling explained, but she's been very ill since May 2023, and was unable to. In any event, he stopped taking the medication and was resistant to any attempts to help him. Eventually, he shut the whole family out, his parents and son included, even though he was close to his family his whole life. So, it's not completely accurate to say there was no plan to provide Card with follow-up treatment after his release from Four Winds. That would be like saying Christopher Columbus set sail from Spain to discover a western sea route to China without some kind of idea of how he would get there. Better to say that there was some semblance of a plan, but it had little chance of success.

Did the struggle he had with his hearing aids after purchasing them in February play a role in his year-long downward spiral? Given the news about the TBI diagnosis, the idea that the hearing aids could have been a major contributor lost traction, but they can't be ruled out as a factor. His son Colby, and ex-wife Cara mentioned the possibility to Deputy Carleton of the SCSO in May when he met them at Mt. Ararat to hear their concerns about his increasing paranoia. Card's purchase and use of hearing aids aligned almost perfectly on the timeline with his claim that he heard various people calling him a pedophile, so the link seemed at the least plausible. Deputy Carleton was intrigued enough about it to do a Google search and see if there was any information that might demonstrate a connection. He then wrote in his report that he did find references alluding to links between hearing loss and paranoia, but there wasn't any scientific data focusing specifically on hearing aids.

Robert had purchased a pair online from a company named Audicus for around $3,000, his sister Nicole explained. Audicus has become a leader in over-the-counter sales of hearing aids since the U.S. Food & Drug Administration lifted the prohibition in 2022. Since that ruling, patients no longer need to go to an audiologist and get a prescription to purchase them, essentially eliminating the middleman and making them cheaper and more accessible for the tens of millions of Americans who suffer from varying degrees of hearing loss.

Critics of the over-the-counter designation say that there's no replacement for an on-site hearing test done by a trained audiologist with specialized equipment. The FDA's ruling made this tried-and-true method of assessing a person's hearing an option rather than a necessity. Instead, online companies like Audicus provide a remote hearing test, which means that the connection between a patient's ear canal and the equipment that records the results passes through the microphone of whatever device the patient uses to connect. This, critics say, can affect the outcome and lead to faulty prescriptions.

Audicus provides online support for patients to adjust their Bluetooth-enabled hearing aids as often as they need to. It's hard to say how often Card sought that support, but Nicole Herling and Hodgson noted that he often struggled to get them adjusted. Hodgson said the hearing aids were a major source of frustration for his friend and he thinks they contributed to his isolation and his state of mind. The sounds of cans and bottles clanging together at the recycling plant were especially disconcerting to him, as was the sound of a dog's collar contacting its metal bowl. His solution was to often shut his hearing aids off, which resulted in him seeing someone's lips moving, but not hearing what they were saying. Both Nicole and Sean Hodgson think that this disconnect reinforced his belief that people were saying terrible things about him.

"In my opinion, they should get rid of online access for hearing aids, because from what I could tell, they're not worth a damn," Hodgson said in a March 2024 conversation.

Card's fellow Bravo Company soldiers also noted the impact the aids were having on him. Master Sgt. Yurek told the Saco police that Card had "Superman" hearing and could hear conversations other people were having from an abnormally long distance away. Other soldiers in the unit told of him leaning in and focusing intently on conversations strangers were having at distant tables in a restaurant.

One thing's for sure: all the people who he thought were calling him a pedophile were not doing that. Was the root cause of this the TBI? Was it a psychotic break brought on by underlying mental illness? Was it his progressive hearing loss, difficulty with his hearing aids, and the sense of isolation that can bring? Or was it a combination of some or all these factors? There's no scientific evidence showing a link between auditory hallucinations and hearing aids. There are a limited number of studies exploring whether there's a connection between auditory hallucinations and hearing impairment. One large study often cited found that 16% of hearing-impaired people had experienced at least one episode in the previous four weeks.[5]

Card's hearing loss was attributed to a hardening of the ear canal, known by its medical designation as tympanosclerosis. It's a condition that's caused by a buildup of excess calcium deposits after an injury like a ruptured eardrum, or acute or chronic ear infections. His repeated exposure to grenade blasts at West Point could well have played a part.

This talk about Card's impaired hearing might seem disrespectful to the members of Maine's Deaf community who were so impacted by his horrible actions on October 25th. Four of the victims killed at Schemengees were deaf, three were wounded, three more in attendance at their weekly cornhole tournament have been emotionally traumatized, and the families and friends left to mourn the loss of their loved ones will never fully recover. But to try and make sense of why it happened, it's necessary to look

---

5. Auditory Hallucinations in Adults With Hearing Impairment: A Large Prevalence Study, *PubMed,* 2018, MMJ Lanzen, GA van Zanten, RJ Teunisse, RM Brouwer, P Scheltens, IE Sommer.

at all the possible factors. The hearing impairment and his struggle to adapt likely played a role. How much of one we'll never know, but there were enough signs to point in this direction.

Dr. Michael Harvey, a Framingham, Massachusetts-based psychologist who specializes in mental health issues related to hearing loss, said in an interview that there is a correlation between hearing loss and depression, anxiety, and loneliness. Long-term progressive hearing loss can be worse, he said.

"Think of it, if you have something precious and you lose it, you grieve that loss. The grieving process for progressive hearing loss is more prolonged, and it can lead to profound depression and anxiety, and a sense of isolation."

But he doesn't believe that Card's adjustment to hearing aids or his hearing impairment was a major contributing factor for his actions on October 25th.

"It sounds like it was a psychotic break independent of any hearing loss. People with hearing loss can have auditory hallucinations and they can have psychotic breaks. But there's no research that shows that A causes B."

There's no explanation that will change what he did or provide a justification for it. Robert Card II shot and killed eighteen innocent people and wounded thirteen more while they were out enjoying themselves with their families and friends. Sick or not, he made that horrible choice. He wasn't alone in life. He had his own son, family and friends who desperately wanted to help him get better. The choice he made instead. cognitively impaired as he was, has devastated more people than he could have possibly imagined.

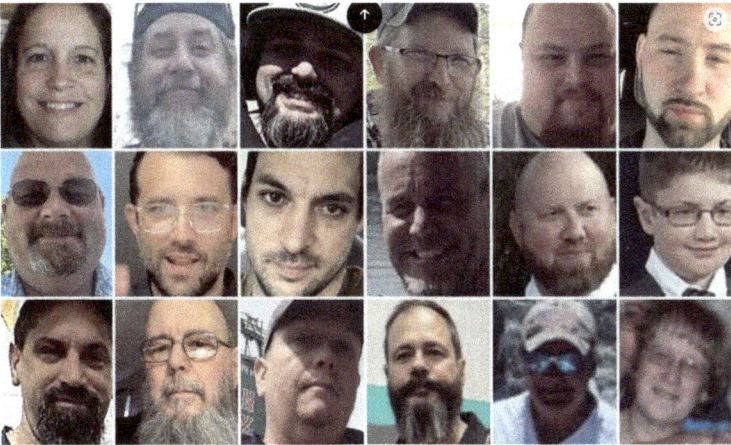

*The 18 victims of the Lewiston shootings. (Photo courtesy of the Maine Department of Public Safety)*

# A COMMUNITY GRIEVES

With the immediate area in lockdown, the community-wide grieving for the victims began on Facebook and other social media platforms as soon as the enormity of the tragedy came into focus in the evening hours of October 25th, 2023.

Once Card's body was found two days later and the lockdown was lifted, it moved outside onto the city's streets, carried by its stunned residents. Anywhere you looked in the days to follow—a front porch on Pine Street, a convenience store on Webster Street, a storefront on Lisbon Street, a playground on Caron Street—you saw a collective sense of shock and deep sorrow pulled from the depths. It was etched on the faces of today's Lewiston: elderly Quebecois-speaking couples, Somali women wearing colorful hijabs, bearded middle-aged men with worn ball caps, children white, black, and brown; a tapestry of innocence lost. In the aftermath, the distant memory of shootings in distant places reemerged: Columbine, Newtown, Las Vegas, Orlando, Sutherland Springs, Blacksburg, Parkland, El Paso, Uvalde. Now Lewiston joined the list.

Nowhere was this sense of loss more evident than on Lincoln Street days after the shootings, where people gathered at a spontaneous memorial of flowers, and placards with photos of the victims, crosses, prayer beads, stuffed animals, cornhole bags, and other mementos stretched along the roadway in front of Schemengees.

Four miles north, a line of pumpkins—painted with messages and framed by signs bearing the names of the victims—lined the road in front of Just-in-Time Recreation Center. When a candle flickering inside a pumpkin blew out in the swirling autumn winds, a smoker would pull out their lighter and relight it. If only it were that easy to bring back a life that had been extinguished so suddenly. The pumpkins served a purpose. Thomas Conrad, the bowling alley's manager, had promised his nine-year-old daughter that they would have a pumpkin carving party for Halloween. Many of the kids who bowled in the youth leagues were still grieving his loss, and the loss of the Violettes, but a week later they gathered to honor his promise.

A thousand people attended a memorial service at the Basilica of St. Peter & Paul on the Sunday night following the shootings, and hundreds more gathered outside, holding candles, and joining congregants inside to raise their arms and hold up their thumb, index finger, and little finger—the American Sign Language sign for *"I love you."*

President Biden and First Lady, Jill, showed up a couple of days later and laid some flowers on the growing Schemengees memorial before hugging and consoling owner, Kathy Lebel. At Just-In-Time, the President told the people gathered there that he and the First Lady had gone to too many mass shooting sites; Buffalo, Uvalde and Monterey Park, California in the year before their trip to Lewiston. *"You're not alone"*, he told the somber crowd. The White House's Office of Gun Violence Prevention beat the president to the city. Formed just the month before, Lewiston was the first incident it responded to. A team from the office arrived on October 29th to steer federal resources to help with funeral costs, small business loans for businesses, and trauma specialists to work in area schools. It also set up a family assistance center at the Lewiston Armory, where it helped facilitate getting enough ASL interpreters for the families of the Deaf victims and survivors. Soon after, the state of Maine and city officials partnered together to open the Maine Resiliency Center, first at the Lewiston Armory, and later at a dedicated space in downtown Lewiston. This mental health resource proved to be invaluable to many of the victims' families, survivors, and first responders as they struggled to cope with the emotions brought on by the horrific events.

The procession of funerals and memorials for the victims began a few days after the shootings. Once they started, it seemed like they'd never stop. Many of the survivors knew multiple victims, and they crisscrossed the city and surrounding towns in the days to come, hopscotching from one emotionally draining service to the next. For some, that's when their anger boiled to the surface for the first time. The shock in the immediate aftermath of the shootings had worn off, and the scale of the human carnage that Card had left behind came into sharp focus.

Danielle Grondin, who fled from Just-in-Time after he had leveled his gun at her, said she "lost it" at Thomas Conrad's funeral, which was one of the first to occur. She had bantered with the bowling alley's manager as he poured her a beer just thirty seconds before Card entered, and she was probably the last person to speak to him. Seeing his devastated nine-year-old daughter crying at his funeral triggered a primal anger in her that she struggles to let go of months later.

For the next two weeks the obituary pages of the *Lewiston Sun Journal* encapsulated the lives of all those lost.

\*\*\*

*Thomas Conrad, 34.* He had only worked at Just-in-Time for a few months, but he made himself indispensable to the owners, and was much loved by the tight knit community of bowlers, especially the kids. His daughter was the bright light of his universe, and as much a fixture at the bowling alley as he was. A former Army combat engineer who cleared minefields in Iraq, he was approaching Card to try and stop him when he was shot and killed.

*Tricia Asselin, 53.* She virtually grew up in the bowling alley and had done every job there many times over. A devoted mother to her son, Tricia was an unstoppable ball of energy. She worked three jobs, raised money for breast cancer research, organized events at the alley and a local golf club, and loved to tell people, 'Sleep is overrated.' She was on her cell phone dialing 9-1-1 when she was shot and killed.

*Lucille 'Lucy' Viollette, 73, and Bob Violette, 76.* They share an obituary because they shared a life and love for fifty years, and they died together protecting the kids they loved at Just-In-Time. The couple met in the offices of the Lewiston School Department in 1973, and they had been inseparable ever since. Lucy and Bob raised three boys together, doted on their six grandchildren, and stayed deeply in love the entire time. Bob stepped in front of the kids he was teaching bowling skills to when Card opened fire. Lucy was by his side in death, as she was in life.

*Aaron Young, 14.* The youngest of the victims, he was a gentle 6' 4" giant who was with the Violettes and his father when he was gunned down. In addition to bowling, he loved to ride his bike and fish. Aaron was a kind-hearted young man who went out of his way to make other kids feel accepted for who they were. He was very close to his mother, Cindy, and idolized his father, who would proudly watch his son become a very skilled bowler at Just-in-Time.

*William Young, 44.* He took his son every Wednesday and Saturday to the bowling alley, and he was with him when they were both shot and killed by Card. Known for his great sense of humor, Bill was a die-hard professional wrestling fan who would sit in the front row of the matches at the annual Fryeburg and Skowhegan Fairs and heckle the wrestlers. He was an Air Force veteran and a skilled car mechanic. His son Aaron wanted to follow in his father's footsteps and work on automobiles when he got older.

*Jason Walker, 51.* His friends thought of him as a true Renaissance man; a man who was a skilled tradesman, played guitar and wrote songs, and made educational videos about vegetable gardening, sausage-making, bread-baking, and the history of his hometown of Sabattus. He was relentlessly curious about how things worked, and fiercely protective of his wife of twenty six years and his family. Jason was shot and killed as he charged at Card with his boyhood friend, Michael Deslauriers, in an effort to disarm him. His courage that night saved countless lives.

*Michael Deslauriers, 51.* You couldn't spend any amount of time in the same room with him without breaking out into laughter at his sardonic wit, his friends and family all say. A network engineer for all his adult life, he was the father of an adult son and daughter, a husband, and an avid Boston sports fan who loved to golf, bowl and fish. Jason Walker, a kindergarten classmate, was his only true friend in life, he would tell people. Michael was shot and killed by Card as he charged him with his friend Jason in an effort to disarm him. His courage that night saved countless lives.

*Keith Macneir, 64.* He came from his home state of Florida to visit his son on his birthday with a bag of stone crabs he had caught before he left. Keith was an architect for part of his adult life before he transitioned to a career with the U.S. National Park Service in the Virgin Islands. He was sitting at the bar in Schemengees waiting for his son to return from a union meeting when Card shot and killed him.

*Joe Walker, 57.* Known affectionately as 'Cue Ball', he was the manager of Schemengees, and an indispensable right-hand man and 'work husband' to the owner. He was also beloved by the patrons of the sports bar and restaurant, and an ubiquitous presence at tournaments and events there. Joe was a loving father to two sons and four daughters and a devoted husband. He yelled out when the first shots were fired, and later first responders told his family that he stepped towards Card with the butcher knife found next to his body.

*Ron Morin, 55.* He was the father of a son and daughter, and a happily married man who loved to tell 'Dad' jokes. Always upbeat, always smiling, Ron loved to play ice hockey, softball and cornhole and make people laugh and enjoy life as much as he could. A Lewiston High graduate and longtime Coca-Cola employee, he and his wife were planning to retire and move to South Carolina to be close to their children. He was playing cornhole when he was shot and killed.

*Arthur 'Artie' Strout, 42.* Known for his infectious humor, goofy laugh, and bear hugs, he was the father of a blended family of five kids with his wife of sixteen years. He was devoted to his family and spent as much time with them as he could. Christmas started the day after Halloween in Artie's house when he brought in the first-cut tree of the season and got the whole family involved in decorating. Like his father, Arthur Barnard, Artie loved to play pool. He was preparing for a tournament when Card gunned him down.

*Maxx Hathaway, 35.* A multi-sport athlete at Lisbon High School, he was busy raising two young girls with his wife. She was pregnant with a third girl when he was shot and killed playing pool at Schemengees. A happy-go-lucky man with a great sense of humor, he loved to spend time with his wife, daughters and his large extended family. He was a devoted stay-at-home Dad who had just completed four years of college courses and received his diploma from the University of Southern Maine on the day he was killed.

*Peyton Brewer-Ross, 40.* Known by everyone who knew him and people who had just met him as a kind and generous man who loved to make people laugh, he was the completely smitten father of an adorable two-year old daughter who still looks down the stairs for her father to play the peek-a-boo game they played every night before she went to bed. A pipefitter at the Bath Iron Works shipyard, he loved pro wrestling, Star Wars, and comic books, and was an avid cornhole player. He was playing at Schemengees when he was shot and killed.

*Joshua Seal, 36.* He was a familiar face to many Mainers as the ASL interpreter for the Maine CDC Covid-19 daily television briefings, but his advocacy work on behalf of the Deaf community was truly his calling. Joshua worked as an educator in a school for the Deaf, started a summer camp for deaf children and served as an ASL interpreter for Vice-President Kamala Harris. He was an avid disc golf and cornhole player, but his greatest passion was spending time with his wife Elizabeth and his four young children. He was playing in a cornhole league game with other deaf players when he was shot and killed.

*William "Billy" Brackett, 48.* The father of a son and young daughter, he had a wide circle of friends in the Deaf community. He was a great all-around athlete—an outstanding baseball and soccer player, as well as a 1000-plus point scorer in his high school basketball career. He loved to hunt and fish and was an avid darts and cornhole player. Billy was playing in the Wednesday cornhole league for deaf players when Robert Card put an end to his life.

*Stephen Vozzella, 45.* Stephen called Massachusetts home for most of his life until he moved to Maine. The father of a daughter, he took to his adopted state like a fish to water. He liked to camp with his wife and daughter and ride his ATV. A U.S. Postal Service employee, Stephen was an accomplished bowler and cornhole player and an avid Boston sports fan. He was playing in the Wednesday cornhole league for deaf players when he was gunned down.

*Bryan MacFarlane, 41.* Bryan attended the Governor Baxter School for the Deaf from the age of two until his high school graduation. He moved out of state after that, living in Vermont, Ohio, and North Carolina before he recently returned to Maine. He was the first deaf person in the state of Vermont to receive a CDL, and one of a very few in the country to be employed as a long-haul trucker. A dedicated motorcycle rider, he also liked to camp, fish and play cornhole. He was playing in the Wednesday night league for deaf players when he was shot and killed.

\*\*\*

The pain will endure for the victim's families and survivors, wounded and unscathed, but the shock was slowly wearing off for the community at large as the calendar flipped into November of 2023.

Some turned it into action. *"Lewiston Strong"* signs began appearing in storefront windows, on digital display boards, on tee-shirts and cornhole bags, in full-page newspaper ads. The *"Strong"* slogan started in Boston in 2013 after the marathon bombing, and since then it's been adopted by towns and cities across the country after a tragedy. Once a part of Massachusetts before it became a state in 1820, Maine and the Bay State share history and support the same professional sports teams. The Bruins, Celtics, and Patriots all hosted families and survivors at games in the weeks after October 25th. All the teams made and wore uniform jerseys designed to show support to the city and its people. The Bruins went a step further by donating $200,000 to a fund set up for families to pay for funeral costs and other immediate expenses. With its deep roots as a hockey town, the team's generosity in both money and spirit created many more new Boston Bruins fans.

Local pro hockey teams joined in. The ECHL Maine Mariners in Portland also created special jerseys, which they auctioned off to raise money for an assistance fund for families of the victims. The hometown NAHL Nordiques also donated to a fund set up for victims and hosted fundraisers at The Colisee. The shootings hit close to home for the Nordiques. Not only is the team based in Lewiston, but a former player and current home game scorekeeper, Kyle Secor, was critically wounded at Schemengees. He received a rousing ovation when he left the hospital in December and showed up on crutches a few days later to drop the puck at The Colisee.

Pro sports teams weren't the only ones to provide financial and moral support. A couple of members of a local softball league batted around ideas of what they could do to help, and on short notice, they organized a softball tournament. The effort took off on social media, and by the time the tournament kicked off twenty days later, twenty-five teams played forty-eight games at fields in Lewiston and Auburn, drawing hundreds of spectators on a frigid November day. The final fundraising tally was $208,000 raised to support victim's families.

A bonus for the spectators—especially fans of *Grey's Anatomy*—was the appearance of Patrick Dempsey, the show's star and Lewiston area native. Fresh off being named "The World's Sexiest Man" by *People* magazine, Dempsey played on a team made up of first responders. Although he's called Hollywood home for decades, Dempsey has maintained strong ties to his hometown. One thing that keeps him coming back is the Dempsey Cancer Center, which sits in a renovated brick building downtown, providing free holistic cancer support for patients. He and his siblings founded it in memory of his mother, Amanda, who passed away from ovarian cancer in 2007, and he returns every year for the Dempsey Challenge to raise millions of dollars to help support the center's programs.

Lewiston High School sports helped buoy the spirits of the community in the months to follow. Three weeks after the shootings the Blue Devils boys' soccer team won the Class A state title in a 3-2 overtime thriller. Tegra Mbele, the Somalian immigrant who scored the winning goal, told the *Sun Journal, "We* just wanted to give back to the city for all they've been through." It was a statement of solidarity between Lewiston's growing immigrant community and its native population. It was the team's fifth state title in the last decade, which coincides with the arrival of the thousands of African immigrants who call the city home now.

The boys' hockey team took home the Class A state title in March. It was a record twenty-fifth state title for the team, which says all you need to know about the importance of ice hockey to the city. Cody Dionne, a team forward, told the *Sun Journal* that he was simply keeping with tradition; his older brother, father, and grandfather all have Class A titles to their name.

Higher up the academic ladder, the University of Maine announced in late November that it would offer free four-year tuition to the children and spouses of the eighteen victims and to the thirty-one people who suffered wounds related to the shootings. The school estimated that over eighty Mainers would be eligible for the tuition waivers.

In March of 2024 the directors of the Lewiston-Auburn Area Response Fund announced that it had distributed $4.7 million to 162 people directly impacted by the shootings. That included heirs, spouses, wounded survivors, and survivors who were at Just-in-Time and Schemengees that night. Coupled with the funds raised by dozens of GoFundMe campaigns, cornhole and bowling fundraising events, and countless other individual initiatives, the money will at least help ease the burden of financial worries for people whose lives were turned upside down in an instant.

In December, city workers gathered up all the memorial items that sat in front of Just-in-Time and Schemengees and brought them to the Maine Museum of Innovation, Learning and Labor, which is housed in the enormous Bates Mill building between the downtown area and the Androscoggin. There, organizers created an exhibit out of the 1000 salvageable items. It will serve as a de facto memorial to the victims of the shootings until the city and chamber of commerce raise enough money to build a permanent outdoor memorial.

And so, the people of Lewiston and the surrounding region are recovering at their own pace. The days and weeks after that awful night disappeared in a fog of grief and disbelief, and now the time past is registered in months, even in larger increments that leapfrog seasons. Like daylight savings; the clock was turned back a few days after the shootings, the darkness at the end of the day a metaphor for the sorrow that descended over the state. For once, daylight savings made sense. The clock moved forward in March, the light at the end of the day a welcome sight after another abnormally warm, but emotionally grueling dark winter. Then came April, with the first bright yellow bursts of forsythia, and May, when the land burst open with sound and color. Time doesn't heal all wounds, but it hopefully makes them less painful for everyone who was scarred by such a senseless and tragic act.

# RECKONING FOR THE SHERIFF'S OFFICE

Until 2023, the town of Bowdoin, Maine and the county it sits in, Sagadahoc County, weren't exactly household names. With just 254 square miles of land mass, Sagadahoc County is the smallest of Maine's sixteen counties. What it lacks in size, it makes up for in variety though. From drop dead beautiful ocean views in Phippsburg and Georgetown, to bucolic farm, field and river views in Richmond and Bowdoin, to the towering cranes of the Bath Iron Works (BIW) shipyard on the Kennebec River and the brick-paved streets of the small city of Bath, Sagadahoc County packs a lot into a little area.

Sagadahoc was the first native Abenaki name for the Kennebec, which itself is also an Abenaki name meaning "mouth of the big river." It's a 170-mile-long river that flows out of Moosehead Lake, the state's largest, and empties out into the Atlantic by Popham Beach, mid-coast Maine's crown jewel of a beach. Aside from a few pocket beaches further northeast up the coast, Popham beach is the last long stretch of sand on the Gulf of Maine, a fact that doesn't escape summer tourists as they fill its parking lot before late sleepers roll out of bed on a sunny summer day.

Lesser known is the fact that Popham was the site of the second English settlement in America, coming just months after the landing in Jamestown, Virginia. Established in 1607, the 125-person settlement at Popham suffered through a brutal first winter, and the death of its leader,

George Popham. Before he died, Popham sent a letter to King James reporting that a large body of water a few days' journey to the west was the Pacific Ocean and the route to China, "which unquestionably cannot be far from these parts." Without the benefit of proper charts or GPS, Popham wouldn't know that he was about 14,000 nautical miles from China. Fortunately for him, neither would King James.

By 1608, what was left of the colony that had survived the winter decided they had enough of the new land and planned their return to England. They mustered just enough strength to build the first ocean-faring ship in the New World for their journey home. Behind them, Popham Colony was forgotten and lost to history until 1888, when their plans for the colony were discovered in a maritime history archive in Spain. There's a stone Civil War-era fort at the far end of the beach, just down the road from the old colony site, which is used now as an overflow lot for beachgoers and fishermen working the incoming tide in the hopes of hooking on to a sweet-tasting striped bass at the river's mouth. A simple plaque with a brief description marks the spot.

Located in the town of Phippsburg, Popham lies at the eastern boundary of Sagadahoc County. On the far western end is the town of Bowdoin. With its rolling fields and hay bales, weathered farmhouses and wooded winding roads, its pastoral setting makes it seem like it could be in another state, not a county town just thirty miles away from Popham's crashing surf and Georgetown's craggy coastal ledges. The quiet little town wasn't known for very much before October 25th, 2023. Now it's known far and wide as the hometown of Robert Card, Maine's forever notorious mass shooter.

Sagadahoc County wasn't all that well known before 2023 either. Now its Sheriff's Office is known as the law enforcement agency that had an opportunity to prevent Card from killing eighteen people, but either was grossly negligent, as critics say, or handcuffed by ineffective gun control laws and limited resources, as its supporters say.

Of course, the critics have shared their opinions online, especially in the days following the shootings. They did again in March 2024 after the independent commission found plenty to fault in the SCSO's failure to recognize how dangerous Robert Card II was to the public. In fact, from the time that the SCSO first posted the video clip image on its Facebook page of Robert Card with the Ruger AR-10 held in a firing position after he entered the bowling alley on the night of October 25th, there's been a public backlash against the agency.

A few comments in the chaotic and confusing early days set the tenor. *"You had the information for months, and you failed to serve and protect. The blood is on your hands SCSO."*

*"This could have been prevented if you had acted. Epic failure on the part of the Sagadahoc County Sheriff. Disgusting!"*

Whether they read these early comments or not, the impact of the shootings would have an immediate effect on SCSO personnel. The strain was clearly evident on Sheriff Merry's face in a television interview on October 26th, the day after the shootings. He looked ashen, and sounded defensive, saying in his clipped Maine accent that his officers "worked within our policy." He did respond by saying, "that's a fair question," when asked whether his officers should have relied on the Card family to remove the ten to fifteen guns they were told he possessed. But the overall impression he left was that he believed his officers acted properly given the circumstances.

He doubled down on that a few days later. In an online statement issued October 30th, Sheriff Merry outlined key points of his officer's interaction with Card and concluded with the following: *"We believe our agency acted appropriately and followed procedures for conducting an attempt to locate and wellness check.*" Under the statement on the SCSO's Facebook page was a disclaimer: "*The Sagadahoc County Sheriff's Office limited who can comment on this post.*" But it wasn't just limited. The comments' function had been disabled. Predictably, this move sparked a backlash.

After releasing the statement, Sheriff Merry said in an interview with the *Portland Press Herald* that his agency was doing "some soul-searching" on whether they could have done anything differently. But he went on to suggest that the state's weak yellow flag law and his office's manpower issues were also factors that contributed to their handling of the wellness check call. He hasn't made the manpower claim since. In fact, he hasn't made any, because he went off the radar publicly, letting the December review commissioned by his agency speak for him.

In the court of public opinion, Sheriff Merry went from a long-serving and respected law enforcement authority to a pariah on social media. "*Resign, coward,*" urged one Facebook commenter. "*The Sagadahoc County Sheriff's Office was cowardly throughout. Sheriff Joel Merry should step down immediately,*" said another on Twitter. He has his supporters, of course, as does the agency. There are plenty of social media posts defending them, but they're less vocal than its detractors

By the end of the first week after the shooting, a petition calling for Sheriff Merry's removal was posted online. By the end of November, some of the criticism had morphed into bitter sarcasm. When the SCSO posted on its Facebook page about its involvement with a program called "Sand for Seniors," which distributes sand for elderly residents to use on icy walkways and driveways, the critics were ready. Under a photo of Sheriff Merry and six officers standing behind a stack of five-gallon buckets at an area Lowe's Home Improvement store, one commenter wrote, "*Best of luck protecting those buckets. You certainly did a bang up job protecting Robert Card...God help us all, because the police won't."*

The impact of Robert Card's actions on October 25th, 2023 will be felt for a lifetime for the families of the victims. The crater it left behind is deep and wide and spreads out from the center into the community. The stain of being associated with the absolute worst crime in Maine's history might never wash off for employees of the SCSO and members of Bravo Company of the 3-304th Battalion who served with Card.

Sheriff Merry is a forty-one-year law enforcement professional. He spent twenty-five years at the Bath Police Department, where he rose to the rank of lieutenant. He's led the SCSO since 2009, after winning in an election over his current Chief Deputy, Brett Strout. He's run unopposed in three election campaigns since then. At sixty-five, he's reached the traditional retirement age, but state law prohibits counties from establishing a mandatory retirement age.

During his long law enforcement career, Sheriff Merry has been the recipient of several awards. Among them, he was awarded the Ed Googins Award for Leadership in Gun Safety by the Gun Safety Coalition in 2021 for "his outspoken commitment to gun safety." This came after two cases in West Bath over the course of six months in which a child picked up a parent's unattended gun and pulled the trigger. The first was when a two-year-old took his father's Glock 9mm from his parent's nightstand next to their bed and squeezed off a round, hitting the mother in the leg, and the father in the head with two bullet fragments. The second involved a four-year-old picking up his stepfather's .40 caliber handgun and firing a round that penetrated the apartment wall into an adjacent unit. No one was hurt in that case. The sheriff lambasted the gun owners in the press for their negligence and urged the public to be more vigilant about storing their guns safely. Both men were charged with endangering the welfare of a child.

Sheriff Merry has also been recognized for his outspoken advocacy for increasing mental health resources in the state. In 2015, he was named the recipient of a lifetime achievement award by the National Alliance on Mental Illness' (NAMI) Crisis Intervention Team. He still serves as the law enforcement liaison for his region on the group's CIT team council. NAMI's CIT team is a collaboration between the mental health community and law enforcement to develop and allocate mental health resources for "complex cases and individuals in frequent contact with emergency services," according to the group's website. Sheriff Merry's mental health counterpart on the council is an employee of Sweetser, Maine's largest behavioral health provider. Founded in 1828 as a resident care home for children, the nonprofit now serves over 20,000 children and adults across the state every year and generates more than $62 million in revenue.

In one of the cruelest of the many ironies that exist in the Lewiston story, in the fall of 2023 the *Portland Press Herald* published an article titled, 'Midcoast police hire mental health liaison to help people in crisis.' The article described how the SCSO, and police departments from Bath, Brunswick, and Topsham drew funding from the state's $235 million opioid settlement award with several national Oxycontin distributors to hire a Sweetser mental health professional to respond to calls with officers for citizens requiring crisis intervention.

"It's the best use of these funds to send back out into our communities to provide critical services that address the crisis we are currently experiencing," Sheriff Merry told the reporter. The article was published on October 24th, 2023, one day before Card's rampage. Did the SCSO miss a golden opportunity by failing to consult the Sweetser liaison about Robert Card when they came on board at the beginning of October? Would a heads-up from Sgt. Skolfield when he returned from his vacation have jump-started a follow-up?

It's one of many questions Sheriff Merry is grappling with in the aftermath of the shootings, and then the subsequent interim findings of the independent commission. He's got plenty on his plate these days. In addition to heading the SCSO, Merry is also the board chair for the Two Bridges Regional Jail in nearby Wiscasset, the president-at-large for the Maine Sheriff's Association, and he sits on the board of directors of the Maine Police Chiefs Association and the United Way of Midcoast Maine. He's also a member of the Maine Deadly Force Review Panel, which is tasked with reviewing incidents of police shootings to determine whether they were justified. The panel was established by the Maine Legislature in 2019 after years of questions about the Maine Attorney General's Office's determination that, of the 175 police shootings in Maine since 1990 they investigated, every single one was justified.

So, Sheriff Merry clearly had a lot of irons in the fire in September 2023, when his agency responded to a welfare check call on Robert Card II. It's fair to ask whether he was spread too thin to be an effective leader, and whether he lost focus on preparing his agency for the current day challenges that law enforcement faces. Unless he decides to retire before the November 2024 election, he'll spend a portion of his workday devoted to defending the agency he's led for the last fifteen years, and another portion doing everything he can to make sure it doesn't happen again.

# INNOCENCE LOST

Many of the survivors of the shootings at Just-In-Time and Schemengees say that they now struggle to make themselves go out in public, and when they do, they're constantly scanning their environment, their fight or flight antenna always engaged. That's true to a far lesser extent for countless Mainers too. There's an underlying sense of wariness here now that feels as foreign as seeing a shooting in a Hallmark TV movie. Months have passed, and for many, a thought bubble still works its way through their bloodstream as they go to church, walk into a store, go to a concert—*What if a shooter came in here? Which way would I go? Where are the exit doors?*

The rest of America may say, *Welcome to the 21st-century, Maine.* The state isn't the idyllic lighthouse and lobster paradise populated by salty, hard-working country bumpkins as it's portrayed to the rest of the country, but this—a fellow Mainer cold-bloodedly mowing down eighteen others—this was never supposed to happen here. But it did, and the fallout is still in the news cycle months afterwards.

The public hearings held by the independent commission investigating the Lewiston shootings have revealed many of the missteps by law enforcement—most notably the Sagadahoc County Sheriff's Office—and the benign neglect of some of the Army Reserve's Bravo Company officers and senior NCOs in not taking care of one of their own.

They've also revealed the massive challenges law enforcement faced in the forty-eight-hour manhunt for Robert Card, as well as some of the communication breaks and leadership decisions that short-circuited what should have been a much quicker resolution.

Finally, they've produced searing, heartbreaking testimony by the family members of the victims and survivors. Their grief and post-trauma symptoms palpable, they courageously shared memories of their loved ones and the horrors many of them experienced on that terrible night.

Who knows what impact the commission's full report will have when it's produced sometime in 2024. The scrap heap of history is full of blue-ribbon panel recommendations after catastrophic events. In the Roman Coliseum-level fights that revolve around firearms, whatever remedy they might recommend will surely be challenged.

That was evident in early January 2024 when gun control advocates held a rally at the State House to mark the opening of a new legislative session. Still raw from the open wounds of the Lewiston shootings, hundreds of people crammed into the building's rotunda to voice support for tougher laws. Waving signs and thunderously applauding the speakers who came to the microphone to make impassioned pleas for change, they outnumbered gun rights advocates by a factor of at least ten to one. Still, in the sea of signs proclaiming, *Mainers for Gun Safety* and *Moms Demand Action,* the signs saying, *People Kill, Not Guns,* and *Technology Changes, Rights Do Not,* were hard not to miss.

"This is not about taking guns. This is about doing the right thing and finding the right politicians who are willing to do the right thing more than they're afraid of losing their jobs," Arthur Barnard, the father of Schemengees' victim, Artie Strout, told the crowd, his voice quivering with emotion.

Never a quiet place to begin with, the State House became an even livelier place after the shootings. Bomb threats in January and March of 2024 emptied the building and the attached office complexes, sending hundreds out into the cold. And for the first time in its history, it was the site of active shooter simulation, which lawmakers requested in the wake of the events of the previous few months.

The disbelief and heartache Mainers felt in the immediate aftermath of the shootings was etched on Governor Mills' face from her first press conference early on October 26th. She's a former Androscoggin County DA, and she met her husband in Lewiston and sent her children to schools there. Her grief was raw and heartfelt, not the faux grief that some politicians manufacture on demand. So, not surprisingly, the shootings prompted the governor to step off the tightrope she's been precariously balanced on and take some decisive gun control action. In her State of the State address in late January 2024 she proposed a package of legislation that would expand the state's yellow flag law—one that she was instrumental in crafting in 2019—to allow law enforcement officers to obtain a warrant to take a dangerous person into protective custody in order to remove their firearms. This option was not available to SCSO personnel in September when they went to Card's trailer to do a wellness check. It was a provision that Mills deliberately avoided when she helped create the law five years before in an effort to appease Republican opponents.

Maine's current law is a cumbersome process that can take officers many hours to shepherd from beginning to end; from determining an individual is a serious risk, to taking them into protective custody, to a mental health evaluation, to a judge to sign an order, to the eventual removal of firearms—it requires a tremendous time commitment for law enforcement agencies, especially undermanned rural ones. Still, it's better than nothing, as the shooting's aftermath revealed. In the three years from its enactment to

October 25th, 2023, it was used eighty times by agencies statewide. In the three months after the shooting, it was used 117 times. It was invoked a dozen times in the week after Lewiston alone, including on four occasions when the subjects specifically mentioned Robert Card or their own desire to do a mass shooting. It might be a horribly bad joke to some, but law enforcement officers are well aware of the documented phenomenon of copycat shootings.

Some specific incidents include a Halloween night altercation, when a man in South Portland threatened to spray a Buffalo Wild Wings restaurant with an AR-15. That threat resulted in him being charged with terrorizing, an option that was available to the SCSO and Saco Police after Card threatened to shoot up the Saco Reserve Center. The next week, a former Mainer living in Oklahoma City was arrested after he posted on Facebook that Robert Card had an accomplice, and that accomplice was going to shoot up Lawrence High School in the central Maine town of Fairfield. The school was shut down for several days as police traced the post to the man, a former student there.

The most curious case occurred in early March 2024, when the Waldo County Sheriff's Office invoked the yellow flag law to seize several firearms that were stashed on the shore of an island in mid-coast Maine by a man wearing a ballistic vest. The man had been spotted on a boat by a construction crew working on a home on the island, which is situated a mile offshore from the town of Lincolnville. Deputies came out and took the man into protective custody but failed to find any guns. A maintenance man on the island was convinced he saw the man carrying firearms, and he and his crew took up the search after officers departed. Three days later they found them stashed on the shore. The find triggered law enforcement to initiate the yellow flag process. Ironically, Cara Lamb, Robert Card's ex-wife, knows someone on the crew who took part in the search. They're convinced that the man intended to return and ambush the crew and anyone with them. Thankfully, they paid enough attention to prevent having to find out whether that was the case.

So, there is heightened awareness now amongst Maine law enforcement agencies and the public in the wake of the Lewiston shootings. That public awareness and the desire to enact meaningful gun control laws prompted Augusta legislators and the governor to pass and sign a number of new laws in late April 2024. Among them was a law to expand background checks for advertised private sales of firearms and to allow for law enforcement officers to apply directly to judges to obtain warrants for a protective custody hold. Another requires a seventy-two-hour waiting period on firearms purchases. Governor Mills did veto a bump stock ban bill that was passed by both chambers, and a proposed red flag law never made it out of committee, but the overall mood was a positive one for Maine gun control advocates at the end of the session.

Predictably, gun owners' advocates were incensed. SAM (Sportsmen's Alliance of Maine) immediately said it would file an injunction to prevent the seventy-two-hour waiting period from becoming law, citing it as a kiss of death for gun show operators. The Kittery Trading Post, a major gun retailer in southern Maine, threatened to move to New Hampshire in protest of the new laws.

Despite the initial change in tone after the Lewiston shootings, Republican political opposition to substantive gun law change hasn't wavered much. House Minority Leader, Billy Bob Faulkingham, told the *Portland Press Herald* that the sister of one of the victims killed in the shootings informed him that her brother wouldn't want his death to be used to enact new gun control laws. True or not, that shameless political point drew a chorus of criticism. Faulkingham has also echoed a talking point that's circulated among gun rights' supporters by claiming that the ability for law enforcement to obtain a warrant for a protective custody hold would not have made a difference in Robert Card's case. That's not accurate. Had the option of obtaining a warrant been available to SCSO personnel, they may well have exercised it. Besides, Faulkingham added, Card was an anomaly, a crazy person thrashing around in a sea of normalcy.

"I don't think the state of Maine should be building a gun policy on the actions of one man who was apparently a paranoid schizophrenic."

This tone-deafness isn't reserved for politicians and special interest groups alone. The Fine Line Gun Shop in Poland, the store that sold Card the Ruger SFAR .308 rifle he used to kill eighteen people, advertised the same rifle on its Facebook page in December, just three months after the shootings. One commenter on the post replied, "*Awesome shooter. Lightest .308 around.*"

Faulkingham's misinformed reference to Card's mental health diagnosis is a blanket fallback argument for gun rights supporters, but it does have some merit. While there is a misconception that *most* mass shootings are committed by someone with a mental illness, studies do show that's the case in close to one out of three shootings that result in four or more fatalities.[6] For example, Columbia University's Department of Psychiatry examined 1315 mass shootings involving 10,877 fatalities in a 2021 study. Some 30%—resulting in over 3,200 fatalities—were perpetrated by someone with a diagnosed mental illness, they determined. That's hardly an anomaly.

There's no doubt that the issue of mental health and firearms is a prime concern to law enforcement officers every time they put on the uniform. That's supported by the most recent Maine Deadly Force Review Panel findings, which "urgently" called for the Maine Legislature to give

---

6. Psychotic Symptoms in Mass Shootings: Findings From the Columbia University Mass Murder Database, Gary Brucato et al., Columbia University Department of Psychiatry, 2021.

law enforcement and mental health professionals more help with resources, and more teeth to laws to help them take dangerous individuals into protective custody. In 2023, the panel reported that nearly 75% of the cases it reviewed since 2019 involved a person in mental distress. Sheriff Merry of the SCSO, who sits on the panel, has been a longtime advocate for increased mental health resources for agencies statewide. So too has Maine Department of Public Safety Commissioner, Michael Sauschuck, another member of the panel.

Governor Mills' 2024 legislative proposals also included expanding a network of mental health crisis centers statewide, building on a model established in Portland and a follow-up center in Augusta. The proposal was only supported by a $1.4 million appropriation though, a modest sum given the needs. She also called to strengthen the mobile crisis program, which responded to nearly 15,000 calls statewide in 2023. The news in early March 2024 that a major mental health provider in Lewiston faces imminent closure unless the state floats $2 million to another agency to take over its operations makes the need even more pressing. The agency serves 1,800 clients, including survivors and family members of the victims of the Lewiston shootings. If it were to close, it would stretch the thin mental health care resources in the state even further.

Like many states around the country, Maine reduced per capita investment in mental health programs in recent years, resulting in a backlog of need and questionable care in the institutions it did financially support. In fact, the state's lack of support for mental health services has been going on much longer than that. In 1989, patient advocates sued the state for negligence in the deaths of ten patients at the state-run Augusta Mental Health Institute, and ended up forcing the state to sign a court-ordered consent decree to meet minimum standards of care. Many of those same advocates are graying now, and they're still waiting for the state to abide by the decree. Rather than seeing incremental gains, they've watched Augusta ignore, and occasionally kneecap the mental health care system. Governor Mills has reversed some of the policies of former governor, Paul LePage, who in 2013 blamed the problem of mass shootings on "mental disease." Mills allocated an additional $30 million for funding a supplemental package of mental health-related policies in 2024, including an additional $422,000 to assist law enforcement in keeping up with the surge of yellow flag orders since the Lewiston shootings.

LePage, who referred to himself as "Trump before there was a Trump" when he was in office, had an ill-disguised disdain for social welfare programs, including mental health care, resulting in significant cuts to access in his eight-year tenure. His views haven't changed much over the years. The man who vetoed the red flag law passed by the Legislature in 2018 reacted to the shootings in his hometown by announcing that he would host a black-tie fundraiser to raise $500,000 for the families of the victims. When asked by a local radio station what needs to change to prevent more mass shootings from occurring, he said, "We have to deal with mental illness." His event was held at the end of 2023 at the Royal Oak Room, an elegant meeting room housed in the former main train station in Lewiston. The communications point person was the former governor's daughter, Lauren LePage, who owns a Sanford-based lobbying and consulting company. Prior to that she was the state's National Rifle Association's director for four years, including the year her father vetoed the red flag law. The fundraiser raised $475,000, she confirmed in the spring, and was distributed to thirty-one families directly affected by the shootings.

And finally, after the series of public hearings that spanned four months in 2024, the independent commission issued its interim report in mid-March. Curiously, they did that unannounced on a Friday at 5 p.m., long recognized as the best time to dump news that you don't want a wide audience to learn about. Their findings, as expected, did not reflect favorably on the Army Reserve's 3-304th Bravo Company soldiers.

*The Army Reserve did not encourage law enforcement to charge Card for threatening to "shoot up" the facility. They failed to divulge Four Wind's recommendations and concerns. They treated Card as a high risk of violence against the unit's members, but appeared to minimize the threat he posed once they were satisfied that Card was not coming to the unit on September 16, 2023.*

That's all they had to say about them. Given all the other damning information that's known and was presented in testimony earlier in the month, it's not much. The commission did follow up this interim report with an April hearing to elicit testimony from Sgt. Daryl Reed and Staff Sgt. Sean Hodgson, the two friends of Card's, who had been inexplicably excluded from earlier hearings. Their testimony, while riveting, echoed what's been previously presented in this book.

The bulk of the commission's interim report was directed at the Sagadahoc County Sheriff's Office and the failure of its personnel, most specifically Sgt. Aaron Skolfield, to take Robert Card into protective custody and invoke the yellow flag law. The seven-member panel left little doubt about whether that should have happened. They listed a variety of reasons why they came to that conclusion:

*The Commission unanimously concludes that the Sagadahoc County Sheriff's Office had more than sufficient information to begin the process of securing a Yellow Flag order against Robert Card II on September 17th, 2023.*

*As of September 17, 2023, the SCSO had information that a member of its community with serious mental illness, had been hospitalized for two weeks related to that illness, had access to 10-15 firearms, had assaulted his friend days earlier, had threatened to shoot up the drill center in Saco and had threatened to "get" his superiors who were responsible for his hospitalization.*

And finally, they left little doubt as to how they felt about the SCSO's decision to rely on the Card family to remove his guns.

*The ultimate response to this information was to leave the responsibility for the removal of Mr. Card's weapons and the assessment of whether Mr. Card needed a mental health evaluation with Mr. Card's family and close the case without any plans for follow up. This responsibility was that of the SCSO, not that of Mr. Card's family.*

The main target of this scathing assessment is Sgt. Aaron Skolfield, the man who responded to the call to do a wellness check on Card on September 15th, and then ultimately left responsibility in the hands of the Card family. While his lack of judgment and initiative was clearly the main driver of the panel's findings, Skolfield's demeanor during the hearing certainly didn't help his cause. His glasses perched on the end of his nose, he was righteous, defiant and unremorseful to the end. For instance, when asked whether he was concerned when he heard that Card had threatened to commit violence, Skolfield matter-of-factly said, "No, I hear it all the time. I threaten to kill my kids if they don't clean their room, but that doesn't mean I'm going to do it." If his performance was graded for tone deaf arrogance and a lack of situational awareness, Skolfield aced it.

But Skolfield is so sure he performed his job admirably he took out papers to run for the position of Sheriff in the upcoming November 2024 election against Sheriff Merry. Merry, who has run unopposed in three elections since 2012, filed papers to run again shortly after Skolfield did. In a later interview with the *Portland Press Herald,* Skolfield laid the blame for his inaction squarely with Bravo Company soldiers, saying they downplayed Card's behavior when he spoke with them. "I can only work with what I have. I wasn't given the complete picture," he told the reporter. For all his finger-pointing in that interview, he fails to mention the fact that he didn't bother to read a 1300-word report written by another SCSO deputy about Card's deteriorating condition months before while he sat in his patrol car for nearly an hour waiting for another officer to arrive. Nor does he mention that he didn't bother to ask how many and what kind of weapons Card had when he was "negotiating" for the family to take control of them, that he was aware that Card had been hospitalized for psychosis two months before, that he was aware of his threats to shoot up the Saco facility, or that he didn't bother to check to see if the Card family has successfully removed the guns before he lifted a File 6 BOLO alert on Card when he returned from vacation.

Skolfield followed up this interview with the release of a defiant twenty-page attack on the commission's interim report by his own attorney. In addition to repeating his assertion that Bravo Company soldiers downplayed Card's condition, he accused the commission of distorting facts and jumping to conclusions to make him the scapegoat. That's two reports commissioned and paid for by either his employer or himself that exonerate Skolfield. That fact triggers a question posed earlier in this book: *Can a review commissioned and paid for by the subject of the review truly be considered an unbiased, independent, third-party examination of the facts?*

Skolfield's entrance into the sheriff's race presents an interesting quandary for Sheriff Merry. If the independent commission's findings had him considering whether to dismiss Skolfield - which he is entitled to do under the collective bargaining agreement signed between the county and the local union representing SCSO officers - would he dare do it after Skolfield's announcement that he was vying for Merry's job? If they both stay in the race, neither one should count on support from any Card family members or their many supporters. Some are outspoken in their disdain for both men, others not, but they'll write in someone else if they bother to participate.

For now, the family members are trying to make sense of what Robbie did and why he did it. The TBI diagnosis helped them be able to forgive him, but none will ever say it exonerates him. They hope that more research by the CTE center will lead to definitive links to his West Point training and ultimately, to policy changes by military officials.

As they struggle with this reckoning, they're also navigating how to live in the community they've called home for so long. The women in the family—sister Nicole, sister-in-law Katie, and ex-wife Cara have faced this issue head on. Janna, who was close to her son, is said to be the exception. She's heartbroken, very ill, and would never share that heartbreak publicly. Nicole is publicly advocating for better mental health support for veterans. Katie makes it a point to "spread love and kindness as best I can despite all the sadness," and both they and Cara have publicly shared the anguish they all feel about the loss of so many innocent lives.

*"We could never come up with the right words to express our devastation for those who lost their lives, for those who lost their loved ones, for those who won't ever be the same because of this. We feel it all. I promise you,"* they said in a Facebook post.

Later in May 2024, all three, plus Nicole's husband, James Sterling, testified at a public hearing in front of the commission. They did so to let the community and the victim's families know that their relative public silence was out of respect to those families, and that they would always carry the grief and sorrow they felt for all of them. Their testimony was raw and courageous, and a real testament to the family's character.

They also testified in the hopes of bringing attention to the challenges facing military veterans, to the shortage of mental health services, as well as the need for everyone - law enforcement, military, health care professionals, and others - to understand what went wrong with the responses to the red flags that Robbie was waving in the hopes that it won't happen again. The other men in the family? They're from a multi-generational farm family, and stoic to a fault. No one is prepared for such a horrible scenario, but some have the tools to deal with it better. They just don't have those tools in the box. Robert Sr. is said to be devastated by what his son did and grieving for him, but he won't likely ever share that publicly. Ryan, his oldest son, is said to be really struggling. After four combat tours, injuries that resulted in a Purple Heart, and PTSD issues, he's been on 100% VA disability for years. He had his own mental health struggles before October 25th. Ryan was close to his brother—as close as two men brought up to bottle their emotions can be—and he was the last person in the family Robbie stayed in contact with before completely separating.

As for Colby, Cara Lamb says her son has done his best to move on.

*My son is an absolute champion, just the best kid I could ever have hoped for and then some, how I got so lucky in who he's become is beyond me. His dad had a part in that too. As hard as that is to fathom, we shared this child for years, on opposing sides, and look who he has become, just a wonderful human being who deserves nothing but the best...and I'm asking for us all to give him just that.*

As for the greater community's feelings, most people seem to recognize that the Card family cared deeply for Robbie's well-being, and they tried to get him help. Say what you will, this wasn't a family that turned their back on one of their own. The community at large isn't going to do that to the Card family either. There are some who might think they fell short of their responsibility. Could they have done more? In hindsight, it's very easy to say yes, but that's looking with rose-colored glasses. The truth is that they reached out to the SCSO and Army Reserve soldiers, and instead of getting help, they were tasked with dealing with it themselves when they were confused, afraid, and frantic with worry. The fact that you're a friend or family member does not make you a qualified crisis intervention professional.

They know they're probably looking at years of litigation. Cara hired an attorney after she came to the realization that lawyers were lined up to pounce on them if they made any probate decisions. She recognizes that it will be a painful and lengthy process that she'll be indirectly involved in, despite having no relationship with her ex-husband for the past sixteen years. But she's prepared to deal with whatever comes down the pike to help her son navigate his future. She's not responsible for what his father did, and neither is he. They both have to live with it and figure it out as they go, because there's no manual for any of the family to consult.

*Elizabeth and Joshua Seal and their four children, Sephine, Jarrod, Jaxton and Jayson (left to right). Joshua was one of four deaf men who were shot and killed while they played in a cornhole tournament at Schemengees. (Photo courtesy of Elizabeth Seal)*

# PICKING UP THE PIECES

There was a lot of activity at Just-In-Time Recreation on a Saturday in late January of 2024. Stacks of new flooring were piled high near the front entrance, the ceiling was opened up, exposing wiring that connected shiny new heating and ventilation systems.

While Justin and Samantha Juray sat down at one of the only tables not covered with building materials, two men were halfway down the lanes installing new bumpers and gutters, while another hammered away near the front desk. It was noisy, and Justin rolled his eyes as he paused in mid-sentence. Annoying maybe, but it was the sound of progress, the sound of a rebirth. The couple had decided they would reopen in the spring. They couldn't walk away. They couldn't let Robert Card II win. He ripped the heart out of their bowling family, but they're going to put it back together as much as they can, and they'll do it together at a newly refurbished Just-In-Time.

In early May, a few months after the interview, they finally reopened. The parking lot was jammed with food trucks, TV news trucks, and radio station tents, while inside, the sparkling renovated bowling alley was packed to capacity. Governor Mills cut the ribbon, and other politicians showed up to speak. The Jurays unveiled a wall memorial featuring bowling pins with the names of all eighteen victims of the shootings. It was a festive day laced with sadness; a day to remember the past, a day to move forward.

In the time immediately after the shooting, they didn't think they could reopen. The thought of going back there was just too painful to bear. Plus, their landlord offered to let the Jurays walk away from their ten-year lease if they wanted. People would understand if they made that decision. Many would be disappointed, but they'd understand. But then they thought of Bob and Lucy Violette. Bob would never let them shut down for good. He'd haunt them from his grave if they did, Justin said with a laugh. Once they made that decision, they were all in. The Violettes' would be very pleased to learn that a Bob and Lucy Violette Bowling Fund has been set up to provide the youth league with financial support so the kids can continue to embrace the sport that meant so much to their mentors.

The community has rallied around the Jurays and their rebuilding effort. Their social media posts showing the progress of the renovation were met with a blizzard of encouraging comments. Not just from customers either. People from across the country offered words of support. In fact, Just-In-Time was named the New England Bowling Alley of the Year by online voters in March 2024.The owners of other bowling alleys across the country were incredibly generous with donations of new equipment too. So was the Bowling Proprietor's Association of America, which donated a new electronic scoring system and flew Justin and Samantha to New Orleans for the association's annual meeting in January 2024, and then put them up at a hotel for a few days so they could enjoy the city. They discovered that their bowling community isn't just in the Lewiston area; they're in small towns and big cities from coast to coast.

The wall memorial honoring the victims of the shootings is a focal point, a visual reminder to make sure that they'll always be remembered. Not that the Jurays need it. "We say hello and goodbye to them every time we're here,"

Samantha said. "They'll never be forgotten." "Never!" her husband emphasized.

Justin still struggles to sleep, he wakes up sweating and crying, and he's nervous about going out in public. The first time he went to the supermarket, he found himself looking for exits. He's not embarrassed to say he sees a therapist to help him deal with the trauma of that night. Samantha doesn't, but she might down the road. She studied psychology in college and feels she's able to self-process a little better than most. But she knows that the horrors she saw might that night climb out of the compartment she's locked them away in at any time.

People were coming and going, the phone was ringing, decisions had to be made about new menu items and a long list of other things. But not before Justin added a final thought.

"Don't take anyone or anything for granted. I used to do that. But I never will again."

Four miles away, Schemengees is beginning to look like the vacant building it is. It wasn't attractive before, but the people, the traffic, the lights and noise, made it welcoming. Now it's a cold empty structure that houses terrible memories.

Kathy Lebel owns another restaurant called Station Grill at the other end of Lincoln Street, and that's where she can be found most of the time now. She told the *Boston Globe* she's not sure if she'll ever reopen Schemengees at its current location. She's looking for another building, but finding a similarly-sized 10,000-square-foot warehouse type building in a good location in Lewiston is a tall order. So, in the meantime, plans are in limbo. She's gone back and forth over the decision to reopen, she said, and finds herself asking her friend and former manager, Joe Walker, what she should do. But the answer still remained elusive. She even searched up, *"What to do with your building after a mass shooting"* on Google, and found some information about schools and churches, but none about restaurants and bars, Lebel told the *Globe*. Even the Internet can't fully explain what to do after such a traumatic event.

Elizabeth Seal's husband, Joshua, died in that building playing cornhole with his friends that night. She knows he would have been laughing and having a good time as he did, because that's who he was and how he lived his life. She and Joshua had known each other since she was two and he was three at Baxter School for the Deaf nursery school. They went in separate directions in the third grade, but connected again when she was fifteen. They started dating, married in 2010, and had four children—Jayson, twelve, Sephine, ten, Jarrod, six, and Jaxton, four.

Elizabeth's face lit up as she explained about how good a father he was. It was early March 2024, and she was signing with an ASL interpreter in a small conference room at the public library in Bath. Despite the author's apprehension, the conversation flowed, in large part because her face was so expressive, and she communicated as clearly as a bell. It helped that she and the ASL interpreter had such an obvious rapport.

"He was a hands-on Dad from the first day. No matter how busy he was, he always found time to spend with them. He fed them, laid on the floor and played with them, slept with them. The day before he died, he spent the whole day with them."

Joshua was busy with so many things: Organizing ASL interpreting services for the Pine Tree Society; planning a new season for the summer camp for deaf children he started; working on his own as an ASL interpreter for clients like Vice President Kamala Harris, and the former Maine CDC director, Nirav Shah. Plus, he loved to play competitive cornhole and disc golf in his down time.

"But that never got in the way of time with the kids," Elizabeth signed. "They'd run to the door when he came home, and he'd take them down to the basement playroom to shoot hoops, play with them, whatever made them happy."

All four of the children are deaf, which is very unusual. She's the only deaf person in her family, and Joshua's deafness was linked to his grandmother. But both she and Joshua had two copies of the gene that causes deafness, guaranteeing that the children would have the same. That didn't slow down the Seal family one bit. They were always on the go. At the end of a busy day, Josh and Sephine would always snuggle before she went to sleep. She's understandably devastated by his loss, and every night she goes down to the basement to kiss a lightbulb that's been flickering on and off since he died. She believes it's her dad talking to her. In fact, they all do, except Jayson, the oldest. He's creeped out about it. He's older, and his grieving is more internalized, but Elizabeth sees it and knows he's missing his dad just as much.

As for the light, she swears that Josh has helped her find tools in the basement to do the home repairs that he used to do, or alert her to a problem that needs looking after. Sometimes she's sure it's her mind playing tricks on her, but then she'll ask the light where a tool is, or how to fix something, and it will flicker like crazy when she gets close to answering her own question.

"Maybe I'm just imagining it. But it helps us to think he's still with us, and that helps us get through another day without him."

Dr. Nirav Shah got to know Joshua when he was the Maine CDC director during the pandemic years. Joshua was his primary ASL interpreter for the almost daily media presentations. Dr. Shah delivered the often-grim COVID-19 updates in an upbeat, meticulous manner, so much so that he became a celebrity in Maine. In fact, he was so popular that the Biden Administration offered him the position of Principal Deputy Director of the U.S. CDC.

Speaking from Washington D.C. as he hurried from one meeting to another, Dr. Shah said he and Joshua hit it off almost immediately. They spent a lot of time around each other in that stressful period, and the discussions they had about his work as an ASL interpreter, and Dr. Shah's work as the state's principal public-facing voice during the pandemic, helped take some of the edge off.

Over time, they'd come to joke around with each other. That was something that came naturally to Joshua, Dr. Shah said, and he never felt ill at ease communicating with him, in part because they were both natural-born communicators.

"Joshua had a way of making you feel very much at ease. His sense of humor was wonderful. He would crack jokes, but at the same time, he was very professional and very skilled as an interpreter. He really was the voice of the Deaf community in Maine, and he will forever be missed by many."

Artie Strout's dad, Arthur Barnard, hasn't let up on his effort to see a national registry for guns established. He spoke to legislators in Augusta in March about it as they were hammering out details for proposed universal background checks and a three-day waiting period.

These are all well and good, he told them, but if you don't have a recorded serial number next to a name in an accessible database, it's like putting lipstick on a pig. He's not interested in the incremental gains that others tell him are the only way to measure progress in the political arena. To Barnard, half-assed measures are for politicians, not for grieving family members of mass shooting victims.

He's been asked to sing his song, *18 Souls,* at a national vigil for gun violence in Washington D.C. in December. Meanwhile, Barnard expects his performance of the song will appear in a PBS documentary about the Lewiston shootings on October 25th, 2024, the first anniversary.

He may go to Vegas in May 2024 to play in a national pool tournament with a Lewiston-based team. A long-time high-level player, Arthur has taken his son's place on the team. They've had some team shirts made up with the names of Artie, Maxx Hathaway, and Joe Walker emblazoned on them. Schemengees' pool players will represent on a national stage, even as their home base remains shuttered, its future uncertain.

As busy as he is, Arthur can see that Artie's kids and his wife are having a hard time without him. He was always there for them, the big teddy bear, and his absence leaves a big hole in all of them that seems impossible to fill.

Arthur and the other victim's family members are having to navigate uncharted waters. How would any of us deal with the unimaginable loss of a loved one killed in a senseless shooting? How do you not fill the void with unbearable sadness, anger, remorse, depression, sleepless nights? How do you find a way to patch it over and carry on? The lucky among us won't ever have to confront those questions. Because, really, at the end of the day it comes down to luck.

Arthur left Schemengees minutes before Card walked in. Artie stayed.

Samantha Juray went into the Just-In-Time kitchen just before 6:55 p.m. to check on dinner orders. Tricia Asselin, who wasn't even working that night, walked towards the front desk to check on a problem. Card walked in.

Keith MacNeir came from Florida to celebrate his son's birthday. He waited at the Schemengees bar for him to return from a union meeting.

Card's gun jammed as it was trained on Danielle Grondin. She managed to escape. It cleared just as Jason Walker and Michael Deslauriers charged him.

Mike Roderick stumbled into a utility room and found the main breaker switch just after Card loaded a new magazine. His son and many others survived as a result.

The lockdown after the shootings prevented the employees of Maine Recycling from going to work the next two mornings. Robert Card II was hiding in a trailer in the overflow lot with a semi-automatic rifle, two hundred rounds of ammunition and a deep-rooted grudge against them.

Eighteen unlucky Mainers went out on a pleasant October evening to enjoy life. They never came back.

## *18 Souls* by Arthur Barnard

Seems like just yesterday
I was driving myself downtown
Just taking care of some business
Wondering if you were around
Then you called me up and said
Dad do you have time
To shoot a few good games
Tell me what's on your mind.

First I thought I was too damn tired
Didn't know if I could
Then I said hell why not
'Cause it was so understood
These were the best times
That we shared our souls
Talk about kids and life
What was making us old

How was I to know this day would change our lives
We'd be picking up the pieces from 18 shattered lives
18 Souls so beautiful all gone in a Flash
From an angry Troubled Man with a gun tight in his hands

I remember that day it's all so Crystal Clear
People laughing drinking and signing All without any fear
There was a mama chasing her baby saying how sorry she
was
Your little girl's not going to bother me I've got 20
grandchildren Love
I was so glad to hear that you were both okay
Just a small little blessing from that tragic day
What I miss the most is your goofy laugh and smile
And that great big beautiful heart that you carried with such
style

How were we to know
This day would change our lives
We be picking up the pieces
From 18 shattered lives
18 Souls so beautiful all gone in a Flash
Like Rubble they're just
memories and heartaches that will last

I hope that we can come together with our hearts and Minds
Make some better choices with these gun bills that we sign
I hope that we can coexist for our families and our kids
So we never have to have another tragedy
Like October 25th

How are we to know this day would change our lives
We be picking up the pieces from 18 shattered lives
18 Souls so beautiful all gone in a Flash
From an angry Troubled Man with a gun tight in his hands

18 Souls
Oh 18 Souls

Yes, my son was one of those 18 precious Souls

# A LONG LIST OF WHYS

On a blustery, cold and damp late March 2024 day, both the Miller Park boat launch and the trail heading south towards Lisbon Falls are quiet. The reeds and marsh grass along the edges of the outlet are withered and brown. The ice that encased it for the previous four plus months is gone, and a family of ducks slalom through, reclaiming their home here where the Sabattus spills into the Androscoggin.

Like most of them lately, it was a winter of wildly inconsistent high and low temperatures. The ground was bare, and the ice was out as the calendar flipped to spring, and then a storm dumped a pile of miserable glop—snow, freezing rain, sleet, back to snow—that took down ice-laden trees, knocking out power for a couple of days or more across the region. It melted soon enough though, power was restored, and now it's a waiting game for real spring to arrive and set the table for summer behind it.

The drivers of two pickup trucks have slotted into spaces facing the ramp and pulled out their lunch. One places an apple on the dash. It stays perched there for a few seconds, then rolls off. His head disappears from view as he bends over to pick it up.

The other has cranked up the volume of Lynyrd Skynyrd's *Sweet Home Alabama* and is thumping to the beat on the steering wheel with one hand while he eats a sandwich with the other. The music carries out of the cab into the swirling wind. These guys must know they're parked feet away from where the vehicle involved in the largest manhunt in Maine's history was found five months before, a rifle and papers identifying the owner as Robert Card II visible to police officers when they discovered it at 10:08 the night of the shooting. Of course they know. They have Maine license plates. They'd have to be deaf, dumb, and sleeping under a rock not to know the full story. Ten minutes after Lisbon police officers spotted the car, the Maine State Police tactical team rolled up in force. When they did, there were already thirty to forty police officers surrounding the car, their vehicles putting on a blue strobe light show that must have terrified every living creature burrowed into the woods around the boat ramp.

There's no sign of that drama now, nothing to indicate it even happened. There's just the wind rippling the water of the outlet, traffic whipping by over the Rt. 196 overpass, and two guys sitting in their trucks eating their sandwiches.

These guys must also know that Card's body was finally found a little over a mile from here. Maybe they're aware that forty-six hours passed from the time the car was discovered until the time they found his body. If they were residents of Lewiston, Lisbon, or Bowdoin, they would have been in lockdown—or "shelter in place," the gentler phrase the authorities like to use—the whole time, going stir crazy and glassy-eyed watching the news, and peering out the windows for any signs of movement.

In a state where 48% of adults own a gun (much higher outside of the cities), they might have had theirs locked and loaded within arm's length. They would have seen the bowling alley video of Card with his Ruger SFAR-10 held exactly how his Army Reserve unit taught West Point cadets every summer in their training exercises. They would know this wasn't a petty criminal on the loose. If they thought about it too much, they were probably more than a little nervous, scared even.

Thankfully, it all ended with no more loss of life. Life goes on here like it always does. Eighteen innocent people have been laid to rest. The wounded are mending—at least physically. The families left behind struggle to varying degrees. Their grief resides on many levels, and it changes day by day. Many are angry at authorities for ignoring all the glaring warning signs that Card displayed. Some are angry that gun advocates continue to resist change. Others don't want their loved one's death used to create new laws. Some of the young children can't understand what happened and why Daddy isn't home with them. The ones old enough to understand have a hole in their heart that will never be filled.

The people who knew Robert Card II the best struggle with a complicated mix of grief, anger, and remorse. They grieve for him, and they grieve for his victims and their families. And they also grapple with the anger they feel at their local law enforcement agency and his Army Reserve colleagues for ignoring all the warning signs, and the remorse they feel over not being able to find a way to get him help before he did the unthinkable.

The hue and cry for tougher gun laws in the immediate aftermath has diminished in volume, but the usual partisan politics' battle lines have been drawn in Augusta. Maybe not the usual; it's more difficult for a Maine politician or gun owner's advocate to give a full-throated defense of gun ownership now that the unthinkable has happened here. Yet, few minds seem to have been changed as a result.

The who, what, when and where questions of the night of October 25th, 2023, have mostly been answered. Ongoing investigations and plaintiff's lawyers could answer most of the rest.

That leaves the why?

Why did the Army Reserves fail to provide Card with long-term help?

Why didn't the law enforcement members of his Reserve unit recognize the danger he presented and utilize their unique training and cross-jurisdiction access to get him help and keep the public safe?

After making the decision not to force a confrontation at his trailer, why didn't the Sagadahoc County Sheriff's Office, specifically Sgt. Skolfield and his immediate boss, Lt. Quinn, come up with alternative plans?

Why was Robert Card II allowed to keep his extensive collection of firearms, despite all the warnings that he was a powder keg ready to explode?

Why did Sgt. Skolfield consider the case closed when absolutely nothing had been done to ensure public safety?

Why do law enforcement agencies and the military put the public at risk by refusing to proactively share information with other jurisdictions?

With all the available training, and all the case history on record, why do these institutional failures keep occurring?

Why do these institutions then circle the wagons and admit to nothing, instead of publicly acknowledging mistakes and working to improve?

Why are so many elected officials so reluctant to find solutions to this horrible scourge on American society? Is there a tipping point, a number? Would it require a mass shooting that takes one of their own family members for them to change their minds?

Does the information contained in this book provide any useful insight to help identify potential mass shooters, hold those who swear to serve and protect to their vows, and maybe help reduce the risks to the public? It's a long shot, but if it helps just once, it will justify the effort.

The Lewiston shootings are a faint blip in the background for most Americans already. Once the next mass shooting occurs, the city will be just another marker in the graveyard of American mass shootings. The attention will shift to the next one. And then the next one. On and on it goes, when it stops, no one knows.

But the pain will live on here. For the victim's families, it will be generational. For the survivors, a lifetime. For everyone else, there's a dull ache that comes with the realization we were wrong: It can happen here after all.

# EPILOGUE

We've reached the one-year anniversary of the tragic Lewiston, Maine shootings on October 25, 2023, but the fallout continues in a steady drumbeat of proposed laws, official investigation reports, lawsuits, political elections, and more.

In terms of impact, the findings of Governor Mills' appointed Independent Commission to Investigate the Facts of the Lewiston Shootings made the biggest. In August, the Commission echoed the findings of an interim report issued earlier in the year that the Sagadahoc County Sheriff's Office made an egregious error in judgment in not utilizing existing laws to take Robert Card II into protective custody to remove his firearms.

The Commission singled out Sgt. Aaron Skolfield, the 25-year veteran who responded to Card's home in September to do a welfare check. Skolfield has vehemently denied he did anything wrong, and is, in fact, running for the position of sheriff in a November election against the incumbent, Joel Merry.

The Commission also took aim at the Army Reserve, noting that its soldiers in Bravo Company downplayed the seriousness of Card's mental health decline when it interacted with the sheriff's office, and that it failed to monitor Card after he was released from a psychiatric hospital three months before the shootings.

The Army Reserve has acknowledged it failed to follow up on Card's mental health diagnosis, and has internally disciplined three soldiers. However, it withheld thousands of pages of documents from its own investigation from the Commission, and has been close-mouthed since, almost assuredly because of pending lawsuits which will be filed by lawyers representing the families of victims and survivors of the shootings.

As a result of the Lewiston shootings, Maine's U.S. Senators, Susan Collins and Angus King, proposed legislation in September called the *Armed Forces Crisis Intervention Notification Act*, which would require all four branches of the armed services to notify states if they determine a member has been declared mentally unfit to use and possess military firearms due to credible threats of violence, and to utilize the states' existing mental health intervention programs. The proposed bill would also require the military branches to provide relevant facts to state law enforcement agencies and judicial branches. This bill would plug the huge gap that often exists between the military and civilian law enforcement in identifying potential mass shooters before an incident can occur.

Democratic Congressman Jared Golden, another Maine politician with ties to the Lewiston shootings, is facing an unexpectedly stiff re-election fight from a first-term Republican state legislator – in large part because Golden announced days after the shootings that he would support an assault weapon ban after being a lifelong staunch Second Amendment supporter. His district includes Lewiston, where that message plays well, but it also includes a wide swath of rural Maine towns, where he's viewed by many as a traitor for his policy shift.

Locally, Just-in-Time Recreation Center underwent a major renovation during a seven-month closing, and it reopened under the ownership of Samantha and Justin Juray. The leagues have returned, and the Bob & Lucy Violette

Bowling Foundation is hard at work raising money to support youth bowlers and honor the legacy of the beloved couple, who were two of the eighteen victims that tragic night.

Schemengees Bar & Grille remains shuttered and with the unexpected death of co-owner David Lebel at the age of fifty-seven in September, will almost assuredly never reopen. However, a local outreach center for the homeless will open a warming center, food kitchen and access to services there this fall. The site will expand its footprint from an existing 2,000 sq-ft. to 10,000 sq-ft., turning the scene of so much hopelessness and despair into a beacon of hope for those who need it.

For more news about Robert Conlin, subscribe to our newsletter at *wbp.bz/newsletter*.

Word-of-mouth is critical to an author's long-term success. If you appreciated this book, please leave a review on the Amazon sales page at *wbp.bz/lewiston*.

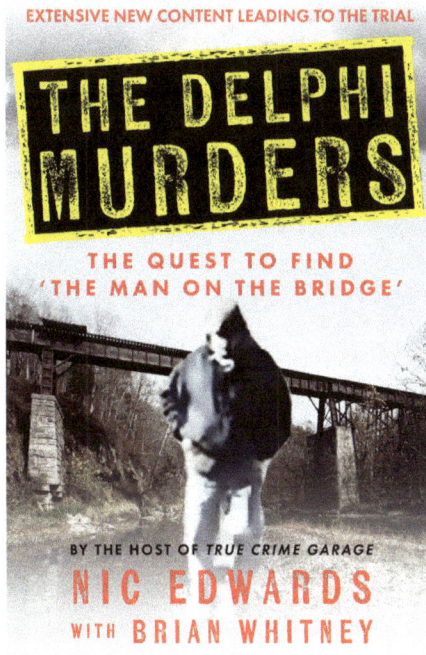

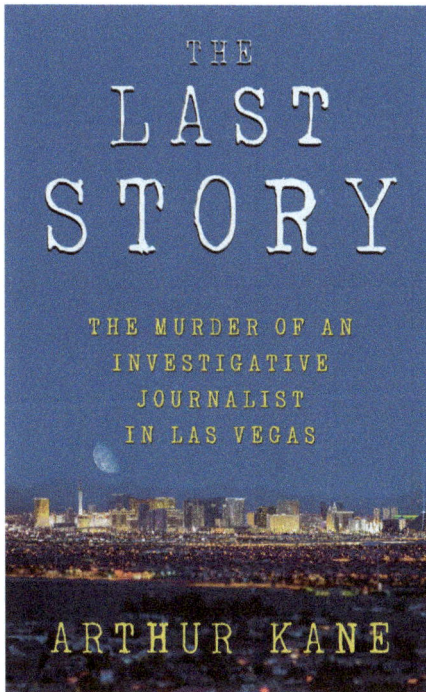

www.ingramcontent.com/pod-product-compliance
Lightning Source LLC
Chambersburg PA
CBHW070056030426
42335CB00016B/1912